The Clash of Modernities

The Clash of Modernities

The Islamist Challenge to Arab, Jewish, and Turkish Nationalism

Khaldoun Samman

Routledge
Taylor & Francis Group
LONDON AND NEW YORK

First published 2011 by Paradigm Publishers

Published 2016 by Routledge
2 Park Square, Milton Park, Abingdon, Oxon OX14 4RN
711 Third Avenue, New York, NY 10017, USA

Routledge is an imprint of the Taylor & Francis Group, an informa business

Library of Congress Cataloging-in-Publication Data

Samman, Khaldoun.
The clash of modernities : the Islamist challenge to Arab, Jewish, and Turkish nationalism / Khaldoun Samman.
p. cm.
Includes bibliographical references and index.
ISBN 978-1-59451-697-9 (hardcover : alk. paper) - ISBN 978-1-59451-698-6 (pbk. : alk. paper)
1. Nationalism—Middle East—Philosophy. 2. Civilization, Modern—Philosophy. 3. Middle East—Civilization—Philosophy. 4. Nationalism—Islamic countries. 5. Nationalism—Israel. 6. Nationalism—Turkey. 7. Nationalism—Arab countries. 8. Middle East—Civilization—Western influences. I. Title.
DS63.5.S26 2010
320.540956—dc22

2010016331

ISBN 13: 978-1-59451-697-9 (hbk)
ISBN 13: 978-1-59451-698-6 (pbk)

Designed and Typeset by Straight Creek Bookmakers.

To my mother,
Shahira Samman Obeji,
And my best friend,
Shoshana Nicole Lev

Contents

Preface

On the Arab Revolutions and the Counter-Revolutions of 2011

The wave of Arab revolutionary movements in 2011 that have spread throughout the Middle East and North Africa are tearing down not only political regimes but also a state of mind that has constrained the social and political imaginaries of people in the Arab world as well as many whites in Europe and the United States. This book covers a long period of colonial ideological expansion from the nineteenth century to our own contemporary period. I argue that this period has been dominated by a colonial script that places the people of the globe into a Social Darwinist world view where civilizations are ranked, in a highly Eurocentric manner, from low to high, with the Arabs and Muslims symbolizing fear, patriarchy, and backwardness. I argue in this book that the usual response by the Arab and Muslim elites to this problematic racial and civilizational script (as is also the case for most of the world's Others) throughout this period is profoundly lacking in political creativity. As we will see throughout the book, the elites of these movements, dressing themselves as oppositional to the colonial regimes of the West, have in actual practice been closely in alliance with this Orientalist script. If we are to have any chance of liberation from the grips of this racial script we cannot look to either secular Arab nationalist or the Islamist movements. I believe strongly that both of these movements are inescapably entrapped within the Orientalism inscribed in colonial modernity. All of these movements are quite comfortable living in a museum-like world of representations where the people of the globe mimic the world's diversity as ornaments of staged authenticities, some dressed as "Western" and Others as Arabs, Muslims, Turks, and Jews, all needing to be transformed to an ideal replica of the culture or religion before the coming of modernity, Enlightenment, or Judgment Day is possible.

This is precisely why I am very excited about these recent uprisings. Their message is clearly a challenge to this old and tiring civilizational and racial script, offering an alternative social justice rights-based approach to their liberationist arsenal while sidelining the old culturalist, civilizational, identity politics that has dominated the thinking of the old vanguard. These movements represent a conscious attempt to refuse to abide by the older colonial scripts of "Islam and the West" and other colonial-era binaries by offering images of the multitude in its actual, lived complexities rather than the rigid, museum-like approach of Arab nationalist and Islamist movements. In these recent uprisings there seems to be an awakening left populism that can realign political identities away from the destructive cultural divides that the holders of power, both in the Middle East and in the "West," want us to have instead. A video produced by Egyptians active in the January 25th movement, which was widely circulated through Facebook and the Internet, said it best: "We will never be silenced. Whether you are Christian, Muslim, or Atheist. Give us back our rights!"

Of course, I am both excited and cautious about these Egyptian and other movements: excited that a U.S.- and Israeli-backed Arab dictator has been forced out of power; cautious that elites in the Middle East (especially the military) and elsewhere (including the Saudis, the United States, and Israel), interested in returning to the status quo, may attempt to use Islamist forces like the Salafis and others in order to kill the movement. These Arab, American, and Israeli elites are searching for ways to curtail the power unleashed by this movement and would like nothing more than to limit the call for equality and worker's rights demanded by the movement. Banning further protests and imprisoning activists are the visible signs of the desperation of these Arab elites, but silently supporting Islamist groups and others is done behind the scenes, often with Saudi, Israeli, and American intelligence and support. The reasons for this is obvious: to revert back to Islamist versus secular, West versus Islam, terror versus order, and other binaries, keeps the public's attention away from the highly inegalitarian political and economic system that has been imported via American neoliberal designs, and to protect the interests of the military elite who have profited greatly from the privatization of the public sector and their so-called peace treaty with Israel.

But this shouldn't keep us from celebrating the ultimate effects these youths will have on the coming of new cultural models of resistance that are changing the geopolitical and geocultural face of the Arab world. Anyone who has followed the events taking place in Tunisia and Egypt in late 2010 and 2011 can easily judge from the protestors that they are careful not to represent the movement as Islam versus the West, Copt versus Muslim, heathens versus the self righteous but an unjust regime and its abuse of the people, especially the poor and other victims of the Infitah years (the so-called opening of the economy to international capital). While the movement no doubt had wide appeal, it began and was made possible by the immiserated majority, the poor urban youths who lived in the shantytowns and who minded the vegetable stands and cleaned the streets. These youths are well aware that their fate in life has been impacted by a global political economy that left them as its victim, and that to express their resistance in terms of Copts versus Muslims, secular versus Muslim, and other civilizational or religious binaries is to miss the target of their biggest culprit: the tyrannical regime that rules over them and enacts the will of the global capitalist class.

The model of resistance that preceded the January 25th movement, which shall be the subject of this book, was largely imagined around the binaric symbols of religion and civilization. It was highly racial and ethnicized, largely stemming from a colonial system that framed the world around racial and developmentalist symbols. The reason, for instance, Islamists came into existence in the late 1970s is precisely because the old populist regimes, in their effort to position themselves as the new vanguards of the people, used national and cultural symbolism that was highly Eurocentric and relegated Islam to the margin of their developmentalist discourse. This made it possible for opponents of these old regimes to find an alternative discourse simply because these earlier movements placed it as its deviant other. So I expect that if these Islamists take power (which I doubt given the small numbers of support for them in Egypt), oppositional movements will be able to move quickly and usurp more secularist symbols to bring down these Islamists. There is no doubt in my mind that if Islamists do come to power their life span will be much shorter than the old populist regimes. One reason for this is obvious: Their rigid cultural ideology will easily produce symbolism of dissent, and thus be easy to attack. But even a more important reason is that the world economy today, being much less prone to upward mobility in wealth than it was in the

1950s and 1960s, will place the Islamists in unmanageable leadership roles. This is, of course, also true for all other movements who will come to power over the next couple of decades.

I think it is important, though, to be careful not to overgeneralize a group of discrete movements under one umbrella, the "Islamist movements." Islamists are different in Palestine than say, Algeria, Egypt, or Lebanon. In Palestine, Hamas has gone beyond cultural politics and is active in the Intifada, largely in a constructive manner, offering many social services in a context in which the Israeli occupation permits no functional state to exist. Fatah, on the other hand, has become, over the past few years, quite corrupt, working closely with Israel and often acting more like a colonial surrogate police force than as an anti-occupation movement. To be fair, in the case of the Muslim Brotherhood in Egypt, they too have done considerable work on the social service front, providing important social services to an impoverished population abandoned by the state. But there is something really disturbing in the manner most Islamists carry out their cultural work and the aggressive nature with which they exert their morality onto the public. They are in effect fulfilling the prophecies of the most Orientalist and Islamophobic sectors of their former colonial masters.

Yet when watching the mainstream American media and reading its newspapers (both high- and lowbrow), the old Orientalist ways of seeing the world that I discuss in this book remain alive and well. I love the message of this revolution, especially the way it continues to focus on social justice issues and refuses, unlike its predecessors, to play into the clash of civilization discourse. But we have to remember that there are powerful rhetors (both European and Egyptian) at work who will try to bend the meaning back into the "war of Islam against the West." I can feel a rising army of neocons, especially in the United States, preparing to interpret the Egyptian revolution in the usual Orientalist and racist fashion as a gift of capitalism and "our" creation of free markets which, according to this Eurocentric myth, has allowed a middle class in the Arab world to develop and press for democratic changes in "that part of the world," when in fact it is the exact opposite, the complete immiseration of a large portion of the Arab population. The best dose of change is to steer away from the neoliberal regimes of the past few decades and find alternative political and economic relationships that can ease the unsustainable high inequalities, both in relative and absolute terms, between the global rich and the global poor.

There are times, however, when the farce is so apparent that even powerful rhetors can't reinterpret the situation in the standard way. This is clearly one of those moments. Over the past few months I've heard a number of "experts" in the American media proclaiming, "Western leaders press for change"! From the perspective of many of those in the Arab movements and their supporters, this would sound comic if it weren't for its tragic consequences. Those pressing for change are clearly not the American administration. More obvious to these protestors is how Western leaders are looking to see what they can salvage of this Egyptian dictatorship and its old regime. The leaders of this Spring Revolution, as it has come to be called, are well aware that there are powerful internal and external social forces at work who possess lots of tricks up their sleeves and who happen to also own the global airwaves. Having a quasi-monopoly over the ideological apparatus, this old vanguard, composed both of Americans and Arabs, will do everything in their power to construct a "silent majority" who is under attack by bad and dangerous Muslims or—in the case of groups like the Salafis—Westerners. It is at moments like this that supporters of the status quo, both in the Arab world and in the United States and Europe, will sharpen their hyperreal tools and attempt to inject their mediated subjects with political fear of the Other and offer them civilizational sound bites so as to undermine the goal of these revolutionary movements. Recently, for instance, on a road trip across the United States I was listening to a rightwing Christian radio with a preacher attempting to do precisely this. Indeed, the American media and satellite stations have acquired a whole army of rhetors constantly flocking the public airwaves so as to paint this revolutionary moment back into the old racial and binaric script.

While the objectives of the United States and the ruling Arab class desires to dampen the demands of the Arab Spring, the Israeli position is even more desperate. Since its very inception in 1948, if not earlier, it has worked tirelessly to portray itself as the only democracy in a region of barbarism. It constantly used this script as it systematically attempted to destroy Palestinian society, offering those under its occupation the most tyrannical kind of regime where absolutely no rights are permitted for the indigenous population under its occupation, all while usurping their land and homes and handing it over to European, Russian, and American Jews. To have a successful revolution occur in a country where the despot that ruled over the Egyptian people was their major ally doesn't speak well for their old script of the only democracy surrounded by barbaric Arabs. Zionists prefer to live in a region dominated by Arab dictators and Islamist regimes for the simple reason that it legitimizes their own atrocities against the Palestinians. Killing the democratic revolution in Egypt and elsewhere and having it revert back to a dictator, even better yet an Islamist regime, would fulfill better their racial policies and the near-total usurpation of Palestinian lands and homes. A strong and democratic Arab regime(s) would no doubt make it ideologically more difficult for them to continue to build their already-erected apartheid state. As one of my friends, Steven Sherman, said to me shortly after the January 25th uprising, "Today, as was the case a month ago, the 'existential threat' to the 'Jewish state' of Israel is not Iran or a radicalized Egyptian government, but a growing global civil society's hostility to the concept of a racial/religious state and the apartheid system it is consolidating." Curtailing and containing the implications of the Arab Spring, especially its democratic character, will surely be one of Israel's biggest goals in the remainder of this decade. I am largely optimistic that the movements underway throughout the Arab world will be powerful enough to offset these powerful counter-revolutionary forces.

Of course in places like Libya, Syria, and the Gulf, the picture is less rosy. Given the clan-like political structures of Libya and the Shi'ite/Sunni division erected by the Gulf states, as we have seen in Bahrain, and the political and military alliances built between the army and the political elite in Syria, one could reasonably argue that the counter-revolutionary forces in these countries may be able to extend the lives of the old regimes a bit longer. Bahrain, for instance, has labeled the protests there as a Shi'ite-led attack on the nation and its people and with some success has been able to receive the support of a large sector of Sunnis who benefit in multiple ways from their confessional affiliations with the ruling regime. This state-subsidized sectarian character of the population that characterizes the Gulf states will make it difficult to reproduce the political victories that we saw in Egypt and Tunisia. The success of the movements in the oil-rich states of the Gulf is made more difficult by the fact that there are ten of thousands of immigrant workers who are refused the most basic rights. They service a privileged, largely Sunni minority dedicated to saving the oil-rich, and heavily American-supported, despotic regimes. As such, forces of change versus forces of the status quo are unfolding around sectarian ethnic and confessional grounds, allowing the state to use the old racial script to maintain its hold on power. But they too will no doubt be changed by this powerful wave.

So in sum, it seems like there is a vibrant pushback against the highly inegalitarian global system that was once offered by local and global elites, and the large majority of the participants of the Arab Spring have recognized that repelling the real danger to them and their families (the corporate, financial, and military-industrial complex) is their highest priority, rather than the cultural politics of the old secular and Islamist movements of the past. Local and global elites who have benefited from this inequality will do everything in their power to revert us back into the civilizational discourse of fear versus order, terror versus security, Islam versus the West, Sunni versus Shi'ite, Jew versus Arab, and so on. We will no doubt see some gains in some of the early revolutions (specifically Egypt and Tunisia) while in other countries smaller, yet important, changes with lots of violence (Libya, Syria, Bahrain). All in all I'm hopeful the region will be better off than what preceded the coming of these movements. The rest of us need to be vigilant and understand the history of this discourse in order to challenge those in our own context (the United States in my case) who want to continue sliding the world further into an unjust and unsustainable political future by challenging them on the airwaves, in print, and in editorials. The counter-revolutionary forces are not just over there, they are here as well, and they will surely continue the civilizational spin of the past (Islam vs. the West) in order to appropriate the emotional sensibilities and loyalties of the already stressed and overworked populations around the highly problematic binaries of American versus Muslims, Christian versus Muslim, moderate Muslim versus bad Muslim, and so on. We will need to offer our support to those social forces trying to push in the other direction. This book is a small attempt in that direction by offering an historical analysis of how this very destructive racial script came to the region we now have come to call the Middle East. The hope with which I offer this book to you is that it will provide a conceptual tool through which you may be better equipped to trace and study how this sectarian, Them and Us racial script came into existence in the first place.

Acknowledgments

THIS BOOK IS, LIKE MANY THINGS IN LIFE, a product way beyond my own initiative. Shoshana Lev has spent literally many hundreds of hours discussing issues covered in this book with me, and without her penetrating insight, the writing of this book would not have been possible. Her deep reflections into issues like the Palestinian-Israeli conflict, the impact of modernity on our psychological well-being, gender, race, class, the environment, and spirituality have all been thoroughly weaved into the details of this book. I'm sure that if she had written this book it would look different, so I am solely responsible for its defects. But what good comes out of it is directly related to our deep and loving relationship. I'd also like to thank Ferruh Yilmaz, whose ideas I'm still digesting and have only partially captured here. No doubt the next intellectual journey I take will be with him at my side.

I have received helpful comments from a number of friends and colleagues: I thank Joan Wallach Scott for reading and critically commenting on every chapter of the book. Andrew Pragacz, Terry Boychuk, and Kara Witt also read an early version of the entire manuscript and provided me with helpful suggestions, which I incorporated into the next draft. Other friends kindly read portions of the book. Kathryn Haddad, Charlotte Karem Albrecht, Willie Nour, Nahid Khan, and Ronald Longstaff provided generous feedback on my introduction. A special thanks goes to Poo-bah for all the daily positive energy she has provided me. I'd like to also thank Dean Birkenkamp of Paradigm Publishers for his patience and understanding. The editorial staff at Paradigm have been exceptionally professional in their work, and I'd like to give special thanks to Jason Barry, Carol Smith, Sharon Daugherty, Linda Carlson, and Thanassis Gournais.

Finally I'd like to thank my mother, Shahira, who has always been there for me, providing me with insights in ways books and intellectual systems can never do. Her stories of her childhood growing up in Jerash and Zarqa and her crisp memory in helping me recollect my first eight years living in Jordan and our family's move from Jordan to New Jersey have added much depth to the analysis found in this book. As with Shoshana, every fiber of this book can be traced back to the special loving relationship I have with my mother.

Introduction

A Personal Example of a Temporal Script

A Personal Example of a Temporal Template

I HAVE COME TO RECOGNIZE that writing this book about historical and contemporary nationalist and Islamist movements is partially a biographical inquiry into my life. The great figures that I deal with in this book speak to me in their psychological quest to negotiate a highly racist script of the modern world, where Jews, Turks, Arabs, and Muslims were placed somehow less up to par than their fellow white men of what has come to be called "the West." Situated to exist in a time before the modern like the main historical characters of this book, I too—being an Arab and a Muslim—would find myself negotiating with a temporal instrument that always placed my family and me as belonging to a culture and a religion that was outdated, behind the times, not modern or progressive enough.

The world that we now inhabit is viewed as containing not only different cultures but people located in different times, with some on top and posited as being the most modern and advanced and others placed lower on the scale, coming from cultures of a different, earlier time. This is now so widespread that it can be said to have become a conceptual "tool" that many of us are coerced to make our own. Being much more than just a structural or material transformation, this powerful temporal instrument, with its highly judgmental ways of looking at the world of difference, creates anxieties and tensions at very personal levels.

The reason I am writing this book is in part related to my coming to terms with how this gaze has lived inside me as well. In me I see the struggles necessary to deal with the deep psychological wounds created by this never ending comparing and judging of one's identity. When reading and researching about Theodor Herzl and Kemal Ataturk, two historical figures I deal with in depth in later chapters, I also recall the desire I had in my youth to remove what I then perceived to be my cultural baggage. As Meltem Ahiska has argued, this way of looking at the world produces anxiety in those construed as "non-Western" and "behind the times" to feel "alienated from their own present which they want to overcome by projecting themselves either to the utopian future or the golden age of the past due to the 'time lag' stigmatized and internalized as 'backwardness' in representations of non-Western modernity."[1]

As I write these words today, I remember so clearly, when I was seven, my father informing my family and me that we would be leaving Jordan to live in the United States. Immediately I started to envision my future life. I imagined myself dressed in white sneakers and white socks, white shorts, and a white shirt. I imagined a sparkling new bicycle and my family and me living in a big house with a green yard and lots of trees. I remind you that I was seven years old, but I understood—although at that time I didn't know the origins of this dream—that I was about to be transformed—color, accent, and all—into the image that I had just begun to see on my next-door neighbor's television set. Excited by the news, all I knew was that I, along with my family, were *moving* West.

Indeed, I had already begun practicing my new self before I even landed in New Jersey, frantically trying to learn my first English words and putting on clothes that I believed would best fit my newfound identity. Dressed in this new clothing, and with the few English words I had learned, I looked into a mirror and tried to act "like an American." In New Jersey I continued down this path in full force, trying to remove my "Arabness" in every conceivable way, even at the expense of keeping my family distant from my friends. When the phone rang when I was expecting a friend's call, for instance, I would run in a frantic effort to get to the phone before my father or mother answered it, because I feared that with their "thick Arab accents," they would demonstrate to my friends and others how Arab we really were. I would plead with my parents to speak more like "Americans." Likewise, when I saw Yasser Arafat appear on ABC's *Nightline* with Ted Koppel, or when pictures of the Ayatollah

Khomeini appeared on the news, I would feel angry that the attire they wore made the region I came from appear "backward." "Why couldn't they wear nice clothing?" I used to complain to my parents, brothers, and sisters, who often watched television with me.

Having pale skin allowed me the privilege to hide my "real" self. Even my school lunch bag was a point of contention between my mother and me. I would request that she leave out any food that looked Middle Eastern. I found creative ways to make myself feel and look white-American, especially through music and partying. Fitting my car with the best stereo equipment available, courtesy of my family's small business, Samman's Discount Electronics, I would pack my car with friends and jam down the streets of Jersey to the powerful rhythms of great rock and roll bands like Led Zeppelin, Lynyrd Skynyrd, and Pink Floyd. The music I heard in my home, like Umm Kulthum and Farid al-Atrash, never made it into my car. Of that I made sure.

Although this pressure to fit in is not unique to Arab immigrants or other minorities but also extends to majoritarian experiences when moving to new countries, there is something unique about the psychological implications for those marked as belonging to a culture that's construed as premodern and behind the times, especially when we add in the special case of being Muslim, which for some Americans is considered a "dangerous" and even possibly "violent" religion. Other children, struggling to fit into a new community, might experience quite uncomfortable issues, but not in the same racialized connotations of those coming from a "backward culture."

It was not until I entered college that I began seriously thinking about why this is the case, with my research becoming the vehicle through which I would make sense of it all. At first my search was unsystematic and confusing. I did not yet have the right questions or conceptual tools to penetrate this unconscious desire to repress my "Arabness." At times, I turned to a crude form of multicultural identity politics. But that felt awkward and unreal, like a museum representation of natives dressed in colorful clothing, chanting to tunes that seemed distant and unreal to my life—in many ways replicating the Orientalist representations that made me want to shed my Arabness in the first place.

Thankfully that project quickly faded away, and in its place, I began pursuing more serious intellectual pursuits. I began reading people like Immanuel Wallerstein and Edward Said, who were arguing that the *world* is in fact politically, economically, and culturally stratified, with race constituting the very epicenter of the stratification. Racism and underdevelopment, Orientalism and its residual "Other," the "West" and the "rest," the rise of Europe and the decline of Southern civilizations were, I was beginning to learn, all a product of modernity, of a "specific manifestation of a basic process by which our historical system has been organized: a process of keeping people out while keeping people in."[2] According to Edward Said, this is a system held together by power. The lens through which we have access to it is *racially* tainted, leading to an interpretation of a world where the "West" possesses some unique trait that legitimates its "rise" above the rest of the world, rendering the Arab, the Turk, and the Muslim racially or culturally inferior, unable to match those refined qualities that are believed to be the sole patrimony of the West.

Through these penetrating analyses, I began to link my desire to assimilate into America along with the highly stratified global system that it constructs, in which some sectors of the world population are seen as superior and others deemed inferior, with the whole organized around an axial division of labor that inserts people into a complex set of unequal relationships. This construct forms the foundation, I now believe, of a world system that shapes, forms, and destroys our very identities. It unfortunately has dire psychological consequences for a majority of this world's population, engendering in many an inferiority complex similar to the one I experienced as a young child.

In the same way that I quickly appropriated a strategy of removing my imagined Arabness in order to travel West, in my recent travels through Turkey, Israel, Jordan, and Morocco, it became quickly apparent that many Middle Eastern elites, including its brightest intellectuals, are struggling with all their might to pull on the rope that hangs between an imagined East and West, using everything in their power to pull in the "Occident"—with the belief that by doing so they can finally "develop" and modernize "their nation" and join the "civilized" West in its time of modernity.

The déjà vu that I experienced upon my visit to Istanbul and other cities was deep, and the parallels between my own biography and the psyche of the Turkish, Jewish, and Arab nationalist were dramatic. As was the case with me, speaking to Turks, Arabs, and Jews and hearing many secular Turkish middle-class intellectuals talk about the veil or Islamism as being a toxin coming from Iran or similarly some Iranian Americans pointing to the Arab world as a source for all their problems, sounded like pages taken straight from my own diary, possessing an inferiority complex so powerful that all effort was made to transform the "Oriental" self into a modern, civilized, and "Occidentalized" self.

The identity crisis that I began observing was a personal reminder for me of the devastating effects this racialized discourse inflicts on individual minds. Experiencing it among Turks, Jordanians, Arab Americans, and others reminded me of my own family photo album, with my siblings besieged by an inferiority complex so deep that you can see it, if you look carefully enough, in their eyes. It is a destructive discourse that compelled my beloved family, as was the case for so many people around the world, "to assert their Western identity by denying and repressing the oriental within themselves."[3]

But fortunately, with my sanity left intact, I have begun to see that these representations have never gone completely uncontested. The colonizer's deeply insulting discourse has proven to be an ambiguous enterprise against which people live their everyday lives. I now see such folks as creative producers of their lives, who make the best of the discourses they are forced to inhabit and live with. Now when I see an Arab American youth struggling to deal with his or her scarred identity, I also am aware of the creative manner by which she produces a life that has dignity. I no longer just see a duped mind but instead one that is constantly and creatively appropriating the dominant discourse, so as to bend it in such a way that it no longer has the same meaning that its powerful originators intended.

So, too, should we be cautious to also see how Kemalist, Arab nationalist, Zionist, and Islamist discourses trickle "down" to everyday Jews, Arabs, and Muslims so as not to essentialize and identify those discourses to a passive mass audience. This study is not about Jews, Turks, Arabs, and Muslims per se. Instead, it concerns itself with a form of representation with which all of us have had to negotiate. Dominant discourses are ambiguously digested by the larger forces of society, in the marketplace, mosques, universities, villages, the streets, and on the body.[4] This is another face of modernity: that even in a world where "all that is solid melts into air," modernity is never a uniform, singular experience.[5] Rather, it is always in a state of crisis and contradiction, offering spaces of resistance and harnessing the creative impulses of a people under great stress. In other words, although it might appear to have a logic as we look at an elite sector of its users, the colonizer's temporal template has otherwise been unsuccessful, owing to the fact that the multitude have found ways of taming it so as to make it possible to live a dignified life. As I walk the streets of my former homes in Jordan and New Jersey, as I visit Istanbul or Jerusalem, it is now apparent to me that people do find a number of ways to deal with this view, some for good ends and others for destructive purposes. Because I am most concerned with the nationalist and Islamist elites, however, my analysis will be focused largely on the destructive side of modernity, where the colonizer's gaze has lived deep in their minds.

The Protean Script of Colonial Modernity: The Colonizer's Temporal Template

This book is about the insertion into our world of a particular way of seeing global difference and power that occurred during the imperial expansion of the West into the global southern hemisphere from the nineteenth century to our contemporary period. It was a perspective that viewed the world in terms of a highly racialized notion of development and progress, where global difference was situated in a hierarchy of races and cultures, in which some (particularly the "West" and the "white race") were temporally farther ahead in time than the Other racial, cultural, national, and civilizational species of the planet. Through the material and ideological arsenal available to the Western powers, which included everything from the diffusive efficiency of print media to the allure and the finality of the language of science, the world was forced into accepting the axioms of this temporal template and to see reality through it. The people of the globe were placed into spatial and temporal islands that were divided along a hierarchical model from low (barbaric, underdeveloped, simple societies) to high (advanced, developed, complex societies) and gave it a stamp of objectivity (laws of nature, laws of progress or history ...) that made it very difficult to imagine or argue outside of its social imaginary. This way of seeing the world became so powerful that people looked around and saw differences, not only in terms of race, culture, and religion, but in terms of time as well. Through this lens people could look across a border and label those on the other side as "distant neighbors," as though they were not just culturally different but also existed in a different time than their own.

The colonial regimes of modernity, as they set themselves to rule over the southern global hemisphere, produced a temporal script that became hegemonic, by forcing all of the agents to negotiate according to the way they structured and perceived their own Self and the Other. Global difference was now situated upon an axiom in which each society, race, nation, civilization, and religion was viewed as an autonomous container, where time moved in accordance to the internal life span of each "national" or "civilizational" specie. But what made this colonial template hegemonic is not that it forced itself upon all of its presumed subspecies but rather that it was protean in nature. As we will discuss, this temporal template did not travel from the colonizer to the colonized unchanged. Indeed, as it moved through geographical space and through multiple layers of power, upon landing in its new home, it was altered so as to make it of utility to its new owner. Indeed, the awesome and alluring power of this temporal template lay in the fact that by structuring time in an evolutionary (cultural or biological) manner, it created the ideological space for less powerful male elites of the global southern hemisphere to pull it out of the colonizer's strong grip and use it as a leverage against their own Others.

Its racial and cultural meaning can thus be used and reproduced in different contexts. We will discuss a number of sites in which this temporal template was sequestered from the colonizer, only to be used later by the colonized elites toward their own Others. Jewish nationalists, upon receiving their own political container, seized the racialized temporal template from the anti-Semite so as to use it against Palestinians and Sephardic Jews. Jordanians similarly would snatch it from their British colonizers and use it to distance the "modern" Jordanian from his Bedouins. So can the Lebanese Christian elite use it against a Muslim majority, in order to claim a leading position to rule the state. Kemalist, secular Arab nationalist, and Islamist male elites, the three movements we will cover in detail, would also clutch it from the hands of the colonizer and use it to sequester power over their own women and others. Although we don't cover it here, the temporal template can be further removed from the original site of power and be used by more subaltern actors, like women, Palestinians, Bedouins, and others, as they attempt to relieve themselves of some of the repression that the more powerful have applied against them. Indeed, this can be done at the very micro level, where the discourse swirls through the public arena and is captured in the minutest situational details.

But just as it is protean in its functioning, this temporal template also restricts the social and political imaginary in which all of these movements and subjects act. Colonial temporality creates a frame through which we see global difference and power, producing certain boundaries of how far we can stretch our view of the world. If it were a completely free-for-all type of discourse, power would not be able to grip the material world but only capture empty air. Edward Said (1979) captured this well in his discussion of the power of certain Orientalist scripts. In his provocative thesis, knowledge of global difference doesn't just explain an inert, pre-given reality called the Orient, the Middle East, Islam, or the West. It produces these constructs so as to structure and *produce* knowledge of Self and Other. In this sense, it is not just a stereotype, as some have misunderstood Said to be saying, because that assumes an essential difference that exists before the "unfair judgment" was ever made. Rather, having the power to produce knowledge of Self and Other creates a file in which we can archive and inventory the world of difference. In other words, global binary civilizational categories like "Islam and the West" were not just "out there" waiting for a historian or social scientist to inventory and describe, but rather, they had to be first produced by knowledge agents who had enough institutional power to make the idea of a "Western" or an "Islamic" civilization stick. It was only after they had been constructed as antithetical, "different" cultures, each having its distinct space-time, separate from the other, that we were able to archive the world and give it a logic that eventually seemed self-evident. If you asked a tenth-century Parisian if she lived in a "Western" civilization, for instance, she would no doubt have difficulty comprehending what precisely such a culture is. This would also be the case when asking a Muslim in the same century living in Damascus or Tehran if he lived in an "Islamic civilization." This is because people's identities were difficult to insert into such large geographical worlds because there were few institutional channels through which to produce such an "imagined community."[6]

To make this clear for my students, I use a personal example of one of the first times I was exposed to a script. It happened when my family moved from Jordan to the United States, when I was eight years old. My seven-member family bought a home in New Jersey that was too small. The house was more suitable for a family of two or three at the most. It had a private septic tank that was not attached to a public sewage system. The tank was too small to meet the needs of our large family, and it overflowed when used too much, creating, as you might suspect, an unpleasant odor in the front yard. So my parents made a rule: Flush the toilet only after having a bowel movement. Thus, it became second nature to me not to flush the toilet after I urinated. This sometimes created problems when I visited homes of people who did not have this issue with their plumbing. Upon visiting one of my first friends in the United States, I used their toilet and didn't flush after urinating. My friend noticed this and complained to his mother, who politely said, "in this country we flush our toilet." Hence, what was simply a plumbing issue in the mind of my family was archived by my friend's mother as an issue of "cultural difference." I bring up this example not to bemoan a stereotype that was used against me, but because I think it highlights well how racial (or cultural) scripts actually work.

Many academics, in a more sophisticated fashion, no doubt archive the world in the same way my friend's mother did, without even realizing it. In the first chapter, I touch upon the issue of honor killing, which is assumed to be a characteristic of cultures deemed as having "honor" codes, which allows criminal justice systems to produce new files that academics can return to and operationalize in their studies. Take the hypothetical example of a "white" Danish man and a "Muslim" Danish man who have both killed their daughters to hide the shame of incest. The police, during their investigation, were able to conclude that this was an incest crime for the white male but were unable to conclude the same for the Muslim male, because the criminal justice system recognized the cultural difference category called "honor killing." The construct was applicable *only* to the Muslim man. As the prosecution for both men proceeds and they are both found guilty of murder, one is filed as an incest crime and the other as an honor crime. Future academics, studying the issue of honor crime, when collecting their data will be able "to show numerically" that honor crime exists on a much greater scale for the Muslim community than it does for "white" Danes. Notice how once a trait is defined as "cultural," belonging to a particular community, the entire group is marked as different from the Danish nation. The opposite, when the white Danish man kills his daughter because of incest, no such grand marking is produced, leaving whites protected from blame because here it is defined essentially as an act of an individual.

This, in its simplest description, is the power of knowledge at work to produce and filter our social and political reality. In Edward Said's brilliant words, "Knowledge no longer requires application to reality; knowledge is what gets passed on silently, without comment, from one text to another. Ideas are propagated and disseminated anonymously, they are repeated without attribution; they have literally become *idees recues*: what matters is that they are *there,* to be repeated, echoed, and re-echoed uncritically."[7].

But what is even more interesting in this example of honor killing is the fact that the Muslim father, who knows he killed his daughter so as to hide his shame from the public, prefers to activate the construct of honor killing, simply because it offers him a way to save face and look less shameful in the eyes of others. However shameful killing one's daughter to uphold the honor of your family may be, it surely beats the level of shame felt for killing her because of an act of incest. This is the other side of the story when power meets knowledge. Edward Said defines this as the productive side of the cultural text. It allows its labeled Other to appropriate the construct in its own projects of power. In this sense, the ideas of "Islam" and the "West" become productive, durable cultural constructs of difference and influence people "who were called Orientals as well as those called Occidental, European, or Western; in short, Orientalism is better grasped as a set of constraints upon and limitations of thought.... "[8] In Said's own words:

> It may appear strange to speak about something or someone as holding a *textual* attitude.... People, places, and experiences can always be described by a book, so much so that the book (or text) acquires a greater authority, and use, even than the actuality it describes.... Most important, such texts can *create* not only knowledge but also the very reality they appear to describe. In time such knowledge and reality produce a tradition, or what Michel Foucault calls a discourse, whose material presence or weight, not the originality of a given author, is really responsible for the texts produced out of it....[9]

It creates an archive for categorizing the world's people into files of difference, both culturally and temporally, supplying both the "West" and "Islam" as possessing a certain "mentality, a genealogy, an atmosphere; most important, they allowed Europeans to deal with and even to see Orientals as a phenomenon possessing regular characteristics ... [which] deepened and even hardened the distinction."[10]

The dominant script that this book is interested in covering, however, is what we will call *the colonizer's temporal template.* It is a way of seeing global difference through the category of time. Our next chapter will define this term in more detail, but for now, let's say that by the mid-nineteenth century, with the rise of Social Darwinism to prominence, the reigning idea among intellectual and political elites in the United States and Europe began to take shape around the idea of evolution and progress. These elites made the astonishing claim that the world consisted of a number of races that can be arranged in accordance to an evolutionary model, with some races still in the grips of the time of the "savage" and other races, namely, whites, in another time—that of the more perfected race. This model of seeing difference was so powerful that it produced in the mind a temporal reality that viewed people in the *contemporary* world as existing in different levels of time. It was only with the eruption of anticolonial movements that this lens was partially disturbed when the colonized insisted that they, too, could maneuver "their cultures" into the time of modernity. Rather than wait for racial evolution, real change can happen at the level of culture. As we will see in the coming chapters, this temporal script led to an array of political projects that still deeply haunt us to this day.

Overview of the Book

What I argue in this book is that movements, stretching from Zionists, Iranians, Kemalists, and Arab Nationalists to present day Islamists, can be understood as products of the racial structuration of the colonizer's temporal template. All of these groups, in a variety of ways, are responding to a globalized discourse that can be described as a way of inhabiting and seeing time that is politically, economically, and culturally marked, so that the "West" and "whiteness" is ranked as the superior race/civilization, while its Other, being "stuck" in an Other time, signifies all those qualities and characteristics in a manner exactly opposite to the Occident.[11] The Islamists, having emerged after all of these movements failed on their promise to create socially just and equal societies by emulating the West, would dramatically pull away from this Eurocentric construction of the world by positing Islam as a far superior system in which to nurture and develop their subjects and offering an alternative path, one that has long existed but was abandoned by the "Westoxified" elites of the Muslim world.

The question that comes up as these movements struggle to free themselves from colonial rule and create in its place "new" societies is how to precisely respond to a discourse that posits them as its child. As Europe gained momentum in the eighteenth and nineteenth centuries, and with the eventual fragmentation of the Ottoman Empire in the hands of these new powers, Arabs, Jews, Iranians, Turks, and Islamists would all search for a strategic response that would allow them to "catch up" to the West. These movements developed nationalist projects with the intention of producing "new" Jewish, Arab, Iranian, Turkish, and Muslim subjects that they believed would match, or, in the case of Islamist thinkers, exceed the quality of those modern people in the West. This is where, I believe, the concepts of Modernizing, Occidentalizing, and Orientalizing identities will prove to be of utility in our effort to make sense of the various strategies deployed by the movements in the Middle East in their efforts to "move" their populations "into" the modern world.

The first chapter will use the examples of the World's Columbian Exhibition of 1893 in Chicago and Disney World's Epcot Center of today to discuss the history of the colonizer's temporal template as it moves from racially based Social Darwinism to culturally based notions of "modernization" and "development" so as to see how the decolonized world, in its efforts to give agency to the male elites of the global South, pulled the temporal template from the hands of their former colonial masters in order to have leverage over their own time-space vehicles. In this first chapter we will also provide some sample remnants of this discourse today in such places as the pages of the *New York Times* with the writings of Thomas Friedman as well as in some mainstream feminist circles over the issues of honor killing and gay rights.

In the second and third chapters we will turn our attention to what I call Occidentalizing projects. Here we will look at major Jewish (chapter 2) and Turkish (chapter 3) nationalists like Theodor Herzl and Kemal Ataturk to see how and why they became so thoroughly convinced of the colonizer's gaze and proceeded to remove anything resembling "oriental-like" qualities from their "new" and—once the changes had been made—improved national subjects. These identities "travel" West in their effort to *completely and totally Occidentalize* the self. Working insatiably to remove themselves from the Orient, these Occidentalizers never look to return to their "original" self, which is now deemed, in its entirety, as a barrier to modernity. This is the path Kemalists, Zionists, and the Pahlavi regime of Iran prefer: Here both the public (exterior) and the private (interior) spheres are viewed by Zionists, Turkish nationalists, and prerevolutionary Iranian nationalists alike as in need of major changes, to be transformed and remade in the image of the West. According to this Occidentalizing paradigm, the nation needs to be radically de-Orientalized or de-Islamized before it can move forward in history. In other words, all "Oriental-like" qualities must be purged and replaced with new—more improved—"Occidental-like" cultural traits. According to these nationalists, transforming the exterior of the nation without also overhauling the interior, Oriental/Islamic characteristics of the nation is doomed to fail and "keep" them lingering in the waiting room of history. If the nation is to be successful like the West and move diligently along the tracks of time, it has to be made, through the disciplinary power of the state, to behave, act, dress, and even speak like those in the Occident.

In the fourth chapter of this book, we will look at how Arab nationalists in the early and mid-twentieth century created what I'd like to call cultural schizophrenia, where they looked admirably toward the West and proceeded to assimilate things they defined as universal values and belonging to *all* "modern" men and "reforming" those Arab and Islamic cultural practices that seemed obsolete, so as to make their new nations more in line with what they understood to be the needs of the modern world. Here I'd like to take Partha Chatterjee's (1993a and b) influential analysis of Indian nationalism and critically apply it to the ways specific Arab, Turkish, Jewish, and Islamist movements responded to this new reality. According to Chatterjee, many postcolonial nationalists understood their new polities as divided into two domains, "the material and the spiritual." The material, he argues, "is the domain of the 'outside,' of the economy and of government, of science and technology, a domain where the West has proved its superiority," and the Indian nation must now adopt it as its own. "The spiritual," on the other hand, "is the 'inner' domain, bearing the 'essential' marks of cultural identity."[12] According to him, the anticolonial movements, in order to challenge the colonizer, produced an "inner sphere" that they understood to represent their "authentic" time-immemorial culture, one that must never, they asserted, be polluted and must be maintained in a state of purity at all costs. The nation, in the view of these nationalists, can therefore only appropriate the exterior realm in its production of a response to the global North, leaving the imagined authentic "indigenous" interior untouched. But I'd like to complicate his analysis in two ways: First, it seems that Chatterjee, when I turn my attention to the Middle East, may have overstated the argument that these nationalists, in their quest to challenge the colonizer's hegemony, created a closed inner sphere so as to protect it from contamination. It seems to me that Arab nationalists, those who fit most closely to Chatterjee's Indian counterparts, were not interested in protecting their Arab "traditions" but were open to the possibility of scrutinizing their past so as to select "proper" Arab and Islamic practices from those deemed "archaic." Second, I'd like to revise his thesis a bit by arguing that there were, not just one, but three very different responses by the anticolonialist movements. Whereas Arab nationalists come close to his analysis, there are in fact two distinct responses that the other movements have used toward this end. In this book I will introduce how Zionists, Kemalists, Iranians, and Islamists differ dramatically from the Indian case Chatterjee describes. Although he opened up a form of analysis that allowed many of us to break free from past essentialist ways of talking and analyzing the Third World, we now have to deepen his contribution by critically analyzing movements that tried to either assimilate entirely into colonial modernity (Kemalists, Pahlavist, and Zionist) or to disassociate themselves from the most stark Eurocentric elements of the colonizer's template (Islamists).

The Islamist response, which will be discussed in chapter 5, will attempt to further deepen and critique Chatterjee's analysis. These identities travel East in what I call the Orientalization path of Islamic militants. Here both the private and public spheres are defined as the interior, so that for these religious militants neither sphere may fall prey to Westernization/Occidentalization. This is the path Sayyid Qutb, Ayatollah Khomeini, Ali Shariati, and Osama bin Laden prefer. It's a form of identity that directly challenges the Kemalist, Zionist, Pahlavi, and Arab nationalist forms, by suggesting that the nation needs to be cleansed completely from the toxins of Westernization and secularization and instead asks the nation to look "back" to the Medinan period *in order for it to move forward.* Rather than Occidentalizing the nation's identity, this path advocates instead a process of Islamization/Orientalization. For the Islamists, both the private and the public spheres are completely collapsed and are "cleansed" of any Western contamination. Thus, no distinction between private and public is needed, for Islam is a total unity of life, so they say. Everything from governance and science to the minutest everyday practices of child rearing and the body needs to be Islamized. If the Islamic *Umma* is to return to its glorious past of the rightly guided Muslim community of the seventh century, it has to be made—through the reinstallation of Allah's sovereignty—to behave, dress, and pray like the original seventh-century Medinan community. Only by adapting the Straight Path of the faith in its entirety, they argue, will the nation ever truly attain the future that it surely seeks.

In chapter 6 we will turn our attention on how these varying projects impacted the category of gender. Nowhere are the consequences of these new competing identities felt more than in the construction of gender. The consequences of the emergence of these new temporal categories, I will argue, had specific ramifications on the construction of gender in the region, specifically, as we shall see, in terms of the nationalist and Islamist responses to this new colonial reality. In attempting to "recover" from their subordinated position, the leaders of these movements believed that with a little help from their newly established vanguardist state, a new Arab, Jew, Turk, and Iranian could be produced *only if their women were properly developed.* Gender was central to this modernization project, where Kemalists, Zionists, and the Pahlavi regimes all used the discourse of "modernizing the woman" and "the progress of woman" as status displays of "*how European and civilized we've become.*" Indeed, the progress of the nation was measured and evaluated against the perceived liberation of Western women. This is slightly different than the gendered discourse used by Arab nationalists in Egypt, Jordan, Syria, and Iraq and radically different than that used by present-day Islamists. For the Arab nationalist, "modernizing the woman" was also used as a status display, but this time to demonstrate "*how well our religion and traditional culture can accommodate itself to the modern world.*" The Islamists, on the other hand, decided to negate the language of progress altogether and refused to use such discourse as a status display. In stark contrast to the other two modernizing movements, Islamists understood the discourse of "modernizing the women" as a symbol of a lost authenticity, of "*how far we've been corrupted.*" But in all three instances, nationalists and Islamists have all appropriated gender as a way to represent the kind of moral and modern nation that they need to become by *using* the woman as a sign of how effectively they have used the time machine. Occidentalizing nationalists, in constructing a nation that is made to look civilized, modern, and European, represent women as liberated by the nationalist vanguard, using a civilizational discourse that is highly racialized. Orientalizing nationalists, on the other hand, construct the nation as contaminated by an impure woman that needs to be replaced with a morally righteous Muslim woman. In this sense, they are all using a discourse that is highly gendered, where women become the symbols of men's desire to procure a society in which they rule. No matter which of the three we choose to look at, the symbol of woman is appropriated in a number of ways to legitimize the authority of male elites.

The book will end by citing at least three ways of thinking about change that do not fall prey to the political and social imaginary that the colonial and nationalist elites use to rule over their Others. This will mean creating epistemologies of change that free us of the time-space box of colonial modernity. The book will conclude by suggesting that we will need a political and social imaginary that allows for a symbiotic relationship between Self and Other so as to make it difficult for any hegemonic power to rule unjustly over its constituent parts.

Chapter 1

The Colonizer's Time Machine and the Discourse of "Becoming Modern"

> Look all over the globe, it is always the same; dark races stand still, the fair progress.
>
> —*Robert Knox, 1850*

> To me, the experience of visiting this place [the Kalahari] and these people was profoundly important, as if I had voyaged into the past through a time-machine. I feel that I saw the Old Way, the way of life that shaped us. . . .
>
> —*Elizabeth Marshall Thomas, 2006*

The Colonizer's Temporal Template

FOR SOME TWO CENTURIES NOW, many of us have imagined global diversity ranging along a historically hierarchical trajectory, as though it were a sloped, ever-ascending mass movement of humanity where cultures, although existing side-by-side at the very same moment, could be located at different points of time. By simply cruising the world, this highly racialized perspective offered the alluring promise that we could see not only humanity's great cultural diversity but its historical diversity as well. It makes it seem as though H. G. Wells really invented his time machine to allow us, as we travel across the world's different cultural landscapes, to visit places of "far-away time."

Americans can cross their southern border and visit their "distant neighbor," as one book's title advertizes. Or we could visit, as a travel promotional brochure claims, Morocco and encounter, on camel back, "ancient ruins" and an "age-old culture," where "life is much as it was centuries ago." Those who accepted this temporal social imaginary believed that they could, at this very moment, for instance, stand in Manhattan, look toward Iran, and declare, because it is ruled by Mullahs, that it is "still feudal" and "stuck" in the fourteenth century, with the slightest hint in the irony of such a claim. They do, of course, realize that Mexico, Morocco, and Iran are all here in their very present. But because of their linear temporal perspective, which separates "societies" as containing their own space and time, this time-like travel myth has, over the past couple centuries, become the dominant frame through which we see difference, to the level that we have now become accustomed to seeing cultures or civilizations as possessing their own launching pads, with some unable to ignite their engines and others being deep into the way yonder.

In this sense, our minds have been colonized by a nineteenth-century, if not earlier, temporal dogma that there exists a linear historical progress to which all "societies"—although at radically different speeds and at varying points of times—must travel through before reaching modernity. This dominant temporal lens makes it appear that some may "still" be at a "traditional," or agricultural/rural phase, while others are "nearer" to modernity, living in the Middle Ages or feudal-like societies. But as soon as "they" get their true renaissance or religious and secular reformers—their equivalents of "our" philosophes, scientists, artists, human rights activists, and Luthers—they too can join the more "advanced" societies.

As we will see, this temporal lens, with its peculiar epistemological ways of seeing the world of difference—in which "they" are in a time of "our" past—has been only slightly revised in the hands of the colonized, with much of it being accommodated by the political and intellectual elites—both secular and Islamists alike. Whereas the colonizer constructed this historical imagination in their desire to dominate the global South, so as to make it appear that their rule over the natives was a natural result of history's call for the realization of rationality, the Spirit, democracy, the liberation of women, or human rights, the colonized scrambled to re-narrate this same discourse, so as to place themselves as the vanguards for the emancipation of their societies. By removing the colonizers from their midst and replacing them with "indigenous" leaders who have the best interest of their people in mind, they will be well-positioned, so they claim, to deliver their societies—which they admit are "still" in the grips of a stagnant mentality—to this glorious future. As Ali Mirsepassi recently argued, the colonizer's gaze "defines contemporary conditions in the [colonized] in terms of abstracted conditions of European historical experience" where the colonized are positioned to embody "aspects of Europe's past (feudalism, etc.) ... [with] the assumption that ... Europe has experienced this path in advance of the non-Western world."[1] In order to make this cosmology of time work for the anticolonial elites, they had to remanufacture this evolutionary and stageist schemata so as to make it feasible to claim that, in the hands of an enlightened elite, they could fix their launching equipment and place a more powerful engine that would propel them through time at a greater speed.

Recently, while I was roaming Epcot Center during a visit to Disney World in central Florida with my family, I was able to see the persistence of this colonizer's narration of cultural differences along this continuum of time. Here I could see how glaringly this triumphalistic vision of an evolutionary and stageist view of the globe has been put on display as an entertainment spectacle—a site not unlike any other major pilgrimage center, except instead of a religious communion, folks here can come together and experience the rites of passage from traditional to modern society. It could be a coincidence that, in 2004, I visited Disney World's Epcot Center shortly after I had read about Chicago's World's Columbian Exhibition of 1893, but the timing couldn't have been better. As I walked through Epcot Center, it seemed like I was in the middle of a plagiarized text that had been written more than one hundred years earlier.

Epcot Center is organized by two central themes. On one side sits Future World which depicts a "highly developed" civilization, composed of science, technology, and progress. This side of the park contains science exhibits and rides like Spaceship Earth, in which passengers travel through time "from the dawn of man to the future." Here, Europe and the United States represent the civilizational location in which science, philosophy, and secularism are assumed to have been invented and, over time, diffused to far-away worlds.

The narrative suggests that only during the Dark Ages have other, particularly Islamic, civilizations lent a hand to the enterprise of human development. The speaker pauses when the ride approaches the stage of Europe's

Photo 1.1 Map of Epcot featuring all of the rides and exhibitions in both Future World and World Showcase, including the bridges that connect both sides.

Dark Ages, when Rome, because of the Gothic, Barbarian attacks, was burning and experiencing a moment of deep illness—a sort of midlife crisis that "Western civilization" was experiencing. But, as we pass into the next display, the narrator says, "But not all was lost. The torch of light was secured by the Muslims of the East" which, he continued, held on to the torch *until* Europe was prepared to take it back, once it had, with the coming of the Renaissance, recovered its health.

Notice here that the manner in which Epcot's thematic structure incorporates the Other within its storyline of progress maintains the prevalent sense that "Islamic civilization" is marginal to the developmental trajectory, in essence acting only to *safeguard* "our" torch of progress, which appears to have been detained in some sort of midlife crisis during the Dark Ages. Once "we" have recuperated from this temporary illness, the Islamic Other simply hands the torch back to its rightful owner, *unchanged,* and the West continues on its path of enlightenment and progress, developing its science, its printing, its philosophy, and its creative arts. It is also interesting to note that the passengers on this ride sit in a moving vehicle that consistently *climbs upward as they pass through time* until they reach the final destination, where AT&T lights up the entire globe and all of man is united under a single beam of light.

Moreover, upon exiting Spaceship Earth and proceeding to the other sectors within this scientific and technological side of the park, one is in constant interaction with hi-tech gadgets and robotic machines. Even the cafés are called "Innoventions," and the shops directly outside the futuristic rides are filled with space creatures and battery- and electronic-run toys and other technological paraphernalia. By contrast, on the other side of the park, where the World's Showcases can be reached by crossing a bridge over a body of water, one may visit many "traditional folk cultures," such as Moroccan, Native American, and Chinese. Here, the visitor is invited to explore other cultures within suggested representative spaces. Morocco, for example, is showcased in part inside of a Mosque, where one can shop and experience the Orient, meeting such figures as Aladdin and observing a sensuous belly dancer perform on stage to Arabic music. In this location, one will have a hard time finding hi-tech gadgets to interact with. Instead, the toys available in these shops are in the form of camels, fezzes, oriental rugs, belly dancing outfits, pyramids, multiple types of plastic swords, and Mummy games and mugs. Indeed, rather than interacting with computers and robots, when it comes to Morocco one has the pleasure of interacting with a belly dancer.

Although it is true that more "advanced" societies like Norway, France, and the United States appear on this side as well, they are usually represented in both their youthful and mature stages, such as the simple Norwegian village or in the shops of Paris, where one can buy "modern" gadgets, like replicas of the Eifel Tower. The Other civilizations are, in contrast, always represented as static, non-evolving entities stuck in a past time through which the West has already traveled. It is taken for granted that those societies belonging to the West that are on this side of the park have evolved and crossed the bridge of modernity to the Future World side of the park, whereas the Others remain in an earlier time.

Thus Disney World, obsessively embodying themes of progress and the future, is an iconic representation of our racialized discourse regarding civilization and progress, providing a Eurocentric understanding of modern global history as entertainment. In a sense, it offers a popular version of the colonizer's model of the world, deploying a clear distinction between the

Photos 1.2 & 1.3 Spaceship Earth at Epcot is an AT&T production, illustrating the ascent of communication from caveman to the world of the future.

Photos 1.4 & 1.5 On the Futureworld side of the park guests interact with computers and robots while on the World Showcase side they dance with a belly dancer in the Moroccan exhibition.

Photo 1.6 On the World Showcase side of the park "Western" cultures are represented along with the others, but they exist in their "folk culture" and childhood before traveling over the bridge into modernity and adulthood.

rational, scientific, enlightened, and "developed" nations of Western civilization and the undeveloped, particularistic, religious, sensuous, and emotional civilizations of Islam and all Others. This narrative implies, implicitly, that the global South sits far behind the West, not because of a historical system organized on an unequal foundation, but simply because of the distinctive political and social characteristics "we" in the West possess.

It is not that such a representation is untrue to history, where obviously steam engines and industry did become most visible in what has come to be called "the West," but presenting it as originating from the heart of Western civilization removes how the Other parts of the world—those who labored in the plantation and slave systems in the colonies—created the fuel through which Europe "rose" to prominence. Reducing the world into autonomous space-time islands of civilizations is an ideological construct by the colonizer to legitimize his rule over the racial hierarchy such a global system is structured around. In this sense, Disney-reality fits nicely into a political project that posits the West as superior to any other past or present civilizational model and, thus, legitimates the extreme inequalities among peoples, civilizations, and nations. This temporal apparatus produces in the mind an answer to the puzzle of why we are wealthier and more powerful, marginalizing or removing all possible other explanations.

Disney's stark imitation of the World's Columbian Exposition of 1893 is stunning. The first thing you'll notice is what the two theme parks, although more than a century apart, share in common. In both Epcot and in the World's Columbian Exposition, "progress" is presented as having been made more acutely on one side of the world, while those on the Other side remained static and frozen in time. This Orientalist representation of the world is, as Edward Said has argued, not new. For Said, "In the system of knowledge about the Orient, the Orient is less a place than a *topos,* a set of references, a congeries of characteristics, that seems to have its origin in a quotation, or a fragment of a text, or a citation from someone's work on the Orient, or some bit of previous imagining, or an amalgam of all these."[2] Orientalism is, after all, defined by its constant urge to plagiarize past texts.[3] Long before the arrival of Disney World, the organizers of Chicago's World Fair, much like future Disney *Imagineers,* divided their exhibition into two categories that looks almost identical to Epcot. Here, the civilized white sector of the city's exhibition, with its commerce, advanced manufacturing, iron, and steel, displayed buildings of Manufacture, Art, Administrations, Machinery, and Electricity, in contrast to the primitive villages of Samoans, Egyptians, Dahomans, Turks, and others.[4] Indeed, as in Epcot, there was a spatial and temporal divide between the civilized and primitive sectors of the Exhibition, and in order to go from one to the other, one had to leave the white man's city and enter through another gate in order to reach the colored man's world.

Of particular note is how, in the World's Colombian Exposition, as well as in Disney's Epcot Center, the industrial, modern, scientific-rational Self is distanced from the Other, both spatially and temporally. Although non-Western and Western civilizations exist on the planet simultaneously, they are constructed as living in different historical times and spaces. The Muslims, in the case of Epcot, live in the time of old Norwegian and German folk cultures, before the latter moved into modernity and evolved into a mature civilization. The Muslims, the Native Americans, and all Others are frozen in time, while the West takes off into space. The Other is distanced from the West, although it actually exists concurrently with it. The implication is that Western civilization, in past epochs, lived in a developmental stage similar to the current stage of Other races and cultures, which are viewed as live examples of a prior Western Self that was in its childhood. However, having evolved and matured into a highly developed human species, the West is understood to have progressed forward in time, *crossing the bridge* to the other, more scientific and mature, side.[5] In short, this Orientalist form of representation "has the explicit purpose of distancing those who are observed from the time of the observer, a denial of coeval time."[6] As one *Chicago Tribune* reporter of the 1893 World's Fair put it in his reflection of the exhibitions, "What an opportunity was here afforded to the scientific mind to descend the spiral of evolution, tracing humanity in its highest phases down almost to its animalistic origins."[7] Others were similarly showing exuberance for the opportunity to witness life as it had "been led by our faraway ancestors or predecessors in the earliest Stone Age."[8] As Raymond Corbey suggests, "World fairs ... were part of a ... landscape of discourse and practice, providing a cultural technology for situating metropole and colony within a single analytic field, thus creating an imagined ecumene."[9] The colonizer's template made the Other appear to belong to an earlier developmental stage, from which it had a great distance to travel before it could reach a level that whites, or American and Europeans, inhabit. "Colonial others were incorporated narratively.... They were assigned their roles in the stories told by museum exhibitions, world fairs, and colonial postcards. They were cast as contemporary ancestors ..."[10] This is also why today a writer from the United States visiting the Kalahari desert could describe her journey in the following manner:

> We found people who called themselves Ju/wasi and were living a lifestyle of our ancestors, a lifestyle of the African savannah that began before we were human beings, changing in form but not in essence as time passed ... To me, the experience of visiting this place and these people was profoundly important, as if *I had voyaged into the past through a time-machine.* I feel that I saw the Old Way, the way of life that shaped us ... [11]

Obviously this author is reminiscing about a lost, innocent past and not offering a demeaning denunciation of those she observed, as did past unapologetic

Social Darwinists. But in her liberal pleasures for her search of an age of innocence, she turns the African savannah into an untouched wilderness that has not been scourged by colonial modernity, one that many analysts of coloniality would contest as a racialized representation that hides the activities of past military, capitalist, and nationalist escapades.

But returning to our analysis of theme parks, it is important to emphasize the *differences* between the 1893 World's Columbian Exhibition in Chicago and today's Epcot. This difference, I argue, has much to do with the move from a biological, racialized form of historical change, as it was understood by Social Darwinists in the nineteenth century, to our own period, in which time is culturalized and perceived to be located in different levels of cultural and political development from "traditional" to "modern" societies. For us, those differences mark the change that the anticolonial movements of the twentieth century brought to our concepts of historical change. The differences are politically very significant, indeed, where in the earlier World's Fair, under the influence of Social Darwinism, the divide was literally a racial and biological one in which "organizers divided the World's Fair into two racially specific areas," with "the White City depicted the millennial advancement of white civilization while the Midway Plaisance, in contrast, presented the undeveloped barbarism of uncivilized, dark races."[12] This would change quite dramatically as a result of a "development" cultural model, pushed in large part by the anticolonial movements who wanted to free themselves from Western colonial regimes. Instead of Social Darwinism, they would put in place an alternative version for understanding this evolution, where one's culture and his capacity to use science, tools, and technology was now understood as the defining criteria upon which his advancement could be measured.[13] Epcot would incorporate this new "postcolonial" script, in my view, offering it a popular normalized site to call its home.

Although the similarities between the two theme parks are interesting for what they tell us about what the general manner of a linear temporal model of development says about the construction of a hierarchy of differences, their differences are also very telling. Epcot offers some differences from its 1893 predecessor in details, like a bridge that *connects* the World Showcase with the future- and scientific-oriented other side of the theme park, as compared with the exiting gate of the 1893 World's Fair, which *separated* savage societies from the civilized people. However, the temporal template that ranks and locates societies on a linear scale of time is evident in both theme parks. That is, in the old version, as illustrated in the example of the 1893 World's Fair, the distance between the civilized White City and all its Others was a racial fact, owing to a Darwinian-inspired schemata, where the "advanced white races worked toward a perfect civilization,"[14] whereas in the Epcot example, by contrast, what divided the two—and what needed a bridge rather than an exiting and reentering gate—was the level of technology a culture was able to display to the world. Indeed, this change was made possible, as we will see, by the struggle of the colonized to rearticulate social Darwinism into a tool that they could use to acquire state power and place them as the new civilizer's of their own people.

This is what I call the colonizer's temporal template, a way of seeing time and the Other that will have a tremendous impact on the way the colonized, in

Photo 1.7 The bridge that connects Future World with the World Showcase side. In my view, this represents a shift away from a racial distinction made in the nineteenth century period of Social Darwinism to a modernizationist model of cultural change that anticolonial movements inspired after World War II.

their attempt to emancipate themselves from the colonizer, understood social change and progress, leading them to think that the only way they could join modernity is through massive cultural, political, and technological overhaul of their societies. As we will see in our comparison of three different kinds of responses to this colonizer's gaze in the Middle East, the colonizer's time of the Other was strategically revised in a number of ways, yet remaining loyal to it as well. Kemalism and Zionism, in their efforts to push "their people" forward in time accepted the narrative almost wholeheartedly and proceeded to eradicate what they perceived as "archaic" characteristics of their Jewish and Turkish cultures, while Arab Nationalists, with a similar desire to get their people to "catch up" to the West, negotiated a more cultural schizophrenic approach on how to appease the colonizer's gaze. But, so, too, as we will investigate, did the Islamists, who likewise wanted to improve their societies. But in order to move forward in time, they prescribed the eradication of Western contamination and reintroduced the prophetic stage, which, they believed, if it weren't corrupted and just had been left alone and remained true to itself—and if the colonizer and their local Arab coconspirators hadn't intervened with their toxic morality—would have produced a "true" Islamic civilization. In this sense, all three movements shared the same temporal epistemology that the colonizer delivered to the region in the nineteenth century.[15]

But before we move on to look at how the colonized appropriated this colonizer's temporal template, it is advantageous to see its earlier manifestation as it was devised in nineteenth-century Europe. In part, this book is a study of the formation and growth of a profoundly influential fiction that many began to accept as true in the period that began with the flowering of global colonialism and Social Darwinism and lasted from the nineteenth century to the present. As Johannes Fabian's analysis of modern anthropology suggests, the two examples of the 1893 World Fair and the contemporary Epcot, existing more than a century apart, seemed to play a bigger role than simply being an attempt by the colonizer to understand the Other's culture. Instead they constructed their "Other in terms of topoi implying distance, difference, and opposition," where their "intent was above all ... to construct ordered Space and Time—a cosmos—for Western society to inhabit."[16]

This temporal distantiation of Western civilization from the Other made it tolerable, even necessary, *to live* and inhabit a world of extreme political and economic inequality. Indeed, the ranking of the globe's diverse populations, especially after the Social Darwinist Herbert Spencer published his double treatise of "Primitive Man—Emotional" and "Primitive Man—Intellectual" (1876), became so commonsensical that by the turn of the twentieth century it seemed second nature to declare the "savage as a creature of retarded development: the savage had 'the mind of a child and the passions of a man'."[17] The colonizer's racialized discourse, in essence, made it possible to juxtapose white men with black men, with the former seen as being able to inherit a biological or cultural advantage from their ancestors, thereby rationalizing why they, the West, hold the torch of light over all Other races and civilizations. This is precisely also why "Black men, in contrast, might struggle as hard as they could to be truly [civilized], without success. They were primitives who could never achieve true civilized manliness because their racial ancestors had never evolved that capacity."[18]

The discursive roots of this colonizer's temporal template can be found in earlier centuries, but by the nineteenth, it fully blossomed, when intellectuals and statesmen alike began to use it with ease, acquiring a commonsensical way of seeing Self and Other. The template allowed prominent philosophers like Hegel to declare that "China and India lie, as it were, still outside the World's history" and that "The Egyptians are vigorous *boys,* eager for self-comprehension, who require nothing but clear understanding of themselves in an ideal form, in order to become *Young Men.*"[19] For Hegel, such civilizations were retrograde, which the *Geist* had long deserted and moved West in its historical march to find true consciousness.[20] "Europe is 'plainly' the goal of history.... The Orientals were the childhood of the world, the Greeks and Romans in its youth and manhood, the Christian people are its maturity'."[21] In the American context, the template made it possible for president Theodore Roosevelt to define Africa and other such "primitive" continents as "waste spaces" in need of a civilized race to set it on the straight path of evolution, spaces that Roosevelt defines as being "void of meaningful human activity" and in need of a people "ready to put them to good use."[22] This temporal template also underlay the literary narrative of the *North American Review,* which "declare[d] with no lack of confidence that the majority of the inhabitants of the British West Indies 'are incapable of independent progress. They can advance only under the pressure of the vigorous influences of northern civilization; without this contract they degenerate and regress'."[23]

By the nineteenth century, terms like *savage, primitive, traditional, underdeveloped,* and *medieval* came to denote the Other "as a fossil of an earlier period,"[24] who are understood to possess a "whole range of attributes" such as being superstitious and reactionary, whereas the European "represented themselves as rational, energetic, in control, progressive-minded, disciplined, punctual, and efficient."[25] What is important to note here is that by positing the Other as located in a distant past, this new way of framing history was able to provide an ontology that made it appear that the Other *is* distant from the modern self, even though they exist contemporaneously with each other. The colonizer's temporal template, having the power of a gifted magician, actually plays a trick on the mind so as to distantiate the *contemporary* populations of the global South from their Western counterparts in front of the viewer's eye.

By temporalizing the world in this way, the imperial relationship between the colonized and the colonizer was rationalized on the ideological basis that the less-evolved Other is not "mature" or "developed" enough for self-rule. As Jacobson sums up the ethos of this generation of American travelers and statesmen, the Other is so drastically "behind" on the evolutionary scale that "we are not beholden to treat them as equals" and we must instead civilize them "in this long process of helping them along."[26]

This temporal lens was an ingenious new social technology for rationalizing the colonial encounter. As Dipesh Chakrabarty has persuasively argued, "Within this thought, it could always be said with reason that some people were less modern than others, and that the former needed a period of preparation and waiting before they could be recognized as full participants in political modernity."[27] He defines this as "the waiting room version of history," where the colonized appear to be lingering in an evolutionary or developmental stage of immaturity, which, with time—and a whole lot of proper rearing by a benevolent superior—will acquire enough maturity and wisdom to join other civilized and advanced peoples. Until then, because the colonized are not yet ready to be left on their own, they must "wait" until they prove to their superiors that they have matured enough. Indeed, what made possible this idea of a waiting room is a temporal scheme of distancing the Other and denying its coevality with more "advanced" civilizations.[28] That is, once the global South was ruled and administered by Western countries, there emerged alongside this new power reality a discourse that placed the Other as a form of property that, with the philosophical interventions of John Locke and John Stuart Mill, was looked upon as land lying unused, awaiting a mature and able soul to make it productive.[29]

The example Chakrabarty provides is John Stuart Mill, who, in his classic texts "On Liberty" and "On Representative Government," claims that in order for the Indians and Africans to be permitted the highest ideals of self-rule, "some historical time of development and civilization (colonial rule and education, to be precise) had to elapse before they could be considered prepared for such a task" and thereby assigning all "rude nations" a waiting period, because they were far from "arriving" at the level appropriate for such privileges. In this temporal imagination it was the colonizer alone who had the rights for self-rule, simply because some "people were to arrive earlier than others."[30] Mill rationalized his argument on the grounds that Europeans had already reached the stage in which they "had 'attained the capacity of being guided to their own improvement by conviction or persuasion'," and "he thought that India, China and 'the whole East' ... had been 'stationary for thousands of years'."[31] Given the fact that "non-Europeans," Mill continues, "were moral and political infants, and thus below the age of consent, a 'parental despotism' by a 'superior people' was perfectly 'legitimate' and in their own long-term interest" for it will "facilitate their transition to a 'higher stage of development'."[32]

Of course, any hierarchy of civilization predicated on skull size, the level of technological gadgets, the quantity of books published, a country's GNP, and so forth is based on the Western, temporalized conceptualizations of global diversity used to legitimate the unequal relationship between colonizer and colonized. Using such standards for measuring the worth of the globe's populations[33] not only legitimized the increasing massive disparities of wealth between the colonizer and the colonized, but also explained why the latter ought to determine whose political structure is civilized, whose human rights are to become the universal standards for the entire globe, and which civilizations or countries are "mature enough" to possess nuclear weapons. That is, placing a temporal template that makes us see the world in terms of differentially and hierarchically located cultures, religions, and civilizations, naturalizes the power relations between the core and periphery, making it appear that the West has more gadgets or a bigger GNP—or the privilege of acquiring weapons of mass destruction and the Others do not—because the West are the adults and the Others are its children. Of course, if the child behaves obediently one may spoil it a bit by giving it a bigger stipend or gadgets to play with, but for the unruly child, strict punishment must be maintained. Indeed, this form of evolutionary cosmology relaxes the colonizer's mind so they can feel self-assured every time they have to beat the child into submission, if not through food and medical boycotts then through military occupation and heavy artillery bombardment.

The Return of the Classical Orientalists: Bernard Lewis, Samuel Huntington, and Thomas Friedman

Unfortunately, there is now a resurgence and a return to the nineteenth century's form of the time machine by Western intellectuals. In the mid-twentieth century West, at the persistence of the anticolonialist movements, a revision of the Social Darwinist model emerged to allow for the possibility of the Other to cross over the bridge of time. Now, once again, the view is emerging that maybe there is something intrinsically dysfunctional about some civilizations so that such crossing, because of the incompatibility of "their" (read Islam) religion to modernity, is not possible at all. Indeed, for many contemporary Western academic writers, such as Bernard Lewis (1990) and Samuel Huntington (1993), crossing over the bridge into modernity means that Islam itself may have to disappear. According to Bernard Lewis, the prophet of Islam and his religion, although having served Muslims well in the premodern world, with some measure of success, now block their development into a better, more civilized world of modernity. Moreover, pundits interpret the rise of contemporary Islamist movements as the natural and essential expression of a religious and civilizational project that stems from some time-immemorial source. This source is characterized as predating modernity and containing a worldview that makes it literally impossible to join the modern civilized world.[34] According to these writers and others, the fact that prior modernization efforts failed in some Islamic regions proves that Islam cannot accommodate itself to the modern world. Indeed, they claim the current conflict between "the West" and "Islam" is due largely to the fact that these are two antithetical civilizations. Islam represents a cultural universe that is in essence antimodern and anti-Western. That is, Muslims, according to this narrative, are culturally indigestible to the modernist project. This is because they have learned traits and mentalities from their seventh-century predecessors in Mecca and Medina that are intrinsically antimodernist.

The problem with this perspective is that it relies on a method that posits "Islam" and the "Muslim world" as containing their own spatial and temporal unity. As I will attempt to show, Islamists, like all of their nationalist predecessors in the Middle East, are engaging in a political project that is exclusively the act of a modern script. The religious symbolism that they use, the appropriation of Koranic text, and the manner by which they select the Prophet Muhammad's *Hadiths* (sayings of the prophet collected over time), is made available to us as it is filtered through the temporal lens that the colonizer made possible more than a hundred years ago. Hence, it is that template, in its modern form, which the Islamists use to interpret key cultural and religious text. Indeed, and what is ironic, is that Orientalists, when interpreting "Islam," confuse this modern lens as the actual lens of some time-immemorial culture in the same way that Islamists do.

Moreover, reading some of the West's most influential thinkers today seems like a revised version of John Stuart Mill's "waiting room of history," where the United States, in its benevolent role as a democratizing agent in a "neighborhood" (read: Middle East) hostile to pluralism and tolerance, if it does its job competently in Iraq, may finally bring modernity to that part of our troubled and backward world by providing a role model for the other Arabs of the region, who remain hopelessly in the grips of despotism. Thomas Friedman, a highly influential *New York Times* best-selling author and journalist among middle-class liberals in the United States, for instance, wrote multiple *New York Times* editorials during the first couple years of the war on Iraq, all the while being in support of the war and only slightly revising his position when American success looked bleak. He assured his readers that "U.S. power is not being used in Iraq for oil, or imperialism, or to shore up a corrupt status quo, as it was in Vietnam and elsewhere in the Arab world during the cold war." Instead, falling back on earlier rhetoric of the White Man's burden, the war is, he asserts, "the most radical-liberal revolutionary war the U.S. has ever launched—a war of choice to install some democracy in the heart of the Arab-Muslim world."[35] If it does fail, he warns his readers, the blame resides partly in the fact that the United States had too few numbers of troops but also because of a time-immemorial "natural tribalism" that defines the Arab world.[36] The discourse of "the heart of the Arab-Muslim world," "the Arab street," or the "infertile soil of the Arab world" are used not unlike the way Social Darwinists rationalized imperial rule during the heydays of imperialism: "In the Arab-Muslim world today the progress-resistant cultural forces seem to be just too strong, especially in Iraq, which is why it is so hard to establish durable democratic institutions in that soil."[37] Indeed, the problem is that "Iraq was already pretty broken before we got there—broken, it seems, by 1,000 years of Arab-Muslim authoritarianism."[38] If there are any fingers to be pointed at the United States, it is that the administration did not prepare the child for it's new civilized way of administrating a democratic society: "Had we properly occupied the country, and begun political therapy," he claims, "it is possible an American iron fist could have held Iraq together long enough to put it on a new course."[39] Again, when reading Friedman one can't help feel it is a plagiarized text taken from some nineteenth-century philosophical work on "the theme of Europe teaching the Orient the meaning of liberty."[40] In Thomas Friedman's own words:

> Iraq was always a struggle of hope against history. After 9/11, and the Arab Human Development Report detailing the increasingly dysfunctional Arab-Muslim world—which produces way too many terrorists—we had a real interest in collaborating with Iraqis to try to build one decent, progressive, democratizing society in the heart of the Arab East.[41]

In short, his analysis falls back on the prescripted Orientalist fantasy that the Arab world is just not mature enough to take up the opportunity that we, the more advanced civilizations of the West, have offered them. Their culture is too tribalistic and feudal, not yet ripe to take advantage of the fruits of civility and modernity. In that sense, Thomas Friedman, as do Bernard Lewis, Samuel Huntington, and the many others whose writings now stock the shelves of our bookstores, share the same episteme of the folks that came before them in the classical imperialist era of the nineteenth century.

The Dialogical Method

The underlying idea behind my book is that the textual and civilizational representations used by Islamists and religious authorities we cover in the chapters to come are products of a global discursive exchange that is expressive of our very present and modern world, of the here and now. To represent the Islamists as "clinging" to a "real" past entity called "pure" Islam requires an Orientalist and colonizing lens that suppresses the dialogical—and very immediate—nature of the actual encounter. Indeed, the method that is contained in a Huntington-Lewis type of analysis takes us back to viewing the world in a manner very similar to the one contained in the 1893 Chicago World Fair, where the Other civilizations and religions are locked in the child's waiting room of history. But this time it's not that their race has to evolve before permitting them to leave their rooms, instead, the complete eradication of their dysfunctional civilization is necessary. Otherwise, Samuel Huntington tells us, there is nothing else we can do but accept the fact that "we" in the West have to hunker down and prepare for a persistent conflict between two antithetical civilizations, one modern and mature and civilized and the Other lost in time, an adolescent who is rebellious and in need of good parenting.

The background methodology of my study is highly influenced by Immanuel Wallerstein's world-systems analysis and Edward Said's notion of a "contrapuntal imagination," in which the researcher remains aware of the dialogical nature in which cultures, civilizations, and religions are narrated and produced. What I find most productive about the methodologies these two provide is that they allow us to apply a new lens in which we could see the dialogical processes at work in which phenomena like "civilizations," religions, and identities do not contain their own temporal and spatial bodies but are instead in constant motion with Others. The time and space of the Other is in fact the very same time and space that "We" inhabit. With this methodology in mind, I hope to show that when Islamists and Arabs or Turks and Israelis produce categories of gender or "tradition," they are doing it through a very modern lens, not through a time-immemorial culture that in some mystical way precedes our present reality. This will become quite clear when we look at, for example, the veil, where it moves from being an unthought customary practice historically to an identitarian symbol of resistance for the colonized in their struggle to deal with the civilizational insult of the colonizer. What for some looks like a "tradition," a time-immemorial religious practice, belonging to "their" culture over there is in fact the product of a very contemporary and unequal exchange of insults on a world scale.

What I find most appealing about this approach is that we are able to see that a nation's (or a religion's, civilization's ...) temporality and spatiality are not isolated within a globe composed of a multiple, yet limited, variety of civilizations, and that to reduce any of them to a crude temporal or spatial island, containing its own *Geist,* is to be fooled by those who have been peddling the time-machine idea. Such a portrayal runs counter to the idea put forward by Wallerstein, Said, and others, that modernity, at the macro level, discursively structures those micro civilizational differences. What appears as an essential expression of difference is in effect the product of power asymmetries that form and constitute those differences.

For those who are entrapped in the temporal and spatial lens that the colonizer invented long ago, each nation, religion, or civilization appears to have its own ethos that is stable within its spatial boundaries and temporal origins. In this sense, the people of a specific group are understood as having a single will, one mind, one race, one Koran, one five-pillars, one masculinist culture, one "unreformed religion" waiting for a Luther or a Newton to bring them into the modern world. The method I am using here allows for an analysis that challenges this highly essentialized notion of difference by positing that all civilizations are the invention of one modernity that all of us, from different locations, are struggling to bend in multiple ways. Such an analysis suggests that actors in different locations of the modern world-system are constrained to act within multiple political containers, which elites mobilize to their advantage through the use of national, religious, and cultural discourses.

Given such strengths, one of the challenges we now ask of world-system scholars is to address the resurgence of colonialist and racist discourses that are emerging in our midst, especially in Europe, the United States, and Israel, three locations where Islamophobia has global political ramifications on a world scale, inciting identitarian politics that are creating, intentionally, a new and lethal social divide between imagined communities. Just as Wallerstein in the 1970s shattered the orthodox theorem that capitalism is reduced to the proletariat-bourgeoisie dichotomies, by illustrating that non-wage labor, including such labor forms as slavery and second-serfdom, are all a product of the world-capitalist system, we also need to shatter present hegemonic discourses that suggest there are certain "cultural systems" that stand outside and even predate modernity. In previous decades, we challenged those who often accorded the industrial working class a leading "historical role" of revolution over other figures of labor (such as peasant labor and reproductive labor). We did so by demonstrating that different labor formations were an intrinsic functioning characteristic of capitalism, rather than being different modes of production belonging to different historical periods of mankind. Similarly, today we must forcefully challenge the belief that Islam stands as the symbol of premodern, feudal society.

As many of us have now recognized, Marxists are not immune to holding this essentialist discourse. The manner by which some Marxists have traditionally dealt with religious movements, especially of the Islamic variant, is congruent with the racist discourse found in Bernard Lewis and Samuel Huntington. The more orthodox variants of Marxist thought tend to see religious identity as "precapitalist," belonging to a primitive, fourteenth-century feudal mentality that has not evolved and caught up with the modern mode of global capital production. Islam, for this strain of Marxism, then, is a preindustrial social structure frozen in time, in which "most people still work in agriculture or in handicraft production." Hence, the lack of a vibrant capitalist class and a vanguard proletariat that moves the system forward, both of which, according to some Marxists, are crucial for modernity, forms the explanation of "what went wrong" and why Islam has been unable to adapt itself to "modernity, industrialization, and representative democracy."[42]

This assertion strikes us as quite odd, for as far as we know, mankind has not yet invented H. G. Wells's time machine. The fact that the holders of this view can characterize and classify people as living in different historical times shows the alluring and racist power of this discourse. As Ali Mirsepassi argues, Marxism does not really differ from liberal or conservative views of the global order because, like its more conservative counterpart, it views history in a linear and evolutionary manner: "The scheme of historical gradation implied in this narrative forecloses the fullness of historical possibility by insisting on the adherence of human practice to an abstract, allegedly scientific, scheme of historical progress."[43] In the same way that Hegel conceptualized Africa as "a continent enclosed within itself ... [where] history is in fact out of the question,"[44] some Marxists, armed with this Orientalist view of history, at times supported nationalist policies that aimed to destroy what they perceived to be archaic institutions acting as obstacles to capitalist or postcapitalist modernity.

What is even more surprising is that some contemporary writers and intellectuals dealing with women's and gay rights seem to be in the grips of the colonizer's template as well. Many so-called progressives are attempting to resolve a whole array of issues—stretching from how we talk about inequalities, gender oppression and patriarchy, "honor killing," FGC (female genital cutting), "tolerance and pluralism," and many other topics—by turning to the colonizer's temporal tool to guide them in framing their emancipatory projects, with many using the usual script of locating the root of the issue in "feudal and patriarchal" relations, where a premodern Arab or Turkish "patriarchy," for instance, is used to explain phenomena like the killing of one's daughter or sister.

Note, for instance, how the anthropologist Clementine Eck, in her book *Purified By Blood: Honor Killings Amongst Turks in the Netherlands,* maneuvers around this culturalized explanation, addressing honor killing as deeply embedded in the immigrant's patriarchal practice. The Turk, by being infected with a historical cultural trait from his homeland, brings with him a practice foreign to our "modern" European culture, the implication being of course that there is something culturally distinctive in his culture that presses men to kill their daughters or sisters when their dignity is at stake. Jealousy killing is posited in such a way that it marks Turks as culturally different than their European counterparts but also temporally behind, practicing a ritual that predates modernity.

Notice also how by culturalizing the killings she creates a category under which data can now be filed and classified. Because honor killing is a Turkish ritual, the police now have access to file it as such, whereas there are no such categories for the remaining Dutch population, whose killings are simply filed into the database as a father/brother killing his daughter/sister. Indeed, the nonimmigrant father or sibling is more likely to be convicted of incest than his Turkish immigrant counterpart simply because the motive has not been culturalized and, thus, open for greater scrutiny. What is most interesting in Eck's analysis of this phenomenon is the way she makes many telling contradictory claims that illustrate the power of the time machine at work in this narrative. Eck is committed to making the issue "stick" so that it is taken more seriously by the Dutch public. She explicitly wants to educate the Netherland's criminal justice system so that it deals more effectively with "honor killing." Indeed, her book seems to be written as a sort of multicultural training manual for the police and the courts so that they are able to better recognize this "foreign" cultural practice. She makes large generalizations about immigrants, assimilation, and Western culture, positing them as temporally and culturally distinct. She also comments on how the Netherlands has to be more effective in providing the immigrants an honorable life, so that they might be more open to "Western culture." Otherwise, they will "cling" to their ancient traditions and act out their honor needs on their women. Moreover, in order to skirt any allegations that her analysis is Islamophobic, she revises the narrative a bit by claiming that the practice is not rooted in Islam but rather in an "ancient tribal or archaic" (Turkish? Arab?) patriarchal practice of controlling women. Interestingly enough, she makes the significant observation that some families might be using honor killing as a rhetorical resource for hiding other issues (like incest), so as to receive a lighter sentence or a relatively more respectable response from their communities, instead of acknowledging the very shameful real reasons for the murders. Instead of analyzing these cases as a product of the social construction of honor killing, where people learn to manipulate *assigned* cultural categories in their situational moments, she leaves these possibilities unexplored and returns to her culturalist and Orientalist analysis, concluding that the Dutch criminal justice system needs *to be able to spot such foreign cultural practices* so as to make sure the victimizer receives a tough sentence for *committing honor killing.*[45]

What is important in this example is the fact that without temporally and spatially distancing the Other, such culturalization of a crime of a foreign immigrant community would not have been possible. In this way, the colonizer's time machine is productive. It *creates* the difference and the divide between "immigrants" and "Dutch/Europeans" in the same way that the bridge and the gates in Epcot and World's Fair function to mark temporal distance globally. Such temporal and spatial distancing becomes part of a nationalist European discourse to separate the pure "modern" self from the contaminants of the Other. *The temporal discourse, therefore, does not simply "deceive" the viewer about reality, it actually produces a visualization in which the difference can be seen.*

This temporal tool can be clearly seen at work in Norma Khouri's book *Honor Lost: Love and Death in Modern-Day Jordan* (2003), which received high acclaim from a number of news sources like *The Jerusalem Post, Kirkus Review, The Weekly Standard,* and *Toronto Globe and Mail,* until it was exposed as a farce containing fabricated stories and events. But more interesting and relevant for us is the manner by which she "exposes" honor killing in Jordan and why the media may have found it eye-opening. Observe her use of the colonizer's temporal tool:

> Jordan is a place where men in sand-colored business suits hold cell phones to one ear and, in the other, hear the whispers of harsh and ancient laws blowing in from the desert. It is a place where a worldly young queen [who is from New Jersey] argues eloquently on CNN for human rights, while a father in a middle-class suburb slits his daughter's throat for committing the most innocent breach of old Bedouin codes of honor. Jordan is a place of paradox. Modern on the surface, it is an unforgiving desert whose oases have blossomed into cities. *But the desert continues to blow in.* Streets are parched and stripped of flowers, trees, or greenery—except for the new steel and glass corporate towers. Unlike the Jordan River, no longer strong enough to flow down to Amman, *the desert drifts up to the city's boundaries.* Like the sand that coats the streets after a windstorm, the *Bedouin code is always encroaching on its urban streets.* Its fierce and primitive code is always nagging at men's instincts, reminding them that under the Westernizing veneer, *they are all still Arabs.* For most women, Jordan is a stifling prison tense with the risk of death at the hands of loved ones.[46]

The use of time here is deeply inscribed into her narrative, making it possible to address the crime as having its foundation in some deep cultural structure, whereby Jordanians, no matter how much they try to appear modern and Western, are forever doomed to remain in the desert, Bedouins of a faraway place and time. No matter how modern they dress, how up to date the technology and gadgets they own, they remain immutable creatures of the past. As Johannes Fabian (2002) comments about a similar tendency in anthropology, Khouri likewise wants to locate Jordanians in a distant time by "pushing the other back in time."

This desire to locate the Other "behind" the West when it comes to human rights is not unlike Joseph Massad's analysis of what he calls the Gay International, where he finds that in gay liberation, as practiced by many Western liberal gay rights groups and their elite "native informants," time is central to the way the issue is dealt with. He notes that these organizations consider the lack of tolerance in the Arab world to be "behind" the rest of the world when it comes to this important issue, where "being gay is 'still' considered [deviant] sexual behavior—the point being that the Arab world has yet to catch up with the liberatory Western model of gayness."[47] His analysis of one gay right's group handling of the issue sums it up quite well:

> Pakistani American founder of a new Gay International organization for gay and lesbian Muslims, the Al-Fatiha foundation, explains to his Western audience how Islam is "200 years behind Christianity in terms of progress on gay issues." … In *Al-Hayah*, Zakharia declared that his group's goals in the Arab world were like those of the feminist movement, namely, to "remove the old and tribalist patriarchal system, which has strangled and continues to strangle our people.… This system is based on the use of "traditions" and honor as weapons to repress pluralism in our societies in order to make democracy practically impossible, and to maintain the tribalist mentality whose effects are very clear in the contemporary Arab world.[48]

Notice that in both examples—of honor killing and gay rights—what holds the discourse together is the temporal framing of cultural difference in sexual rights, without which these two interventions would make absolutely no sense. This form of gay and women rights, by culturalizing the issue, stigmatizes a particular group by marking it as somehow different than "our" world, where such issues have been resolved in some past time, which we have transcended and corrected. One could, of course, make a particularly non-Orientalist analysis of human rights discourse, but the culturalization of such projects, with their temporal and spatial divides, would have to be dropped. Otherwise, these types of feminist and queer politics, rather than producing liberation, become yet another tool the colonizers use to dominate and persecute (as well as bomb) their subaltern.

This is in fact where world-system and Saidian scholars can have much to say by showing that, within the constitution of the modern world, an "outside," external, self-containing set of civilizational islands standing next to, but somehow spatially and temporally disconnected from the other more modern civilizations, can no longer be posited to exist. As Georg Simmel, a German sociologist, recognized during the time in which the colonizer's spatial and temporal template was most prevalent, "The border is not a spatial fact with sociological effects, but a sociological fact which takes a spatial form."[49] Such a view allows the public, especially in the West, to take another look at these temporal categories and see that this constant discourse of distancing the Other is a myth that serves the dual purposes of fear and ridicule and is the greatest obstacle to the ideals that they posit as a central core of "Western" belief. The first step is for the writers and intellectuals, by commanding posts of privilege to the way the Other is constructed, to begin to unthink the temporal and spatial lens that they have acquired from the Social Darwinists of the nineteenth century and to begin building a new house, where all of the members can share the space (and time) equally.

The Colonized's Appropriation of the Colonizer's Time Machine

As we will discover in the coming chapters, although one has to be careful not to reduce the colonized to dupes of this colonialist gaze and overlook the creative nature by which the colonized incorporated the colonizer's form of Social Darwinism, it seems plausible to argue that they did accept, for political reasons of their own, a good chunk of the colonizer's template. Like H. G. Wells's memorable story of the time-traveler who invented a machine with a lever that propelled man into the future, many of the intellectual and political elites of the newly emerging nations of the global South saw that they could bypass, or even skip, the waiting room and, by pulling on the appropriate levers, move their newly independent societies along at a faster pace than the old colonial regimes.[50] The Islamists would likewise accept the time-machine idea, but they complained that their predecessors pulled on the wrong lever, which they now want to correct by returning to the "fundamentals" of their faith, so that they, too, may launch their communities into a future utopia that they believe Allah has prescribed for them.

The leaders of the anticolonial movements, both intellectual and political, wanted to tame the colonizer's rigid and fixed evolutionary lens by positing that, under the leadership of an enlightened indigenous elite, their feudal and backward societies could be remade with the injection of a proper dose of shock therapy. Toward this end, they began to develop a variety of social engineering manifestos, which, they thought, would identify a whole array of programs, both technological and cultural, that would permit their societies to quickly and swiftly replace their traditional, precapitalist, feudal existence with one that would hasten their arrival into the modern world. Unlike the colonizers, they used the time machine notion by adding the insinuation that they need not "wait" until some inevitable law of evolution worked on them. With the proper intervention they, too, Michael Adas explains, "not only could but would 'develop' along the scientific-industrial lines pioneered by the West."[51]

An entire lexicon of scripted questions relating to the subject of what are the central characteristics of being modern, and how to get there, soon began to appear. Consider the kind of questions they readily, and still, are asking: What type of economic system should one have if they are to be considered modern? Does a country need to have a proletariat and a bourgeoisie to be considered modern? What about peasants, Bedouins, large landowners, a big agrarian class—are they appropriate for a modern society, or do we have to replace them with new classes? How much of "our" culture can we keep if we are to be considered modern? Can one be modern yet still Arab, Ottoman, Japanese ... or do we have to give up our culture altogether? What type of school curriculum is appropriate for our "new" modern societies? How much should we include the Koran into our classes, relative to scientific material so that we can ensure that our youth are prepared for the modern age? Is it appropriate to use Sharia (Islamic law) in a modern context? Have we had a "Reformation" or Renaissance that we can call our own? Questions asked even went to the extreme of focusing on what type of clothing (veiling, the fez, pajamas in public ...) is proper for a modern woman and modern man, as well as on proper toiletry, proper ways to eat, and so forth, all of which were now discussed in terms of modern versus traditional. Notice all these questions are possible only if one accepts linear conceptions of time and progress as a commonsense way of understanding history. There is an ascending track, just like in the Epcot's Spaceship Earth, that one can get on and move through time. But what the colonized revised from the Social Darwinism of their colonizing predecessors is that more torque and power can be delivered to the engine by those mechanics who have the genuine interest of their subjects in mind, those, of course, being them.

These types of questions made it obvious that this cohort of leaders would not "stand still" in some waiting room until their paternal father gave them permission to enter into the living room to join the other adults. On the contrary, they believed that such immutable barriers were figments of their superior's imagination, something that they were set on proving otherwise. With hard work, determination, and a creative imagination, they proceeded to develop program after program that would "move" their society up the ladder of time to "catch up" with their already modern Western counterparts. As Michael Latham (2000, 2003) and Nils Gilman (2003a, 2003b) demonstrate, in their discussion of a similar tendency in Leninist and Wilsonian principles of development to see all the problems of the "Third World" as stemming from technological issues that could be solved by cultural reengineering, so, too, did the intellectuals and political figures of the new emerging nations admit that there were many problems to solve before the launch was possible, not least of which were those rooted in their women, sexual practices, religion, culture, and mentalities. Yet such difficulties could be overcome by introducing, through a class of intelligentsia, an array of carefully thought through remedies that permitted their societies to quickly pass "through historical stages [that] . . . would engender a new consciousness as well as a new society."[52] Once they eradicate those things they considered backward and standing in the way of progress, like feudalism or "archaic superstitious" beliefs or primitive mothering that their subjects are "clinging" to, full political and social modernity will be assured.

Colonial Hegemony and the Remaking of the Middle East

Yet after all is said and done, and especially after considering the awesome power of the colonizer to trample all those undermining what it perceived as their God-given right to rule over their dominion, one has to be moved by the courage and creativity with which the colonized and others revised, however slightly, the colonial narrative. It was not just the military power of the colonizer that stood in the way, but the way that the temporal template seemed so natural, that to resist it or claim it false would have made one look like a fool, even irrational. Indeed, this is the test of how hegemony works, that the ontology—ways of seeing the world—becomes so commonsensical, that one is unable to simply discard the lens that they see through or to start a completely new and fresh way to view time. The colonized—being bombarded by massive amounts of texts, technology, planes, mass manufacturing, scientists and other experts, all of which are packaged as belonging to a certain type of civilization or race or a "type" of "modern mind"—had very little public space to even articulate an alternative. Ideas and concepts do not float out of our heads from nowhere. They have to be externalized, reflected upon, reworked, and so on, before they can come into fruition and reorient our thinking. Having very little access to the public sphere, including printed texts, the subaltern is constantly flooded in an environment that is heavily manufactured by the colonial *Imagineers* themselves. This does not mean, as we will see, that the less privileged have no means to resist the given discourse, but the manner by which this is done will be largely constrained by the dominant discourse in place.

As Ernesto Laclau and Chantal Mouffe (2001) persuasively suggest, hegemony is a constantly changing articulation of forces, but in each articulation, a dominant peg tends to come into being, toward which all others are forced to bend.[53] Others, too, force the peg to bend, but rarely enough to cause the whole discourse to come tumbling down. The colonized is forced, by the sheer gravity of the dominant peg, to articulate a counter narrative, by selectively using some of the prevailing discourses as rhetorical resources to resist that very hegemon.

As in the case of the success of the anticolonial movements to drive out the colonized and shape a new world order, such struggles did change and cause a revision and a new articulation to come into the political arena, and that change has allowed us to see the temporal template in ways that are significantly different than it appeared under colonial Darwinism. Even though it is not a completely new break or a new ontology, it allows some new forces—in this case, of course, being the colonized—to become actors *inside* the political arena rather than remaining on the outside of "human history." Under the post-colonial world order, they are now "permitted," by the power of the privilege of being creators of their "own" time and are now accepted by historians and others as "moving" (or not moving, for some "dysfunctional" cultures) toward modernity. This is a significant change. The Other is no longer expected to wait, in a passive manner, for an invisible, slow-moving, evolutionary process to occur. All they need is good leadership, a sophisticated intelligentsia, and a thirst to eradicate all cultural and political obstacles and, once all that is done, they will be well on their way to a new age. Recall the bridge in Epcot that connected Morocco and Native Americans to the more advanced world, as compared with the completely divided landscape of Chicago's World's Columbian Exposition of 1893. Note how in the 1893 example, the colonized and the enslaved were placed in altogether separate parks, which required exiting a gate marking the civilized in order to enter the other designated for the uncivilized. There are no such gates in Epcot, only a bridge. Epcot's bridge is the new social peg that anticolonial movements, through their impressive resistance to colonial Darwinism, had built themselves, so to speak. They are now also, although at a very marginal level, part of the political international order. Yet, even with this impressive shift, notice that, although the Other—or at least their elites—is allowed to enter as a civilizing agent, we are still left with a temporal template and its epistemological assumptions that is in keeping with the more racist formulation found in the 1893 World's Fair.

As our analysis proceeds, we will explore how a number of different actors in the postcolonized Arab, Turkish, Jewish, and Muslim world forced the hegemonic peg to bend in different ways, with each bend, although failing to cause it to break, offering a slightly new way of seeing cultural difference and time. As we proceed to compare these varying responses, it is important to keep in mind that the discourse of civilization and progress are never absolute ideologies that trickle down from the powerful to the subaltern untouched. They always run up against resistance, altercations, conflicts, and contradictions. People of varying locations will influence them in a number of ways. Gail Bederman has addressed this issue, in her discussion of the way civilizational discourse was accessed by different people in late nineteenth-century United States:

> "Civilization" was protean in its applications. Different people used it to legitimize conservatism and change, male dominance and militant feminism, white racism and African American resistance. On the one hand, middle- and upper-class white men effectively mobilized "civilization" in order to maintain their class, gender, and racial authority, whether they invoked primitive masculinity or civilized manliness. Yet as effective as "civilization" was in its various ways of constructing male dominance, it was never totalizing. People opposed to white male dominance invoked civilization to legitimize quite different points of views. Feminists pointed to civilization to demonstrate the importance of women's advancement. African Americans cited civilization to prove the necessity of racial egalitarianism.[54]

The purpose of this study, therefore, is not to ridicule the colonized for accepting the insult given them by the more powerful, but to take note of the powerful legacy of the colonizer's gaze and the equally enticing and creative manner by which the decolonized nibbled away at it, so as to provide the next generation the capacity to see farther into the fog than they were capable of under colonial rule. Given the thickness and stability of the myth, the colonizing elites of the West created an awesome peg, which Nederveen Pieterse and

Bhikhu Parekh[55] identify as "colonial imaginaries," that was extremely difficult to bend in new ways. Under such conditions, even the slightest bend is a huge and impressive accomplishment. How these anticolonial elites maneuvered in this heavy fog is the subject matter of the chapters ahead.

Chapter 2

The Anti-Semitic Gaze and the Occidentalization of the Jew in Zionist and Israeli Nationalism

We are in the Orient only geographically.

—*David Ben-Gurion 1949*

IN THE MANY TIMES THAT I'VE VISITED ISRAEL over the years, it has shown to me, all too clearly, a nation obsessively imagining itself as European, part of Western civilization, and on the move to remove all that is Eastern, Oriental, Arab, Palestinian, and Sephardic from the state of the "new Jew"—and always at the expense of the "Other." As I will argue in this chapter, Jewish nationalists, in their response to the gaze of the European anti-Semite—who accused Jews of being "infected" by the Orient and thus out of tune with the space/time of Christian modern Europe—agreed and, ironically, ran straight east into Palestine in order to create a state in which a "new Jew" with an updated time/space could be produced. By doing so, these Jewish nationalists, otherwise known as Zionists, proceeded to remove everyone and everything that they defined, in Eurocentric fashion, as primitive and Eastern, including indigenous Palestinian inhabitants. Arab Jews would also be targeted as in need of de-Orientalizing and cleansed of their Arabness.

The emergence of Zionism, therefore, needs to be understood as a nationalist movement that sees the location of Jews through the eyes of the anti-Semite, a movement that strategically positioned itself so as to resolve the

Jewish Question by transforming the Jew from an Oriental Other into one that Christian Europeans could accept as a respectable and civilized member of an "advanced race." As we will explore here, in the case of every Zionist leader, the objective was to search for ways by which the Jew could look and feel European, to shed his Oriental skin, and to be allowed an entrance ticket to European civilization.

Rather than viewing Zionism as a Jewish nationalist movement that broke off with European nations so as to create their own culture, it has become obvious to many scholars today that it is more accurate to describe it as an assimilationist state that appropriates the racial classifications in European Social Darwinism so as to remove those Jewish characteristics that the anti-Semite found most appalling. In that sense, the identification of the Jew as Oriental must have been quite unsettling for this emerging Zionist movement, and it was this concept of the Jew as outsider that they aimed to change. The consequences of this cannot be underestimated. Defining themselves in opposition to the Orient and as part of the Occident will have major repercussions for not only European Jews but for both Eastern Jews and the now very Orientalized Arabs as well. Zionists took it upon themselves to embrace and adopt the Western racist discourse about the "Oriental Other," by strategically placing the Jew and his interests as European.

The influence and penetration of European Orientalist thought, the Enlightenment, and Western articulations of race on Western Jewish intellectual developments, I contend, initiated this process by which a minority of European Jewry in the nineteenth century appropriated the ontological framework of East/West and used it to overturn the longstanding European legacy of categorizing the Jew as "Oriental." This overturning was an essential aspect of the Zionist movement, one that solidified and made possible the almost commonsensical notion today of a *Judeo-Christian civilization,* a term that would not have been possible until very recently. It was a complete rupture, where the Jew was dislodged from the East, with which he was traditionally identified. Jews thus came to be seen as "outside" of their "Oriental" location and placed as an organic component of the "West." As Ivan Kalmar and Derek Penslar have argued, "to many Zionists the *realpolitik* of alliances with *goyim* [non-Jews] was never more than a means to realize a radical ... physical exit to the Orient ... as a means of becoming a 'normal,' i.e., Western-style, nation." Deploying this strategy places Jewish nationalists as colonizers who, ironically, throw "off the yoke of gentile domination while assuming a *mission civilisatrice* to revivify an allegedly barren land as a means to regenerating the Jewish people."[1]

We will begin this chapter with first tracing the anti-Semitic gaze and then analyzing its effects on the racial political articulation of Jewish nationalist elites and the eventual formation of Zionism. As in the mind of many Orientalist today who write about Muslims, the Jewish people, until recently in the last century, were not allowed to cross the bridge into modernity and were viewed as frozen in time belonging to the biblical era. The debates that Jews encountered in modern Europe on whether or not their religion or race was up to par with modern Christian Europe, as we will discuss in this chapter, placed them outside the gates of civilization and produced many debates about how and if they could be permitted to enter into the more advanced parts of the world. Yet in the aftermath of the Holocaust and the establishment of the state of Israel, Jews were permitted to finally take a seat along with the other "advanced" races and cultures, to the point now where it has become commonsensical to call the West a Judeo-Christian civilization, a notion that just a few decades ago would have seemed outrageous.[2] How this came about will be this chapter's topic of concern.

Anti-Semitism and the Jew as Non-European

Christians in the "West" and Europe historically have had difficulty accepting the Jew as an insider. It needs to be noted here that many European Christians identified the Jew as essentially a radically alien, Oriental outcast, living in the midst of a Western world. A case in point is the nineteenth-century debate that emerged around Benjamin Disraeli's policy toward the Ottoman Empire. Disraeli's attempt to delay the dismemberment of the Ottoman Empire was seen by his British Parliament opponents as "Jewish," because they felt that, as a Jew, he was bound to rally automatically to the Turkish side. Nissim Rejwan, the author of a book that deals with this topic, makes the comment about this incident that is to the point: "A Jew, even a baptized Jew, they argued, remained an Oriental, and therefore, in the struggle over the Eastern Question, Disraeli's loyalties were necessarily with Asia against Europe, with Islam against Christendom."[3] He cites at length one of Disraeli's most bitter opponents, T. P. O'Connor:

> [T]here has been among large sections of the Jews the strongest sympathy with the Mohammedan peoples.... In the time of the Crusaders, the Jews were the friends who aided the Mohammedans in keeping back the tide of Christian invasion which was floating against the East, and in Spain the Jews were the constant friends and allies of the Moorish against the Christian inhabitants of the country. [Disraeli's] general view then upon this question of Turkey is that as a Jew he is a kinsman of the Turk, and that, as a Jew, he feels bound to make common cause with the Turk against the Christian.[4]

The equating of the Jew with the Orient was so taken for granted that a British author of an 1877 book could confidently complain, "Throughout the East, the Turk and the Jew are leagued against the Christian.... Throughout Europe, the most friendly Turkish part of the press is largely in Jewish hands. It may be assumed everywhere, with the smallest class of exceptions, that the Jew is the friend of the Turk and the enemy of the Christians."[5] Major European intellectual figures shared these same ideas. Johann Gottfried Herder, for example, calls the Jew "an Asiatic people alien to our continent." Arthur Schopenhauer extended this anti-Semitic idea by claiming, "they are and remain an alien, oriental people, and must therefore count only as resident aliens." Werner Sombart later would appropriate this into his own work by calling the Jews "an Oriental folk transplanted into an environment both climatically and ethnically strange, wherein their best powers came to fruition." Many Jews residing in Europe also accepted this same anti-Semitic notion. Walter Rathenau, for instance, perceived the Jewish people residing in Europe as "an Asiatic horde on the sands of the Mark."[6] Similarly the Jewish Arnold Zweig accepted the fundamental description of the Jew in the anti-Semitic notion that Jews are unsuited to European life: "We cannot do without Asia. We shall never be redeemed until we are back home there." For him, a Jew assimilated to Europe has betrayed Asia, "the inner Orient in which he is rooted."[7] In his book, *The Face of the Eastern Jew*, Arnold Zweig further expands on this idea by arguing that the customs and habits of Jews found to be strange in the Occident can only be intelligible if seen as Oriental: "anyone who was ever allowed into a mosque in an Islamic country during prayer will recognize the Jew as an Oriental."[8]

The liberal philosopher Voltaire concurred by arguing that "the [ancient] Jews were vagrant Arabs infested with leprosy."[9] Max Naumann, in his treatise on the Jewish Question some years later, also made the claim that Jews maintained "moral views of sub-Asia foreign to the German spirit" and warned his fellow Christian citizens that Jews threatened the integrity and health of their German values. [10] Such views included intellectuals and political writers who were advocates of Jewish integration, like the Christian Wilhelm Dohm, who identified Jews as a "nation" of "unfortunate Asiatic refugees."[11] Karl W. F. Grattenauer, a German lawyer, in his popular pamphlet, *Wider die Juden* (1803), explained that the most learned and enlightened of the Jews "may talk about Goethe, Schiller, and Schlegel all they please; they nonetheless remain an alien Asiatic people."[12] As Noah Isenberg observed, "Jews [were] viewed within the basic framework of the *shtetl* as a kind of 'oriental' landscape," as was the case with German soldiers who were placed in Eastern Europe and noted that being there was "as if they had 'entered a totally different world of the Orient'."[13]

To many European Christians, Jews inhabited a life of a bygone age that is unprepared for the modern world. The invention of the "compulsory ghetto" that they were forced into functioned not unlike that of John Stuart Mill's version of the waiting room of history that we described in chapter 1, where Jews were "typically subject to strict population control and a multitude of economic and legal restrictions designed to keep them apart from, and under the control of, the Christian majority."[14] But unlike the colonial overseas possessions that Mill was referring to, in the case of European Jews, it was an internal colonization where "the Jews were cut off by the walls of the ghetto as though stricken with some loathsome disease that might carry misery and death unto others."[15] Ever since the sixteenth century, if not earlier, Jews were regularly isolated to such a degree that they developed a distinctive language and culture, making it easier for Christian Europeans to mark them off as a primitive Other who is alien to the more advanced European Christian civilization.

Germany of the late eighteenth century is a prime example of this internal colonization and how it was expressed in the Jewish Question. Elite German and French intellectuals inquired about the possibility of permitting Jews political and social emancipation, but with the understanding that Jews would "'prove their fitness for equal rights,' by shedding their 'backward' traditions, dismantling their separate communal infrastructures, and moving forward into 'modernity'."[16] Like the Orientalism that has long defined how

Western scholars, statesmen, and men of letters understood and constructed the Muslim Other, we see the proliferation in the late eighteenth century of "knowledge" production by an army of writers, philosophers, and theologians, creating a mass textual representation of Jews, all ruminating "on the possibility of a moral, political and physical 'regeneration' of the Jews and grappled with the question of how participation in a modern, secular state could ever be compatible with the Jews' stubborn adherence to an antiquated, Oriental [Judaic] religion."[17] As Aziza Khazzoom (2003) explains: "Christians demanded that Jews ... reform their lifestyle, values, and social, economic, and educational structures. Friends and foes alike were disgusted by their dark, disorderly ghettos ... Jewish appearance, particularly the beards and sidelocks, were attacked."[18]

Given the fact that Jewish Zionists would draw on these anti-Semitic debates, it may be helpful to discuss how Christian Europeans attempted to address what they perceived to be Jewish backwardness. European Christian intellectuals were divided into two camps concerning how to resolve Jewish "primitivism." On one side stood the racist anti-Semite, who saw Jews as inflicted by an immutable, biological defect, and on the other side was the liberal, who believed that Jews' backwardness was a product of the environment. All those things they found most appalling were "a product of the material conditions within which Jews had to live." Notice, that, although they both disagreed on whether or not it was possible to "regenerate" the Jew, they agreed that the problem facing the Jews was the decadent nature of their culture, race, and religion and the fact that they have held "on to a primitive and Oriental way of life."[19] Yet, although they both agreed that the Jewish Question/problem is due to the decadent nature of Jews, liberals, like the German Christian Wilhelm Dohm, proceeded to devise a program that would require Jews to give up such primitivism and provide them the opportunity to advance quickly and assimilate into a more civilized society. In his highly influential treatise *On the Civic Improvement of the Jews* (1781), Dohm proposed that in order to "regenerate" Jews from their "degenerated" present, there must be a systematic political will on the part of the state to grant "Jews civil rights [and] requiring them to perform military service, and moving them away from the 'dishonorable' practice of trade—hitherto their chief means of livelihood—to transform them into productive farmers and artisans."[20]

Dohm's greatest opponent was Johann David Michaelis, who insisted that, given the fact that "Jews were a product of the 'southern' climate of ancient Israel,"[21] they are of an entirely different stock of race that cannot be transformed by some magical environmental solution, that "'even in ten generations' would never have the proper bodily strength to perform military service for a German state."[22] For Michaelis, Jews were frozen in the time of Talmudic Judaism, a religion that persists in the present but belongs to another time and place, and he "felt that Dohm was far too optimistic concerning the Jewish potential for improvement and that the emancipation of degenerate Jews would only bring harm to Christian society."[23] Interestingly enough, however, he still did believe that the Jews, given their true nature, can still serve an important role in German society. Because the Jews are in a similar evolutionary level to the primitives of "southern civilizations,"

> Such a people can perhaps become useful to us in agriculture and manufacturing, if one manages them in the proper manner. They would become even more useful if we had sugar islands which from time to time could depopulate the European fatherland, sugar islands which, with the wealth they produce, nevertheless have an unhealthy climate.[24]

Indeed, for Michaelis, the Jewish Question can be finally resolved with colonial expansion itself, where Jews can be resettled in a native soil proper to their true time and place. This will allow the Jewish race to relocate "to a climate that would enable Jews to become economically productive, to 'colonies ... where one might send malefactors and degenerates'."[25] Hence, for Michaelis, given the fact that Jews of Germany are in a culture of a more advanced civilization than the time of their own, they ought to be moved to a part of the world that is more in line with their own civilizational time. As Jonathan Hess observes:

> As a "southern race" descended from the ancient Israelites, the Jewish Diaspora apparently needs to be displaced once again, sent to a Caribbean climate analogous to its place of origins where Jews might become colonial subjects promoting the wealth of the European fatherland. Dohm's central goal—the integration of Jews into the German economic and political order—can best be achieved, Michaelis implies, by deportation to a German Jamaica or Haiti,

> by a model of colonial expansion that would both serve Germany and put the Jewish "race" in its proper place.[26]

Others like a pastor named Schwager agreed with Michaelis and similarly claimed that Jews were "a completely foreign nation," who possess a culture that is "completely different" and who are inassimilable to "our" Christian Germanic culture. To do justice to their race, we must abide to the actuality of the "Real Jew" before us and admit that they would be better off being relocated to an area of the world where they were more fit for citizenship like "in Asia, and as an independent nation." He goes on to provide further evidence that Jews were quite distant in time and place from Christian Germans: "The Jew reveals in his hair and physical features just how far he stands from us (whether above us or below us is not the question here) ... and his spirit is equally different from ours."[27]

What is most telling of these reflections on Jews is how European Christians position contemporary Jews into the time of the "Old" Testament. As we will explore in the coming chapters, like the Arabs and Muslims, Jews, too, belong to a childhood age to which European Christians, standing in as the adults, pronounce the Other as stuck in a period preceding the great rupture represented in the coming of a new society by the figure of Jesus Christ. Herder, for instance, in his essay on Jewish history, describes Jews of his time with biblical Judaism,[28] where Jews are textually reproduced as living-day remnants of the biblical era, and, who, because they failed to hear and follow the message of Christ, have been "superseded by the victory of Aryan, Indo-European culture."[29] From there it is easy to conclude that the reason Jews are placed in a time and place incongruent with their actual development is largely because of Judaism itself.

The German Jacob Friedrich Fries contributed to precisely this idea by arguing that Judaism, because it belongs to an era that has long been made archaic with the coming of Christ, needs to be abolished in order for the Jews to cross the bridge into civilization. Hence, neither by reforming their religion nor changing their environment will Jews be placed on the track of progress. As James Pasto paraphrases Fries's conclusion, "'Judaism' was the real obstacle to Jewish emancipation.... Judaism had no place in present German society because it was a 'remnant from a primitive time which one should not merely restrict but completely wipe out. The civil situation of the

Jews will improve exactly when Judaism is wiped out'."[30] Moving forward in time and being allowed a place in European Christian civilization will only be possible once Jews stop clinging to a doctrine long outdated by a more enlightened Christianity.

But it was not until Michaelis's polemic against liberals—like Dohm's insistence that Jews could overcome their Oriental and backward ways—that we begin to see the more insidious discourse of a distant Judaism as the cause for the "backwardness" of the Jews. In his very successful book on Mosaic Laws, Michaelis revises Jewish history by positing Mosaic Laws as Oriental in heritage and having characteristics that are "foreign" and "Asiatic," where the laws of Moses are made to appear distant from Occidental history, which he claims Christianity represents. As Jonathan Hess has suggested, such revisions allow Michaelis to narrate Jews as distant Orientals in relation to Europe, "by relegating Mosiac law to ancient Jewish history."[31] Notice, the power of this narration creates a still and unmoving image of Jews, where history locates Jews in an "exilic period" belonging to an era, which Christian Europeans have long overcome, thus, in essence, functioning to place *present Jews* as stagnant remnants, while European Christians, with the coming of Christ, have progressed and moved away from in millenniums past.[32] Indeed, as Jonathan Hess has pointed out, Michaelis did a number of comparative studies, where he noted the similarities between ancient Israelites and other contemporary alleged childlike people. In one instance, he corresponded with a friend of Benjamin Franklin, urging him to ask "questions to Franklin about property law among native Americans in the hope of finding illuminating parallels that he might use in *Mosiac Law*."[33] Thus, Michaelis, like other Christian biblical scholars of his time, "projected Jews into an allachronic Time, a Judeographic present, from which all forward chronological movement could take place only through the fulfillment of Judaism by Christianity."[34] For these thinkers, Jews living in their midst were imagined as having no historical development and no change since the Old Testament days, and, although they might live in the Occident, their true origin continues to belong to the Orient, from which they were imagined to have come. Indeed, one can argue that spatially isolating Jews into ghettos was rationalized on the basis that they were in a space (Europe) and time (modernity) not authentic to who they "really" were.

For many Jews, especially the assimilated, living in Europe and being exposed to this insult must have been very difficult to experience. The constant negative images, including the nonending debates about whether or not they were up to par with "real" Europeans, and especially being marked and stigmatized as Oriental, caused many of them to internalize the anti-Semitic gaze and produce within their communities movements that had as their goal to de-Orientalize and produce a "new Jew."

In some cases, West European Jews dealt with this by claiming that it was the Eastern Jew that remained Oriental, whereas they, living and being exposed to Western culture, have been completely Occidentalized. There were multiple ways of dealing with this anti-Semitic gaze. A particularly stunning response by some European Jews was to use the preferred biblical account of the anti-Semite toward the Jews of the East. With some editing, they took the narrative biblical structure of Christian biblical scholars and added the adjective *Ostjuden*. Nowhere was this more effectively used by Western Jews than in the legend of the "Lost tribes of Israel," where they replaced the anti-Semite's universal category of Jews with Yemenite and Oriental Jews, which were now designated as "the 'lost brothers' from a far distant biblical era, for whom time had stopped and in whom ancient traditions were preserved as they were." As Dalia Manor has suggested, these Ashkenazi Jews made claims that sounded suspiciously like their anti-Semitic predecessors, as in this example by the Jewish scholar Eliezer Ben-Yahuda: "we still find among them the social condition of Israel as it was at the time of *mishna*," suggesting that Oriental Jews, rather than Ashkenazi Jews, were the one's who were trapped and lingered in an earlier time.[35] Indeed, as Manor further argues, for these Ashkenazi Jews, "Arab and oriental Jews from Jerusalem seemed to preserve a biblical way of life."[36] In such accounts, the Mizrahim, as these Arab Jews would later be called after the establishment of Israel, were now "perceived as upholding the ancient traditions ... [with] the oriental Jews in Zionist discourse [becoming] 'The Jews' in Christian theology."[37]

But those more sympathetic to Eastern Jews had yet another way of dealing with the anti-Semite. Arnold Zweig, a Jew who was indeed attracted to the "Oriental" qualities of Eastern Jews, constantly made a distinction between the inauthentic Western Jew and Eastern Jewry. For him, the Eastern Jew is characterized as defying "modern (i.e., Western) conceptions of time: he remains suspended in mythical and literary realm.... He is a figure of utter simplicity, of premodern grace and spiritual guidance, of authenticity and naturalness." The Eastern Jew, for Zweig, is spatially and temporally distant from Western Jews, "removed from the *jetztzeit* (newness) of European big-city life."[38] Notice how in the following excerpt from his book, *The Face of the Eastern Jew*, he uses time to differentiate Eastern, Oriental Jews from Western Jews:

> He turns his eye away from me and into the distance, a distance that is nothing but time. His profile leads like a waterfall into his beard, which dissolves into spray and clouds.... And his gaze draws upon itself a distance about which we know, and is nothing but time. Is this the Jew of the East? Is he an old man, who, *almost entirely removed from the present day and certainly removed from the future,* lives a life that is limited to the most oppressed and narrowest form, a life that scatters itself once the pressure that forced it into that form lets up? *We know that our forefathers were relatives of the men we find today in the cities of Lithuania, Poland, and Galicia*; we know that they lived in the Franconian hill regions and the German plains like us. Thus, today we speak different languages, think different thoughts, live a different kind of Judaism, eat different dishes, measure according to different standards, and we [Occidental Jews] have traded part of our soul with Europe, giving up part of our Jewishness. In not quite five generations it has shaped us, this European fate and its freedom, its new air, its wonderful and artistic values, its integrating and liberating aura.[39]

Whereas Christian biblical scholars imagined their contemporary Jews as frozen in a time and place of millenniums past, Zweig similarly sees Lithuanian and Polish Jews as living contemporaries of what Western Jews were many centuries ago.

In other instances, assimilated Jews would turn to a more self-hating type of response, one that obsessively attempts to free itself from any Oriental contamination. Walter Rathenau, in his 1897 essay *"Hore, Israel,"* for instance, asks his fellow German Jews to accept the anti-Semite's accusations of Jews and to finally leave behind all of their oriental ways:

> Look at yourselves in the mirror! This is the first step toward self-criticism. Nothing unfortunately, can be done about the fact that all of you look frighteningly alike.... Neither will it console you that in the first place your east Mediterranean appearance is not very well appreciated by the northern tribes.... As soon as you recognize [these faults] you will resolve to dedicate a few generations to the renewal of your outward appearance.[40]

It is in this self-hating tradition that Zionism and its brand of Jewish nationalism was born. The negative energy that was produced through anti-Semitism was the same energy that fed and nourished the Zionist movement itself. Zionism was the response to Rathenau's call to look in the mirror and wipe out all blemishes that made them negatively stand out and be detested by European Christians. To that end, Zionism's major objective was to "regenerate" the Jew by freeing themselves from the grips of Jewish traditions, manners, and customs that kept them from progressing forward and "destroyed their people's potential for technical and scientific progress."[41]

Theodor Herzl and the Desire for an Occidentalizing Jewish State

Zionism, as practiced by its best-known proponents, in their response to a European anti-Semitic conception that posited the Jew as alien to Europe and belonging to an Oriental race, was strategically positioned to resolve the outsider status of the Jew, to transform the Jew from an Oriental Other to a respectable and civilized inhabitant of "Western civilization." In the case of every Zionist leader, as will be shown, the objective was to search for ways by which the Jew could look and feel European, shed his Oriental skin, and receive an entrance ticket into European civilization. Indeed it was the concept of the Jew as outsider that the early Zionists aimed to change, to finally be accepted by the anti-Semite. This would all come at a price, because, creating this "new Jew" meant the repression and removal of all those elements that were viewed by Zionists to be tainted by the East.

Although having precursors like Moses Hess, Zionism appeared many decades after Dohm and Michaelis had set out to propose strategies to deal with the Jewish Question, finally becoming an active doctrine in some Jewish circles by the late nineteenth century. It became seriously considered by a small circle of Jews, especially among those who were highly attracted to being integrated into Germany and other European countries, but who soon were convinced that emancipation would not be forthcoming and that the only way to be accepted into the club of the moderns would be to find a land that they could settle and prove that Jews, too, could finally shed their Oriental qualities and leave behind all vestiges of medieval culture. Obsessed with the need to create a new culture, they decided on a path that, rather than challenging the anti-Semite, instead would demonstrate that Jews, too, if given the chance, could be lifted from the degenerated state that they found themselves in. The best route for this would be the creation of a state that would take it upon itself to identify with all "images and ideals attributed to the 'West,' distancing [itself] from the negative characteristics attributed to the 'East'," and where Jews become the "generators of the European gaze upon the Orient."[42] As Raz-Krakotzkin persuasively suggests,

> From the outset, Zionist discourse was premised upon the adoption of Orientalist attitudes, and Orientalism was essential to the nationalization of the Jewish collectivity and the ways in which the nation was imagined ... Zionism can be read as an extreme expression of the desire to assimilate the Jews into the Western narrative of enlightenment and redemption.... Generally, Zionist thought ... did not challenge the dichotomy between Europe and the Orient; rather, it was based on the desire to assimilate into the West.[43]

This assimilation can be clearly observed in Zionism's best-known personality, Theodor Herzl. Viewed by many today as the founding father of Zionism, his life work seems to have been marked by an obsession to resolve the otherness of the Jew, to find a new mode of assimilation that would bring Jews self-respect and honor in the eyes of Gentiles.[44] Daniel Boyarin is correct in concluding that "Herzl had come to the conclusion that anti-Semitism was essentially justified by the behavior of the Jews, especially of course the despised *Ostjuden,* and that only a radical act of self-transformation would win the esteem of Christendom for his degenerate compatriots." His main disagreement, however, was with those anti-Semites like Michaelis and others who viewed Jews as inherently unchangeable. Indeed, Herzl agreed with all of the charges that the anti-Semites of his day leveled against Jews, including "charges of crookedness, lack of ethical seriousness, and parasitism," and wanted to demonstrate that all of these were "entirely the product of the Jewish environment."[45]

The rejection of Jews by Europe was thus viewed as a natural consequence of the failure of the Jews to emancipate themselves from the time and space of the East, and it would take a state to develop their own society that would give them the means to travel out of the Orient and out of their feudal-like condition. In order to negate this European rejection and to solve this Jewish dilemma, therefore, Herzl viewed it as essential to create a state in which Jews could finally pull themselves out of an Oriental-like existence.

The resolution of this Jewish dilemma came to him in the notion of the Jewish state. To remake the Jew on a Gentile model, and finally to solve the "Jewish Question," Herzl proposed the notion of a separate and independent Jewish state. He blamed the fact that Jews had been despised and entangled in a web of Oriental-like characteristics on their statelessness.[46] In Daniel Boyarin's telling words,[47] "For Herzl it seems to have been ultimately the vulgarity of the Jews and the way that it prevented their full acceptance by the gentile elites that disturbed him." For Herzl, the central objective of creating a future state was not only to emancipate the Jews from the grip of the ghetto, pogroms, and other forms of persecution, but also to create and fashion a new Jew on the model of a European: "I understand what anti-Semitism is about," he declares, and goes on to argue:

> We Jews have maintained ourselves ... as a foreign body among the various nations. In the ghetto we have taken on a number of anti-social qualities. Our character has been corrupted by oppression, and it must be restored through some other kind of pressure.... All these sufferings rendered us ugly and transformed our character which had in earlier times been proud and magnificent.[48]

Only with the creation of a modern state could the Jew finally be recognized as the equal of his European colleagues. After the election of 1895 in Vienna, for instance, Herzl declared, "In the election the majority of non-Jewish citizens—no, all of them—declare that they do not recognize us as Austro-Germans.... All right, we shall move away; but over there, too, we shall only be Austrians."[49] This inverted logic made much sense to Herzl, because it captured his desire to be accepted by his beloved Germans. As a contemporary biographer of Herzl explains, "Only by evacuating Europe would Herzl come to be recognized as an Austro-German. Concurrently, only by leaving would Jewish bitterness toward their European homelands dissipate and turn once more into love."[50] "The anti-Semites will become," Herzl declares, "our most dependable friends, the anti-Semitic countries our allies."[51]

Indeed, the manner in which the state idea came to him, in the streets of Vienna, provides us with all of the elements of a man deeply scarred by the Orientalist and anti-Semitic gaze. As Jacques Kornberg tells us, in June 1894:

> The state idea had taken hold of him. He felt possessed; elaborations of the idea raced through his mind out of control while at work, walking, when in a conversation. Gripped by an obsession, he feared he was losing his sanity. Everything came together for him in the notion of a Jewish state.... Eliminating Jewish defects through emancipation ... making Jews independent, masters of their own fate. From this experience he would put down his idea of a Jewish State, a national home for the Jews that would one day remake the Jews "on the gentile model ... gaining honor in the eyes of Gentiles."[52]

Departing from Europe, therefore, was Herzl's way not of renouncing Europe and claiming his difference from the German and European self, but rather of identifying as a European in order to eliminate once and for all the distinction between Jew and Gentile. Kornberg's remarks on Herzl are telling in this respect: "Even spit and polish 'Aryans' now admired Jews."[53] The new Jewish state, as Herzl envisioned it, would not make a decisive break with Europe. On the contrary, its establishment would bring Jews respect and would initiate a new era of "forgiveness, peace, and reconciliation" between Gentile and Jew. The solution that Herzl would devise to bring this about is what is now called Zionism.[54]

When we turn our attention to Herzl's fictional utopian novel, *Altneuland* (Old-New Land), his desire to uplift the Jews to the standards set by the anti-Semite becomes even more clarified. In this novel, Herzl takes us on trip from Germany to Palestine with a German Jew and a German Christian in two time periods. We get to see Palestine being transformed from an Oriental cultural landscape to an Occidental one, a landscape where "a process of regeneration will lead, ultimately, to the creation of 'a Europe in the Middle East'."[55] In his novel he portrays several distinguished "Aryan" characters admiring Jews for their great achievements in a once-barren land. His two characters first visit Palestine in 1902. Upon their arrival at the Port of Jaffa, they are repulsed by the miserable condition in which it lies. The port is described as an Oriental backwater, a place of dirt, squalor, idleness, and filth: "The alley was dirty, neglected, full of vile odors."[56] He has no difficulty concealing his dislike for the inhabitants, including the Jews, which he similarly sees as being too Oriental for his taste. The inhabitants are not only poor but dark and repulsive as well: "Poor Turks, dirty Arabs, timid Jews lounged about—indolent, beggarly, hopeless. A peculiar, tomblike odor of mold caught one's breath.... The inhabitants of the blackish Arab villages looked like brigands. Naked children played in the dirty alleys."[57] So displeased is the novel's Jewish character by these sights that he proclaims "If this is our land ... it has declined like our people." The German Kingcourt agrees: "Yes, it's pretty bad.... But much could be done here with afforestation, if half a million young giant cedars were planted—they shoot up like asparagus. This country needs nothing but water and shade to have a very great future." The Jew, intrigued by his statement, asks the German for a clarification: "And who is to bring water and shade here?" The German replies, somewhat annoyed by the obvious: "The Jew!"[58] Then after twenty years of Jewish productivity and hard work within Palestine, the European characters return to the same port and find a completely modern, magnificent city, one very similar to any found in Europe: "Kingcourt, big things that we don't know about have happened while we've been away.... What happened to old Palestine? ... How changed it all is," cried the Jew Friedrich:

> There's been a miracle here.... Thousands of white villas gleamed out of luxuriant green gardens.... A magnificent city had been built beside the sapphire-blue Mediterranean. The magnificent stone dams showed the harbor for what it was: the safest and most convenient port in the eastern Mediterranean. Craft of every shape and size, flying the flags of all nations, lay sheltered there.[59]

Stunned by this complete turnaround, the two characters are satisfied by how closely the new Jewish state resembles the European civilized world: "The people ... seem more civilized than we do.... Just look up at the cosmopolitan traffic in the streets. And all the well-dressed people!" The cosmopolitanism and diverse population of the renovated port, however, do not distract the visitors from its now very European-like semblance: "Brilliant Oriental robes mingled with the sober costumes of the Occident, *but the latter predominated.* There were many Chinese, Persians and Arabs in the streets, *but the city itself seemed thoroughly European.*"[60]

In his many diaries, Herzl clearly indicated that he wanted to transport the very idea of Europe to the Levant, where along with football and cricket, "I shall transport over there genuine Viennese cafes. With these small expedients I ensure the desirable illusion of the old environment."[61] In his *Jewish State* he expands on this point by reassuring his readers that living in an Oriental sector of the world does not mean that "we" have to give up "our" European habits, customs, and comforts:

> Whoever has seen anything of the world knows that these little daily customs can easily be transplanted everywhere.... There are English hotels in Egypt and on the mountain-crest in Switzerland, Viennese cafes in South Africa, French theatres in Russia, German operas in America, and best Bavarian beer in Paris. When we journey out of Egypt again we shall not leave the fleshpots behind. Every man will find his customs again in the local groups, but they will be better, more beautiful, and more agreeable than before.[62]
>
> Dull brains might... imagine that this exodus would be from civilized regions into the desert. That is not the case. It will be carried out in the midst of civilization. We shall not revert to a lower stage, we shall rise to a higher one. We shall not dwell in mud huts; we shall build new more beautiful and more modern houses.[63]

A discussion with his German Jewish friend Richard Beer-Hofmann shows how fully he envisioned his new Jewish state to be a European transplant: "We will have a university and an opera [in the Jewish state] and you will attend the opera in your swallow-tailed coat with a white gardenia in your button-hole."[64]

Notice the systematic way in which Herzl projects the Jew into the European, civilized, modern construct and always at the expense of the "Oriental" Other, a strategy that we see in the very similar case of the Irish immigrants upon entering the United States in the nineteenth century, when, as Noel Ignatiev reminds us in his *How the Irish Became White,* they constructed themselves in opposition to the black slaves in an assimilationist project "to enter the white race."[65] Herzl and the movement that has come to be known through his work as Zionism clearly positioned the Jew as a member of the Occident, sharing no qualities with the Oriental and thinking of himself and his interests as European.[66] By fusing the Jew with the German/ European/ Western/ civilized amalgam, Zionism established a precedent that would help cement its newly acclaimed Occidental status.[67]

Indeed, all of the founding fathers, from Herzl, Weisman, and Jabotinsky to Ben-Gurion, the first prime minister of Israel, would share these same tendencies to produce a Jew in the Orient that assimilated, not into the region they moved to, but into a far away continent. Like his predecessor Herzl, Ze'ev Jabotinsky, writing in a 1927 article entitled "The Arabesque Fashion," declared, "We are going to the land of Israel in order to advance Europe's moral boundaries to the Euphrates."[68] For Jabotinsky, as it was for Herzl, the "East was a primitive expression of Western culture—the historical equivalent of Europe of the Middle Ages."[69] Marcus Ehrenpreis, in his discussion of the new Hebrew literature, similarly asserts, "Aspiring to a national Renaissance in our historical homeland does not mean that we wish to be Asian again. We are Jews but European Jews; hence our culture, which is an extension of ourselves, must be both national and European."[70] David Ben-Gurion highlighted this in the founding of Israel in 1948: "We do not want Israelis to become Arabs. We are today bound to fight against the spirit of the Levant."[71]

Joseph Massad sums up this Zionist tendency quite lucidly: "The objective of the Zionist movement was not simply to transplant European Jews into a new geographical area, but also to transform the very nature of European Jewish society and identity as it had existed in the diaspora until then."[72] Zionism is the effort by Jewish nationalists to negate all that was considered Oriental while at the same time to narrate Jewish identity as congruent with modern Euro-civilization. The actual act of moving from West to East, ironically, is the path through which Jews can finally overthrow their "Eastern-ness."

Appropriating this discourse in their quest to create a Jewish state, we can see from our discussion above that Herzl and the Zionist movement accepted only half of the equation of their anti-Semitic Gentiles: the need for the Jewish people to return to the "Promised Land." Ironically, they readily accepted the highly anti-Semitic notion of Jews as alien to any Western nation along with its corollary, that Jews have a natural, national identity of their own. What they rejected, however, was identification with the "Oriental Other." After settling in what they regarded as an ocean of barbarism, they worked tirelessly to negate their "Oriental" stigma and to construct an identity informed by European supremacy over the "Oriental."[73] For Zionism's most significant thinkers, the European Jewish settlers constituted a nation like France or Germany, radically unlike the "Oriental" inhabitants of the region they wished to remove. The "Jewish Question," therefore, was resolved by placing the Jews as a race in a nation of their own away from Europe while still holding on to the idea that the Jew belonged to the Western, or civilized, world. It is by this means that Herzl and his Zionist followers transferred the Jew from a status outside the Western concept of the self to one inside, a change that is clearly apparent in Herzl's writings.

In this way, the state of Israel would come to be seen as a floating space in an ocean of barbarism, one that was somehow geographically located in the Orient while remaining in Europe. Although embedded physically in the hard, tough soil of the East, its *Geist* was somehow oblivious of this environment, belonging instead to Western civilization. Ben-Gurion's statement that "the State of Israel is a part of the Middle East only in geography" recalls the image, described by G. H. Jansen, "of the hydroponically-reared plant, its roots floating in a chemical solution, not embedded in the earth."[74] The problem, however, is that Israel is on earth, just not in the Orient, according to Zionists like Herzl.

Zionism and the Silencing of the Arab Other

Zionism and the Project to Make Palestinians Invisible

Zionism thus sees itself on a civilizing mission, first and foremost directed by European Jews at other Jews and only then at "whatever natives happen to be there, if indeed, these natives are noticed at all."[75] By settling in what they assumed to be an ocean of barbarism, they tirelessly worked to negate their "Oriental" stigma and constructed an identity that was informed by European supremacy over the "Oriental." For Zionism's most significant thinkers, Jews are a nation like France and Germany, radically unlike the "Oriental" inhabitants of the region they wish to settle. The resolution of the "Jewish Question," for Jewish Zionists and their European allies, is thus resolved by creating a Jewish race and nation that is a member of the Western/civilized world. It is by this method that Jewish Zionism would transform the Jew from being outside of the Western concept of the self. The procedure that they devised to produce this new Jew was threefold: First was what they called the "conquest of land and labor," by which they meant the establishment of farming and agricultural settlements of Jews, free from native Arabs. They would slowly take over the Palestinian's land and force them to leave their land and communities. The second was aimed at Arab Jews and was at times referred to as "the magic carpet ride," in which Jews brought in from Arab countries would be cleansed, through educational and other "civilizing" modes, of their Oriental pollutants, so as to make them fit for a European-like society. The last and most significant step was to marginalize all traces of Palestinian life in the Holy Land, by silencing the historical and archaeological record of longstanding, non-Jewish communities in traditional Palestine.

The conquest of land and labor was the policy of the early Jewish settlers. Although the official establishment of Israel would have to wait until half a century after Herzl's death in 1948, the process of changing facts on the ground in Palestine was already taking place, from the late nineteenth century to the time of Israel's creation. Indeed, the process is still going on today, as Israel continues to appropriate Palestinian lands in East Jerusalem and the West Bank, by converting them to massive Jewish-only settlements and slowly caging Palestinians in to ever decreasing plots of real estate.

This strategy depended on a three-tiered structure, in which Ashkenazi (European) Jews were the most preferred candidates for citizenship, the Mizrahim (Arab or "Oriental") Jews were second in line, because they were assimilable, and Palestinians were least desirable, because they were cast as Israel's inassimilable Other.[76]

In this display of power to conquer the land from the indigenous Palestinian people, the settlers produced the highly racialized communal farms known popularly as the kibbutzim. Under the guise of a Socialist utopia, these were "Jews-only" cooperatives and accepted "no employment of outside labor."[77] Consequently, the Zionist movement, following an agenda of complete segregation from its inception, created a "dual society" with an economic development policy devised to construct territorial partition and an employment program designed to refuse Palestinians jobs and create exclusively Jewish kibbutzim. As Theodor Herzl, the founding father of Zionism, proclaimed:

> We shall try to spirit the penniless population across the border by procuring employment for it in the transit countries while denying it employment in our own country.... Both the process of expropriation and the removal of the poor must be carried out discreetly and circumspectly.[78]

Such policies were based on the precepts that David Ben-Gurion had articulated in his statement that "Land with Arabs on it and land without Arabs on it are two very different types of land."[79] These ideas informed the Zionist colonies and were a major characteristic by which the Zionist entity maneuvered to displace native Palestinians from their land. As Raz-Krakotzkin suggests, "the dominant culture was established on the basis of distinguishing itself sharply from the actual Arab, and negating Arab history and present ... [by] the total negation of the destruction of Palestinian entity and the ethnic cleansing that was associated with the establishment of the state of Israel."[80]

Jews and Arab Palestinians were strictly segregated so as not to mix, in a sense, recreating the same ghetto structure that the anti-Semite applied to Jews in Europe, with the added element of slowly displacing the Palestinians with Jews. As a result, Palestinians were not only spatially isolated from Jews, but were administered by settler and, later, Israeli authorities so as to prepare them for eventual political and legal disenfranchisement.

In order for this segregation and removal policy to work, the Zionists had to make sure Jews and Arabs did not assimilate into one compound. They were kept apart culturally, spatially, and temporally. Remember that Zionism envisioned European Jews traveling East in order to create a new Occidental Jew, one that, although located in the Orient, would remain distinct from and superior to his/her surroundings. As a result, like their anti-Semitic predecessors, Zionists "developed a range of attitudes toward the Orient and toward the Arabs," where Jews were racially far "above" and temporally more "advanced" than the Arab hordes who surrounded them.[81] Besides labor and land policy, Zionist developed other programs and strategies to produce a racial, spatial, and temporal divide, as in the decision to use Hebrew as the new language of the new Jew as well as other cultural distinctions like music and art. As Jabotinsky insisted before the establishment of the state, Jews needed to do all they could to set themselves apart from the people they were conquering, including the accent by which they spoke Hebrew. As he had argued in his essay entitled "The Hebrew Accent":

> There are experts who think that we ought to bring our accent closer to the Arabic accent. But this is a mistake. Although Hebrew and Arabic are Semitic languages, it does not mean our Fathers spoke in [an] "Arabic accent." ... We are European and our musical taste is European, the taste of Rubinstein, Mendelssohn, and Bizet.[82]

It was this combination of Jewish settlement policy with novel racialized representations of Jews as "advanced" and Arabs as a temporally and spatially distant Oriental Other that served to provide a dramatic shift in social relations between the now segregated two populations. Zionist approval of using once anti-Semitic claims on Jews toward Arabs would further fan flames as the movement enacted a series of "Judaization" projects, while simultaneously "de-Arabizing" the land.

In the very first weeks after the proclamation of the state of Israel in 1948, we saw the initial massive flight of some seven hundred thousand panic-stricken Arabs, who abandoned their homes, villages, and farms after the massacres of Deir Yassin, with the hope of returning upon the end of the conflict. Many of these Arabs believed that they would soon return, but in the end remained, as many continue to do today. They are refugees, because Israel refuses to allow them to return, for the sake of maintaining a Jewish majority in a land they now call their own. It was in this context of emptying the land of its initial inhabitants that Israel proceeded to "make the desert bloom," making sure to leave no trace of the expelled Palestinians, including their 418 villages, all of which were completely destroyed.[83] As Israel Shahak wrote,

> The Truth about Arab settlement which used to exist in the area of the State of Israel before 1948, is one of the most guarded secrets of Israeli life. No publication, book or pamphlet gives either [the] number [of Arab villages] or their location. This of course is done on purpose, so that the accepted official myth of "an empty country" can be taught and accepted in the Israeli schools and told to visitors.... This falsification is specially grave in my opinion, as it is accepted almost universally, outside the Middle East, and because the destroyed villages were—in almost all cases—destroyed completely, with their houses, garden walls, and even cemeteries and tombstones, so that literally a stone does not remain standing, and visitors are passing and being told that "it was all desert."[84]

Indeed, as the Palestinian scholar Joseph Massad informs us, "For Palestine to be 'a land without people for a people without a land,' the Israelis expelled the majority of the Palestinians to render their vision a reality."[85]

But, although the Israelis completely destroyed hundreds of Palestinian villages, they allowed many other villages, containing large numbers of expensive homes, to remain standing. Israeli authorities took over many of these homes and redistributed them to army and political officials. Other homes were either looted or given away to new Jewish settlers. Some of these lootings were of such a large scale that even high officials commented on them: "The only thing that surprised me ... [was] the mass robbery in which all parts of the population participated.... Soldiers who entered abandoned houses in towns and villages they occupied grabbed whatever they could. Some took the stuff for themselves, others 'for the boys' or for the kibbutz. They stole household effects, cash, heavy equipment, trucks and whole flocks of cattle.... From

Photo 2.1 The Israeli occupation of the Palestinian city of Hebron and the West Bank is slowly economically choking its Arab residents. One can argue that this is a continuation by Israel to decrease the demographic numbers of Palestinians.

Lydda alone the army took out 1,800 truck-loads of property."[86] The looting by Jewish settlers and soldiers spread from town to town throughout Palestine, at times taking quite gruesome turns, like when a number of Jewish looters entered a town and proceeded to "forcibly remove rings from the fingers and Jewelry from someone's neck.... The finger of one of the dead had been cut off to remove a ring."[87]

Ben-Gurion, after consulting with the minister of finance of Arab private property, which was being taken from the banks of Haifa at an estimated "1,500,000,000 pounds of deposits belonging to Arabs," permitted such expropriations, leading Israeli historian Tom Segev to note that "the government, too, took a hand in the division of the spoils."[88] This looting went hand in hand with Israeli officials expelling Palestinians from their homes and farms, even while many Palestinians retained legal rights over their property:

> The authority of the military governors was also utilized to expropriate lands. The military governor would issue an order to expel villagers from their homes, or forbid them entrance to their fields and thereby prevent them from cultivating them. Then the Minister of Agriculture would declare the lands to be uncultivated and use his authority to hand them over to others to cultivate. In this way Arab farmers lost their lands without actually losing their title to them.[89]

Sometimes these evictions would include entire Palestinian cities, like that of Tiberias in September 1949, when Yigdal Yadin "recommended that the entire city be destroyed in order to prevent the Arab residents from returning,"[90] or in Jaffa, a major economic Palestinian port, where Ben-Gurion in that same year proclaimed, "Jaffa will be a Jewish city". and permitted "whoever grabbed them first" to have official jurisdiction over said property.[91]

Interestingly enough, however, although many Arab Palestinians did leave their homes and were never able to return, some of them, to the disappointment of Israeli Zionists, remained in the outlying areas, still within the new borders of Israel. These "internal refugees" were able to find ways to survive and build massive refugee settlements. These remaining Palestinians have one of the world's highest birthrates, leading many Israelis to express racist concerns over the demographic ratios between Jews and Arabs. Of special concern to Israeli nationalists is the fear that the so-called Jewish character of the state of Israel would be lost, a fear that is not unlike the concern the Nazis had about the "Aryan" character of Germany.

Palestinian-American anthropologist Rhoda Kanaaneh, in her book *Birthing the Nation,* demonstrates the deep anxieties many Israelis felt about these demographic issues. From the time of Israel's founding to today, leading officials have been trying to reduce Arab birthrates, while simultaneously increasing those of the Jews. In most cases, they would expound freely racist concerns like Golda Meir, who slept every night with the fear that more Arab babies were being born, and then "cried in relief when Russian Jews began arriving in Israel in the early 1970s: 'At last real Jews are coming to Israel again'."[92] David Ben-Gurion likewise in his visits to the Galilee in northern Israel would protest the large numbers of Palestinian Arabs he encountered there and made the comment, "Am I traveling in Syria?" and then shortly thereafter ordered the creation of a Jewish settlement named Karmiel.[93] A recent article in an Israeli paper states the same concerns in even more clear language, with the title of the article giving away the substance of the essay: "Battle in Bed Still Favors Arabs."[94] The so-called dove of Israel, Shimon Peres, participated in the same racialized demographic discourse, when he recently alluded to the "Palestinian demographic danger" in reference to the rising numbers of Palestinians on the 1967 Green Line, separating Jews from Arabs. He was concerned that this could possibly lead to a blurring boundary between Israel and the West Bank Palestinians. His fear was slightly put at ease as "he hoped the arrival of 100,000 Jews in Israel would postpone this demographic 'danger' for ten more years, as ultimately, he stressed 'demography will defeat geography'."[95]

But given the fact that they were unable to completely depopulate the Arab population, Zionists were forced to deal with them with the second-best option available to them—one that allowed Jews to manage the Palestinian natives while keeping them spatially and temporally distant. Indeed, the racialized brand of socialism that many Zionists carried with them to Palestine advocated for an interjection of modernity into the Orient so as to awaken the despotic Other from their precapitalist long sleep. This came in the form of modernization discourse so essential to their simplistic notion of socialism. Equipped with the Marxist theory of history as an unfolding telos toward a progressive end, the Western Jew was seen as playing a necessary role in setting a backward region in a forward motion, helping to place the all-too-bogged-down feudal-like Palestinian back on the track of progress so as to serve history's purpose. As Ahmad Sa'di has persuasively argued, "the Zionists' self-perception as bearers of higher culture, and civilized values ... [has] endowed [Zionists] with a moral right and even with an obligation to spread civilization among the natives."[96] Here, the European Jew represents Karl Marx's British colonial regime breaking down the walls of China so that it, too, may be allowed to experience the unfolding of history as it is freed from the shackles of despotism. In this racialized form of socialism, Jews become likewise the current agents of history who have been called upon to deliver the poor, backward Arabs to rise up from their sad Oriental backwardness and be saved by the advanced Europeans.

Socialist Zionists often see the native Palestinians as thankful to have the settlers in Palestine saving them from their deep sleep of barbarism.[97] Indeed, nonsocialist Zionists like Theodor Herzl also used this civilizing discourse, in which he would describe the Palestinian as ever grateful to the civilizer. Indeed, in his futuristic novel that we discussed earlier, even though he stated his preference for European Jews over Arabs, the Arabs that his two characters meet in Palestine are portrayed in the following manner:

> "Just look at that field! It was a swamp in my boyhood. The New Society bought up this tract rather cheaply, and turned it into the best soil in the country. It belongs to that tidy settlement up there in the hill. It is a Moslem village—you can tell from the mosque. These people are better off than at any time in the past...."
>
> "You're queer fellows, you Moslems. Don't you regard these Jews as intruders?"
>
> "You speak strangely, Christian," responded the friendly Reschid. "Would you call a man a robber who takes nothing from you, but brings you something instead? The Jews have enriched us. Why should we be angry with them? They dwell among us like brothers. Why should we not love them? I have never had a better friend among co-religionists than David Littwak here. He may come to me, by day or night, and ask what he pleases. I shall give it him. And I know that I, too, may count upon him as upon a brother."[98]

In another novel, *The Sons of the First Rain,* by E. Semoli, the theme is almost the same as Herzl's. In this case the character is a Palestinian teacher who wanders into a Jewish school and is utterly impressed, not only by what he sees there but also by the great knowledge that he could bring back to his less-developed and knowledgeable community:

> In the name of God there are many things we have to learn from you, the Jews. This place was barren and deserted and you came and through your energy, you transformed it into paradise, vegetables, flowers, shade-giving tress. There are numerous such plots even larger than this in our village and they serve as lair to donkeys and camels without anyone growing anything on them.... I always say in my heart: God sent the Jews here to serve as an example for us. We shall observe them and do the same. The main thing is that we live in peace as good neighbors. Here you paid us a visit and also we came to see you at school.... We have benefited from your capital, your energy and your good example.[99]

The famous socialist Zionist Lenni Brenner likewise wrote in 1920, "It was for me to enlighten you, to let you taste human relations."[100]

In other cases, Zionists would use civilizing discourse in the same way John Stuart Mill discussed how land and governance should be distributed to the most civilized and capable peoples, and those more primitive should be kept waiting until they have matured enough to make claims to such rights. In full agreement with these imperial philosophers, Zionists would use the idea of their Christian European predecessors to argue that land acquisition should be based on who is ready to make it productive and has the means to develop it, not who actually lives on it.[101] Similarly, these Jewish nationalists converted the views and policies that the anti-Semites used against Jews in Europe, who argued that only through agricultural labor could the Jews be saved from the corrupt trades that they have historically occupied. The logic of this type of argument permits Zionists like David Ben-Gurion and others to claim that owing to the fact that Israel has the capability to make the "desert bloom," then "there is no moral principle according to which Jews could be prevented from developing the country. Their ability to develop the country gives them the right over it."[102]

Nowhere was this civilizing mission made more clear than in the 1939–1940 New York World's Fair, where Zionists created the Palestinian Pavilion. Like the white planners of the 1893 Chicago World's Fair, "American Zionists sought to use the Jewish Palestine Pavilion to show off the good works and the civilizing role taken on by Jews in Palestine."[103] Besides narrating traditional Palestine as the land of the Jewish people, where one could find references limited only to Abraham, or "the return of Jews" from exile in Egypt and Babylonia, with no mention or references to the larger span of the Arab and Muslim period, the pavilion is set up so as to display the progress European Jews made in Palestine. In almost the exact format of Epcot's Spaceship Earth, visitors "ascend a 'staircase of rising immigration,' which was inscribed with the names and dates of Jewish settlements" and then enter an exhibition hall with "animated dioramas depicting 'the transformation of a backward and neglected land into a thriving modern country by the devoted labors of heroic Chalutzim [pioneers]'":

> In these dioramas you will see how the countryside had grown arid because of the dying up of the wells and springs, how sand dunes covered fields once fruitful, hills stood bare of timber, valleys were marshy with the unguided waters of streams which once had nourished grain and fruit-trees. A primitive population lived a semi-nomadic life in this land, which you could barely provide them with a meager sustenance.... Into this land came Jewish settlers, inspired with the hope of establishing there a new home for the oppressed.[104]

In such narratives of modernization, visitors get to watch the pioneering spirit of Jewish settlers transform major Palestinian cities into modern metropolises, where these cities advance from "tiny villages" and "marshy waste" into "the great metropolis [they are] today." The pavilion ends with the slogan: "For centuries this ancient land lay barren and neglected, ravaged by wars fought over its holy sites."[105] Justice Louis Brandeis, for whom a university would be named, added to this discourse by arguing that the Palestinian Pavilion demonstrates Zionism's "mission in the wilderness" and how such a movement by the Jews would bring "enlightenment to the far reaches of the globe."[106]

To Make Palestinians Disappear Biblically

Although demographic policies were a semi-effective way of making Palestinians disappear from the land, there were other options available for Zionists to pursue. The two that stand out most are the production of a Christian-Judeo biblical narrative, and the other is a monopoly over an archaeological representation of the Holy Land. In both cases the Muslim, Arab, and Palestinian historical record was marginalized, if not silenced.

From its earliest days, the Zionist movement recognized that its successful creation of a Jewish state in a territory populated by others depended on the sanction of current imperial powers that were colonizing the region. Such forefathers as Herzl, Weizmann, and Ben-Gurion, for example, regularly appealed to Great Britain and the United States. Because their political project was in search of an imperial sponsor for a new Jewish state, these Zionists recognized early on that an effective means to that end would be to gain the attention of Western powers by appealing to the latter's Christian obsession with the Holy Land.

During the fledgling years of the Zionist movement, many European and U.S. leaders had, for some time, already been showing enthusiasm for the creation of a Jewish homeland in the ancient Middle East. Indeed, as Donald Akenson argues, the appeal for a Jewish state up until the late nineteenth century, "was more widespread among Bible-reading Protestants—especially those of the British Isles—than among diaspora Jewry."[107] By the twentieth century, the Holy Land had become a largely recognized element of popular European and American self-perception. Although the typical imperial ambitions of cheap labor, new markets, and natural resources had played a part in the colonization of Palestine, the emergence of a national and religious identification with the region, particularly with Jerusalem, felt by many Western Christians, formed a unique factor that set it apart from other colonized territories. In this sense, Palestine had formed an unusual part of the colonial imagination, principally because it was not perceived as an ordinary colonial outpost of Western powers. As Edward Said explains, Palestine embodied "an almost mythological territory saturated with religious ideology and endowed with overwhelming cultural significance ... weighed down with historical as well as political meanings for many generations, peoples, and traditions."[108]

It is within this context that Zionists began, during the early years of the twentieth century, to explore the possibility of a coalition with Christian evangelicals, first in Great Britain and soon thereafter in America, in their efforts to establish a Jewish state.[109] Christian Zionists—embodying a tradition older than its Jewish counterpart—thus became essential to the Zionist movement. Today, evangelical traditions of biblical prophecy still form one of the key supportive discourses regarding Israel's occupation of Palestinian territories, specifically East Jerusalem and the West Bank.[110] By seeing the Holy Land strictly through a Biblical lens, Israel's non-Jewish population not only becomes textually missing from the land but is, more significantly, understood as the illegitimate occupiers of it.

This revision of Christian attitudes toward Palestine, coupled with the growing influence of Europe, particularly Protestant Britain, over the affairs of the Middle East, represents a significant paradigmatic shift that would in time make it possible for a small sector of European Jews in the nineteenth century to invent Jewish Zionism, while it provided fertile soil for a sympathetic attitude within Europe regarding the movement's proposal for a Jewish homeland in Palestine. Without such a shift, any notion of a physical return to the Holy Land would have been very unlikely. As the Old Testament was adored by Protestants who had memorized prophetic writings describing struggles and triumphs in Palestine, Zionists would find in them a useful ally in their goals of building and establishing a Jewish state.

This shift in Christian discourse was a tremendously useful tool for Zionists to appropriate toward their goals of building and establishing a Jewish state. Long before the arrival of Theodor Herzl and other prominent Jewish nationalists, as Regina Sharif has so persuasively argued, there had already existed a significant non-Jewish Zionist movement within Europe.[111] Had such a historical context not been available in the nineteenth century, Jewish nationalism and its vision of the Holy Land would surely have taken a very different form. The fact that a modern Zionist template had been developed and nourished by Bible-reading Protestants is highly significant, for when the time was ripe for the Jewish proposal of a Jewish state, amid a fully deflated Ottoman Empire in the grips of Europe, the idea of Israel had already seemed "obvious." The memory of a Land called Holy and the intrigue it inspired in the European imagination played a major role in the development of Jewish Zionism. As Walter Eytan announced in 1958, "the very name 'Israel' is so much part of the Christian heritage" that "when the Jewish State was established and called Israel, it did not have to explain itself."[112] In order to understand the development of Zionism, therefore, it is pertinent to locate its discursive property as emanating from and latching onto the religious changes taking place within imperial Europe.

The founding fathers of the Zionist movement were aware of the potential appeal their ideas would hold for Christians, and many often consciously appropriated European Protestant notions as they developed a mythology of the land of Israel. In this manner, they employed a script with which the British could sympathize and identify. As Jewish settlements and Zionist ideas flourished within the context of British colonial maneuvers in the Holy Land, the success of the Zionist movement would come to depend greatly on its alliance with Christian Zionists, as well as on British commitment regarding the Jewish "return" to Palestine.

By 1900, it had already been made evident in a speech Herzl delivered in London that a clear recognition of the alliance between Jewish and Christian Zionists was fully in play. During the fourth Zionist Congress, he addressed the assembly acknowledging with full confidence the role of Great Britain: "From this place the Zionist movement will take a higher and higher flight.... England the great, England the free, England with her eyes fixed on the seven seas, will understand us."[113] Herzl had been made well aware of Christian Zionist wishes a decade earlier when an influential U.S. evangelist named William E. Blackstone learned upon his visit to Palestine in 1889 that Herzl had been considering Uganda and Argentina as possible sites for the Jewish homeland. Immediately, he sent Herzl a Bible, "marking every passage which referred to Palestine, with instructions that it alone was to be the site of the Jewish State."[114]

As Barbara Rossing contends, the consequence of Evangelical practice is that "Palestinians in the West Bank, Gaza, and East Jerusalem—many who have been refugees with their families since 1948—feel the crushing weight of this triumphalistic understanding of biblical prophecies."[115] According to Father Michael Prior, this form of Christian Zionism is "insensitive to the human rights of the Palestinians, demonizes Islam, and assists in the immigration of Jews to Israel."[116]

Evangelical Zionists adopt one of the earliest tenets of Zionism, maintaining that the indigenous Arab population has no rightful claim of nationhood and ought to be transferred to Jordan, but they add the variant that the Bible promises Israel's right to all of East Jerusalem and the Occupied Territories.[117]

In this biblical narrative, the entire history and existence of a people is suppressed so as to create a political project that favors one imagined national

Photo 2.2 This part of the wall Israel has built is intended to cage the Palestinians in ghettos, and it goes deep into the heart of the Palestinian city of Bethlehem, taking with it large chunks of Arab farms, olive trees, and homes.

community at the expense of another. Michael Prior echoes this sentiment in his examination of Zionism: "With the controlling voice exercised by them the wider history of the region was effectively silenced."[118] Just as Israeli archaeology marginalizes other histories for the sake of bringing forth a Jewish nationalist narrative, Evangelical and Jewish Zionists render Palestinians invisible in order to invoke their Christian Endtimes narrative, in which Muslims do not make the stage.

At the center of this idea, Zionist Israel and the West were bound together and informed by a shared vision for the Holy Land, and the Arab Palestinian inhabitants were relegated to be its illegitimate inheritors. In a short period of time, this rationality made possible Jewish settlements, and the Arab Palestinians were in turn resettled in their "natural" Arab habitat in that Other Oriental land that lay outside of Zion. Hence, the Palestinians remained Eastern and Oriental, and the new Jewish settlers and the Land called Holy were appropriated as an integral part of the West. The Palestinians were relegated to belonging to an Oriental ocean that lay outside the frontiers of the Holy Land. If any actually lived in Palestine, they were there as a result of an illegitimate invasion of days past. It was the genius rethinking of Jewish history that made the Zionists able to use the significance of this Christian reading of Arab Palestine to their own articulation of *Eretz Israel* as the natural homeland for the Jews. It was also this same idea that would claim the Jew and his land were situated outside of the Orient—they were a people who were modern, European, and civilized. As Raz-Krakotzkin explains,

> "The Land" had no history outside its place in the Jewish-Christian theological myth, and was imagined as the land of the Bible in accordance with conventional Orientalist imagery. The land itself was considered to be in exile, until its return to its original "husbands," the Jewish people who came to "redeem" it/her. Palestine was imagined solely as the source of the Jewish-Christian civilization, through the denial of its Arab-Islamic history.[119]

Indeed, the imagery and symbolism of the Holy Land was, and remains, an essential part of the Western conception of the self, where the Scriptures (both the New and the Torah), Jesus' life, his crucifixion and resurrection, as well as the lives of the twelve apostles and the tremendous outpouring of pilgrimage literature and other artistic visual representations of the Land called Holy, all provided "the West" with a vibrant and living historical memory of the Holy Land. The Land called Holy, the need and desire to identify with it, the feeling and belief that it is part of "our" past, solely belonging to "us," has come to be viewed as an essential property of the "West."

The impact of this historical memory has provided the source by which Palestine would come to be viewed not as the property of the "Oriental Other" but as an internal property of Europe itself, with Jews as the rightful biblical keepers of it, a perspective Zionism was quick to make its own. The symbolism of the Holy Land's sacredness in Scriptures and popular memory provided the Zionist movement with a powerful and convenient discourse in its ambitions to displace Palestinian claims over the land.

To Make Palestinians Disappear Archaeologically

As for archaeology, recent scholars critical of Israeli archaeology have argued that a large number of past digs contributed to Israeli nationalist policy designed to silence the Palestinian experience, while simultaneously promoting a Jewish historical narrative. As Massad has persuasively argued, "the Israelis, who have a monopoly on [archaeological digs], are in a constant search for archaeological 'proofs' of pre-diasporic Hebrew 'settlement' in all parts of historic Palestine to further authenticate European Jewish claims to Palestinian/Israeli space and time."[120] As Nadia Abu El-Haj has argued in her book, *Facts on the Ground: Archaeological Practice and Territorial Self-Fashioning in Israeli Society* (2002), one example of how this has been accomplished was in the immediate development of archaeological excavations following the capture of Jerusalem's Old City in 1967, with the attempt to promote the legitimacy of a Jewish nation's "return" to its original homeland. These digs emphasized, in a nationally skewed manner, not the city's many centuries of Muslim history, but rather the era of the Israelite Temples that represented an ancient Jewish national claim. In this manner, Israel pursued a narrative suggesting its revival of an original community that has always been linked with the land of Palestine.

The significance of this strategy to accentuate a biblical past at the expense of the more recent, and much longer, Islamic period should not be underestimated, for as the historian Michel-Rolph Trouillot argues in his *Silencing the Past*, the production of a historical narrative between competing groups is always biased toward the groups that have greater access to the means of such production. Although the consequences of this silencing and nationalizing power might not be as visible as military escapades, it is nonetheless equally effective in forming yet another arsenal the state uses to ethnically purify national memory. This is especially true today, as the overwhelming majority of "research" digs are those perceived to be of national significance to the state of Israel, despite the fact that such efforts only represent a window on one chapter of the great Palestine saga.

In this sense, we can employ the analogy of the bulldozer as a machine that devours not only Palestinian homes but also Palestinian history. Bulldozers are regularly used in Israel to both remove Palestinians in a physical sense from traditional Palestine as well as to dig through many layers of traditional Palestine, leaving the latter's historical artifacts poorly recovered, if not completely destroyed. In the latter case, this has the devastating effect of casting aside, or perhaps possibly destroying, significant Islamic archaeological treasures in favor of the Iron Age, as well-funded archaeologists search particularly for remnants of the First and Second Temples that are at once recognized as important "national" artifacts. Such archaeological narrations create a past in which Palestine is associated not with the natives who inhabit it, but with a "Judeo-Christian" civilization. Hence, it produces a narration in which thirteen centuries of Arab Muslim and Arab Christian history in Palestine is perpetually marginalized. "In this context," Raz-Krakotzkin suggests, "the East—the concrete Arab existence on the land—was deemed inconsequential, and subsequently rejected to the point of obliteration. This mythical concept of the land continues to inform Israeli culture today, and the history of Palestine since the Second Temple is ignored in school curricula, both 'secular' and 'religious'."[121]

Over the years, as I visit Israel's museums in Jerusalem and elsewhere, I am always stunned to discover how small its showcases of the Islamic period are, in comparison to the abundant and extensive Jewish showcases, even though the former ruled over historical Palestine many centuries longer than their Christian and Jewish counterparts *combined.* Yet one would not know this by looking at the archaeological record or watching the PBS documentaries on the historical Holy Land, where usually only a few minutes are dedicated to Islamic history in a sixty-minute documentary. They show just the Islamic Al-Aqsa mosque, but extensively discuss many of the Jewish and Christian sites outside of the basic and central sights of the Wailing Wall and the Holy Sepulcher.

Photo 2.3 The third holiest site for Muslims is the Harim al-Sharif in Jerusalem. It is marginalized in Israeli and Western museums, tourism, literature, and films as compared to the religious sites of Christianity and Judaism.

While archaeologists continue to gain funding, prestige, and media coverage as they focus on eras of "national ascendance" and "glory" in the ancient or medieval pasts, the historical memory of Islamic and Palestinian history will continue to be marginalized and silenced, unless postnationalist archaeologists are permitted to dig the land so as to uncover its more encompassing and symbiotic nature. We need to focus some of our energy and funding toward those archaeologists who can offer us a more nuanced and balanced understanding of traditional Palestine. These archaeological representations "left no room for the Arabs themselves, their contemporary reality, and their rights. By appropriating the 'nativeness' of the Arabs, the Zionists assumed the role of natives and rendered the indigenous population obsolete. Evidently, the real [native] Arabs ... from the outset were considered alien."[122]

Zionism and the De-Arabizing of the Arab Jew

How We Forgot the Arab in the Jew

Yet what is most interesting about the discursive nature of Zionist discourse is the manner by which they set out to de-Orientalize a large portion of Jews from Arab and non-Western lands. As these Zionists traveled East to Palestine and encountered the Jews of the East, they applied the standard insults anti-Semites used against them in Europe and elsewhere toward Eastern Jewry. Jews who have inhabited for several centuries the Near East (the Mediterranean, the Fertile Crescent, Africa, the Islamic Empires, the Levant, Spain, and elsewhere) were discursively racialized as belonging to the lost and antiquated tribes of Israel, frozen in time and in need of rescue by the more advanced Jews of the North. In this way, the objective was to detox the Oriental Jew from what Zionists perceived to be their despotic and cultural contamination of the Arab and Islamic world, a cleansing that would require the latter to be removed from their historical roots, with their Arabness erased, all while in the process of regenerating them as new, Occidentalized Jews. Whereas the Christian and Muslim Palestinians were to be historically, archaeologically, and demographically silenced, these Jews were seen as being possible candidates for Israeli citizenship. But this came at a cost. In order to be accepted by Euro-Jews, who saw themselves as representatives of a superior Western culture, Arab and other non-Western Jews had to "abandon their traditions, deny their past, and erase their memories."[123]

The problem that confronted Arab Jews was the fact that Zionists and Arab nationalists created a dichotomy of Jew and Arab, leaving the Mizrahim (as Arab Jews were later called in Israel) with little option to create an identity outside of this taxonomy. Because the new Israeli state defined itself as both the representative of world Jewry and as radically distinct from the Arabs surrounding it, the terms of citizenship entailed the erasure of any hyphens that linked Jews to the Arab-Islamic world. As Ella Shohat eloquently suggests,

> Fearing engulfment by the East, the Euro-Israeli establishment attempted to repress the "Middle Easterness" of Mizrahim as part of an effort to Westernize the Israeli nation and to mark clear borders of identity between Jews as Westerners and Arabs as Easterners. Arab Jews were urged to see Judaism and Zionism as synonyms, and Jewishness and Arabness as antonyms. Thus Arab

> Jews were prodded to choose between anti-Zionist Arabness and a pro-Zionist Jewishness.[124]

After the establishment of the state of Israel in 1948, and with the mass migration of Arab Jews into the new state, what were historically interlinked identities, Jew and Arab became two distinct and separate categories of people, a rupture so complete that today, within a short period stretching only a couple generations, many people are surprised to learn that many Jews were once Arab.[125]

Hence, the Sephardic and the "Oriental" Jew in the process are erased by these new developments, and their history is separated, extracted, and removed from its Mediterranean, Levantine, and North African context.[126] Whereas Palestinians were relegated as aliens to the Jewish State, "Arab Jews, trapped in a no-exit situation, have been forbidden to nourish memories of having belonged to the peoples across the River Jordan, across the mountains of Lebanon, and across the Sinai desert and Suez Canal. The persuasive notion of 'one people' reunited in their ancient homeland actively deauthorizes any affectionate memory of life before the State of Israel."[127]

Because Israel is founded on the basis of its rejection of the Orient, it not only attempted to de-Arabize native Christian and Muslim Palestinians, but also to reject any cultural traditions tainted by that part of the world, including those that came with the Mizrahim.[128] In order to appreciate the gravity of such change, it is important to emphasize that before the coming of Israel, with few exceptions, the inhabitants of traditional Palestine, especially its Muslim, Christian, and Jewish communities, not only intermingled in the streets, but lived, played, and prayed in a neighborly fashion far more closely than can be imagined today. In no place was this more evident than in Jerusalem, where, as S. D. Goiten, among others, note, homes and other residential compounds were often shared to the extent that Muslims and Jews occupied different rooms under the same roof.[129]

Current formations of identity permit such familiarities precious little room. Even contemporary temples of knowledge house library stacks that are shelved in different sections, according to Jewish or Arab affiliation, "studied by different scholars, and are taught by different departments even though in some cases they come from the same place and time."[130] Indeed, in complete contradiction to modern notions of progress that champion tolerance, exchange, and inclusive societies, the nearer to the present the lens is focused, the sharper the view of exclusivity becomes. As if obsessed with a newfound skill, nations are more efficient than ever at policing their borders, always choosing to reinforce them at any sign of tension or breach. In Israel, this has translated into an ever-maturing image of Jews and Arabs as of two chemical compounds that may combust if mixed together. This insistence upon separateness that has engulfed Jew and Arab alike has served to implicitly suggest a sense of ideological, social, and political volatility, leaving little space for the production of a symbiotic culture.[131] This rupture is so deep that when major Jewish intellectuals like Maimonides, Yehuda HaLevi, and Iben Gabriol are discussed, they are decontextualized from their Arab environment and made to stand as representatives of one unitary Jewish history, under the sign of a dominant Euro-Israeli stamp.[132] The culture that Maimonides and other Arab Jewish intellectuals possessed was silenced and made invisible so as to heighten and expand the Occidentalized version of the Jewish nation. As such, "Israel has taken upon itself to 'cleanse' the Sephardim of their Arabness and redeem them from their 'primal sin' of belonging to the Orient."[133] This is indeed how we forgot the Arab in the Jew.

The Preference for European Jews

Indeed, when Jewish settlers from Europe came into direct contact with the Jews living in the East, they responded very similarly to the way Christian European anti-Semites looked suspiciously upon their Jews as Orientals, who, because of their race, can't help but act and behave in ways opposite of the time and space of the modern society they reside in. They were repulsed and rejected them outright, as does the Zionist Israel Auerbach, who complains that the Asian Jew

> is the pure Oriental. Contended, because lacking in aspirations; peaceful, because indolent; uncomplaining, because submissive; dying with reverence before money, splendour, dignity, titles, because of centuries of despotism; cautious, indeed mistrustful and devious, because used to being surrounded by spies; mainly poor and uneducated, because lacking social organization; unpolitical, unenterprising, unfree, because politics, courage and freedom were forbidden by the lords of the Orient.[134]

These ideas were widespread within the Zionist movement, as in the case of Vladimir Jabotinsky, who loudly proclaimed that "We must put an end to any trace of the Oriental spirit in the [native] Jews of Palestine" and in an article goes on to explain that he opposed the idea of mixed-marriages between European and Arab Jews as well as integration of the latter into the new state on the premise that "he did not know whether this would result in 'a brilliant people or a dull race'."[135] Ben-Gurion made similar pronouncements when he stated that "The Jews of Europe were 'the leading candidates for citizenship in the State of Israel'." He was willing to bring in a race of such low quality as the Arab Jews only under the most pressing needs, and he compared Arab Jews "with the Africans who were brought in as slaves to America."[136]

Indeed, the leadership of the Zionist movement targeted Jews of the Arab world for immigration only when the reservoir of the preferred Euro-Jews were not enough to fill quotas of Jewish numbers in relation to Palestinians. They were regarded as necessary to ensure a Jewish majority. Also, in fear that native Palestinians would fill jobs required to run the new Israeli economy, they sought out Jews in the surrounding Arab countries to make sure that they retained the complete segregation of Palestinians. In this sense, Jews "were regarded as the human reservoir that would ensure a Jewish majority in Palestine. Their mass migration was rationalized in almost purely demographic terms."[137] To make such a supply available to Israel, Zionists collaborated with a few Arab regimes, like that of Iraq's Nuri al-Sa'id, so as "to place a wedge between the Jewish and Muslim communities, for example, by placing bombs in synagogues to generate panic on the part of Jews."[138] They also supported such Arab regimes in "legislation that revoked the citizenship of Jews, in order to force them to emigrate."[139]

It was with this new and relatively large immigration of Arab Jews that many Euro-Israelis became concerned about the civilizational orientation of Israel. They were especially concerned about whether or not Israel would become European or a victim of the East and melt into the Orient. As the following excerpt demonstrates, terms like *Levantization* became the words through which this fear was expressed:

> The ascendance of this Levantine type will finally signal the end of great social dream; the wish to create "good society" will sink under the sheer weight of Middle-Eastern numbers. And indeed... the cynicism and signs of moral decay already present in Israeli life attest to the growing influence of this Levantine spirit.[140]

Jews of the Arab world, including those who were of the upper class, upon their arrival in Israel were forced into extremely poor settlements, whereas

Jews from Europe were provided with the best housing and employment available at the time. Also, unlike Euro-Jews, these Arab Jews "were sprayed with DDT (Dichloro-Diphenyl-Trichloroethane) to 'disinfect' them and 'delouse' them."[141]

The hope of the Zionists lay in the anti-Semitic notion that Arab Jews, if given productive labor, could be salvageable and remade in the image of their more civilized Jewish brothers and sisters. Indeed, Zionist intellectuals like Brenner, Mapu, Borochov, and Katznelson made arguments similar to the European Christian intellectuals, who advocated for Jewish integration, claiming that it is indeed possible to pull such Jews out of the dustbins of prehistory, by providing them productive labor, especially agricultural labor. These Ashkenazi Jews likewise "advanced *avoda ivrit* as a necessary precondition for Jewish recuperation."[142] The newspaper *HaTvzi* expresses this sentiment well:

> This is the simple, natural worker capable of doing any kind of work, without shame, without philosophy, and also without poetry. And Mr. Marx is of course absent both from his pocket and from his mind. It is not my contention that the Yemenite element should remain in its present state, that is, in his barbarian, wild present state.... [T]he Yemenite of today still exists at the same backward level as the Fellahins.... [T]hey can take the place of the Arabs.[143]

Jewish labor recruiters were sent from Palestine to Arab countries like Yemen, as early as 1909, to find Arab Jewish workers to hire in the new Jewish-only agricultural settlements. The objective here was to bring an end to Arab Palestinian labor, which, up until then, had been cheap wage workers. Jews from the Arab world, because they were understood by European Jewish settlers to be backward and not in need of much outside of what is necessary to survive, were thought "to be the ideal solution to satisfy both nationalist and capitalist interests as 'they were Jewish workers who were to be paid Arab wages'."[144]

Uplifting Arab Jews

But if the Arab Jew was a necessary alternative to the Palestinian Arab, then the Oriental culture that they both shared had to be undone, with the Jews of the Orient uplifted from their backward state. For many Israelis, these Arab Jewish immigrants, in order to be brought into modernity, had to be acculturated into the new time-space of Israel, via a sort of time machine that projected the Jew out of antiquity and into the new. In this new and modern society, these

Arab Jews would have the opportunity to learn the benefits of using modern sanitation and toilet paper, as one newspaper claims.[145] As a commentary by Arye Gelbum in the Israeli newspaper *Haaretz* explains,

> This is a race unlike any we have seen before. They say there are differences between the people from Tripolitania, Morocco, Tunisia and Algeria, but I can't say I have learned what those differences are, if they do, in fact, exist. They say, for example, that the Tripolitanians and Tunisians are "better" than the Moroccans and Algerians, but it's the same problem with them all.... Have we given sufficient thought to the question of what will happen to this state if this should be its population?—And then, in addition, [other] Oriental Jews will eventually join them, too! What will happen to the State of Israel and its standards with this type of population? Obviously all these Jews are entitled to come here no less than others, and they should be brought over and absorbed, but if it is carried out without consideration for our limited capacities and if it is not done gradually, they will "absorb" us rather than we them.... To raise their general standards from their communal depths would take generations.[146]

Indeed, as far as Zionists saw it, the task of the new state was to Occidentalize all Jews, but especially the Jews of the Orient, who needed special care to ensure that they were properly civilized and "raised" to the level of their European patriots. The task became especially urgent, given the fact that these Oriental Jews came in large numbers and could cause the racial and cultural stock of Israel to devolve to the level of the Arabs surrounding them. This is clearly expressed in David Ben-Gurion's fear that

> Those [Jews] from Morocco had no education. Their customs are those of Arabs.... The Moroccan Jew took a lot from the Moroccan Arabs. The culture of Morocco I would not like to have here. And I don't see what contribution present [Jewish] Persians have to make.... We do not want Israelis to become Arabs. We are in duty bound to fight against the spirit of the Levant, which corrupts individuals and societies, and preserve the authentic Jewish values as they crystallized in the [European] Diaspora.[147]

Similarly Abba Eban made it known that the resources of the state should be used so as "to infuse (the Sephardim) with an Occidental spirit, rather than allow them to drag us into an unnatural Orientalism'," otherwise there "is the danger lest the predominance of immigrants of Oriental origin force Israel to equalize its cultural level with that of the neighboring world'." Golda Meir also feared that the presence of these Jews might force the new Jewish society back into the time of the Middle Ages, rather than advancing it forward.[148] Sometimes nontemporal descriptions were used, as in the case of H. Tsvieli, an emissary for the Jewish Agency in Libya, who "described the Jews he met there as if he were trading in horses: 'They are handsome as far as their physique and outward appearance are concerned, but I found it very difficult to tell them apart from the good quality Arab type'."[149] In all cases, Jews from Arab countries should be "handled like dangerous, potentially polluting substances" where "maintaining control was key."[150]

But the dilemma in this strategy was that the state, being a body for all Jews, needed a way to place responsibility for the backward nature of these Arab Jews on something other than their Jewishness. Because this was a Jewish state, Arab Jews' inability to evolve to a higher stage could not be seen as caused by the characteristics that they shared with Euro-Israelis. Doing so would make them in agreement with those anti-Semites who believed that the cause of the degenerated state of the Jews lie in their religion or race, not in their environment, an admittance that would be too painful for a society that identifies itself as Jewish. The simplest way out of this dilemma was to appropriate the Orientalist conception that their "fallen" state was a result of the despotic nature of the Arab-Islamic world that they had been trapped in. And exposure to a civilized society like Israel would speed up the process in which they could regain time and evolve into an Occidental-like people. In the provocative words of Gabriel Piterberg,

> Orientalism is then used again, this time to extricate the Oriental Jews from their cultural context, so that the blame for the fact that they are "intellectually frozen, primitive and degenerated, superstitious, lazy, poor and filthy, physically unfit and unhealthy, uneducated and uncivilized, and humiliated and inferior" would not be pinned on their Jewish essence, but on their host societies, that is, the essentialized Orientalist notion of "Islam." … It makes it possible to represent the Islamic context as "responsible" for the alleged predicament of the Oriental Jews. The implication that in a different—essentially national—environment the Oriental Jews can be introduced to Western modernity is rather obvious.[151]

Notice how this racialized discourse, as Ella Shohat argues, places European Jewry as the Sephardic Jews' saviors "from the harsh rule of their Arab 'captors'," who graciously have taken "them out of 'primitive conditions' of poverty and superstition and ushered them gently into a modern Western society characterized by tolerance, democracy, and 'humane values,' values with which they were but vaguely and erratically familiar due to the 'Levantine environments' from which they came."[152] A good example of this can be found in one of the most widely used history textbooks (Haifa: Ha-Re'ali School, 1937) in Israel:

> While European Jewry was amidst a process of turbulent revolution and across the Ocean a new Jewish centre, very powerful and important, was gradually emerging, there were in the underdeveloped Islamic countries of Asia and Africa—previously fortresses of Jewish culture—Jewish collectives whose ways of life were frozen and fell into spiritual slumber.... In the margins of the annals of the Jewish people ... it was as if they were undergoing a historical slumber.[153]

In other similar venues, the blame is placed on a "shortage of textbooks in Yemen," and at other times the backwardness is owing to the fact that some of the Jews of the Arab world were forced to dwell in caves,[154] living a life so primitive that such Jews, when transported from Yemen and other Arab countries by airplane, were described by European Jews through the lens of Ali Baba and *A Thousand and One Nights*, as seeming to be on a "magic carpet" journey to the promised land.[155]

Hence, it was their "Arab environment," not their Jewishness that kept them from evolving in a civilized way. Karl Frankenstein, for instance, clarified this even further by arguing that their "retardation" and lack of development originated from their Oriental and Arab environment and not from their race or religion. He even went further to claim that whereas the "primitive mentality" of these Arab Jews can be compared with "the primitive expression of children, the retarded and the mentally disturbed," their children, nonetheless, "could be rescued were they to be physically extracted from their traditional environs."[156]

Conclusion

The desire to Occidentalize the Jew, as we discussed here, is directly related to the anti-Semitic gaze of Christian Europe. In the case of Israel, the insult led to a massive campaign of ethnic and religious repression, where the Palestinian and Sephardic Jews were asked to bear the brunt of the anti-Semitic gaze. Ashkenazi Jews, in mimicking this anti-Semitic insult, turned their pain onto the weak, so as to be permitted to cross the bridge of time and enter the gates on top of the world. In the process of doing so, as they settled the promised land, they proceeded to seriously scar all those Arabs (Jews and non-Jews) that were indigenous to that land, to the point of causing a completely new racial landscape in what has now come to be called Israel. Indeed, this is why today many Palestinians and other Arabs consider Israel alien to the Middle East, not because they have hated Jews from some time immemorial, but because of the *new* racial project that such a movement brought to the region, one that produced a new social divide between Jews and Arabs.

This dramatic story of Jewish trauma at the hands of the anti-Semite is similar to the one we will explore in the next chapter on Turkish nationalism, as it dealt with the highly judgmental Western appraisal of its religion, whereby it placed Islam on the lower end on the scale of civilizational development. In both cases, Jews and Turks, in dealing with this insult, proceeded to remove the Oriental qualities that the Occident judged as inferior and as an obstacle to progress and enlightenment.

Chapter 3

The Kemalist Acquiescence to the Colonizer's Time Machine

> If our bodies are in the East, our mentality is oriented toward the West.
>
> —*Kemal Ataturk*

> We shall skip five hundred years and not stand still.
>
> —*Ziya Gokalp*

In my reading of the literature on the formation of Zionism and Turkish nationalism, I'm struck by the similarities in the biographies of the "founding fathers" of these two movements. Both Theodor Herzl and Kemal Ataturk in their adult life came to be obsessed with assimilating into European culture. They both found their "cultural heritage" to be lacking, too Oriental, and not up to par with the new challenges of the modern European world. Indeed, they agreed with their most racist and anti-Semitic opponents: The Jew and the Turk were of an inferior culture when compared to other Western nations. But, although they agreed that their respective cultures were of a lower type, both Herzl and Ataturk understood this as a transitional moment in history, waiting for the spirit of progress to be injected into the social body by an enlightened "indigenous" state. For Herzl, as we saw in chapter 2, the Jew could be made in the image of the European only if the Jew had access to a state of his own. Similarly, as we will discuss, Ataturk believed that with a strong dose of European adaptations, the Turk could remove those antiquated traditions that the Turks acquired in their contact with the Muslim and Arab world and march forward in history to join in the riches and progress of Europe. Indeed, the underlying similarity that these two fascinating political elites share is that, in their response to European racist constructs of the Jew and Turk, they accepted the Eurocentric temporal template and proceeded to transform their subjects in accordance to the racial paradigm that underlies the Orientalist script.

The making of the "new" Turk, as it was for Jews and Arabs, thus followed a certain Orientalist representation that placed him on the side of backwardness, in dire need of a radical makeover. In this sense, the power of the discourse of being backward, uncivilized, traditional, premodern, intolerant, nonscientific, and lacking innovation and free-thinking is not so much that it is a negative stereotype, but that it *produces,* in a creative manner, an ontology of difference, where the Muslim is scripted to have certain attributes and the Occidental as having other characteristics, and that to be modern, one has to give way to the other. In Edward Said's provocative summation, "When one uses categories like Oriental and Western as both the starting and the end points of analysis, research, public policy ... the result is usually to polarize the distinction—the Oriental becomes more Oriental, the Westerner more Western." This temporal and Eurocentric script has the power "to channel thought into a West or an East compartment,"[1] forcing the colonized to choose one or the other. As we will explore in this chapter, like the Zionists before them, the Turks—in being designated by the colonizer as having attributes unfavorable to modern civilization, where Islam is essentialized as superstitious, fatalistic, reactionary, irrational, and anti-reason—would attempt to transform their society from head to toe to look like the West, in an effort to decontaminate the Turkish subjects from the toxins of the Orient. If Jewish nationalists traveled East to become Western, Turkish nationalists, under the leadership of Mustafa Kemal, attempted to run West, while standing in the East, but only to find themselves being labeled as incomplete Europeans and not permitted to cross the bridge to the other side.

The Time of the Muslim in the Modern Western Imagination

In contrast to Orientalist historians like Bernard Lewis and Samuel Huntington, other scholars have critiqued the popular notion that "Islam" and the

"West" have historically understood each other as two separate, and antithetical, civilizations. We have become so accustomed to talking about Europe and Islam as distinct civilizations that we forget that up to the early modern period, with the end of the Reformation in Europe, Islam was understood by the Christians of Medieval Europe not as being in its own world, but as a *deviant* sect within the family of monotheists. In contrast to this view of civilizational clash, distinguished scholars like Albert Hourani, Maxine Rodinson, Samir Amin, and Hichem Djait, all of whom are leading figures in Middle Eastern and Islamic studies, have long cautioned against such generalizations, demonstrating that such a history is much too nuanced to be viewed through this modern temporal and spatial lens. Indeed, as Maxine Rodinson has pointed out, Muslims and Christians, up until early modernity, rather than viewing each other as two irreconcilable civilizations, instead perceived each other as conflicting sects, whose origins come from the same source:

> In the Middle Ages, Islam had been considered a schism, a kind of perversion of Christianity. This was, for example, how Dante regarded it. It was a time of an increasing number of schisms in the Church, expressed not only by religious differences but by political ambitions as well. This was the case with Islam, and indeed, it could now be seen as a mere schism, one of many.[2]

Christians residing in what would eventually be called Europe, rather than defining Islam as a civilization unconnected to Christendom, instead perceived it as a heretical innovation of Christianity. Islam was not, as it will become after the Enlightenment, seen as completely outside of the Christian self, where a strict ontology of difference would produce an understanding that Islam possesses a time-space perimeter that is radically different than the time-space of Europe.

As Rodinson suggests in the previous quote, although Medieval Christians perceived Islam as a deviant faith, it nonetheless remains inside the time-space of the self, for even a deviant, no matter how misdirected, has access to the truth but has perverted it. In the words of Hichem Djait, "As excessive as these judgments may be, they arose from the possibility ... of admitting Islam into the body of Christian truth. Christian apologists simply wished to show that Islam was in error according to the canons of the Church, to deny the Prophet's claim to be a real prophet, and to prove that the word of God was the word of God. From this standpoint, therefore, Allah is God ... but he did not speak to

Muhammad."[3] A good case in point is St. John of Damascus (675–749), who incorporates Islam as one of many *Christian* heresies, but with the defects of denying some of Christianity's essential truths.[4]. In this sense Islam invoked a common tradition for "they too worshiped God in their own way, even if in doing so they were totally in error."[5]

In this pre-Enlightenment conception of civilizations, the modern temporal template of civilizations, in which each is perceived to have a distinct time-space module, was far from the minds of the elites. For those Medieval Christians who resided in the European continent, Muhammad, the prophet of Islam, was an imposture, a fake prophet, who peddled Christian ideas but distorted them so as to attain power. In this sense, he was like the Pope for the Protestants of the sixteenth century, acquiring an unwarranted post of privilege by deceptively placing himself as the keeper of the keys of heaven. Indeed, in the words of Martin Luther, "the Pope and the Turk are 'the two arch-enemies of Christ and his Holy Church,' and if the Turk is the body of Anti-Christ, the Pope is the Head."[6] In Hichem Djait's words, Islam's "point of departure," for these Christians, "was a deep anger at the Prophet for having blocked humanity's evolution toward universal Christianity by his 'false prophecy.' . . . Muhammad was a false prophet, an imposter, and a hypocrite."[7] For our concern here, no matter how disparaging these remarks may be, they nonetheless placed the Muslim as one who has access to eternal truth, but was deceived by a false prophet.

This would radically change in the post-Enlightenment period. Beginning in the late seventeenth century and becoming dogma by the late nineteenth, Islam would become more and more relegated as something quite separate from "Western civilization," a *homo islamicus*, a civilization sealed off in its own allotted time-space, endowed with its unique and essential nature.[8] As this new ontology of civilizational difference consolidated itself into a systematic worldview, the Islam-as-a-sect of Christianity argument gave way to a more rationalist, historicist, evolutionary, progressive, and secular philosophy. The East and Orient in general, and Islam in particular, came to be understood in secularized and laicized language. This was not a quick transition from one system of thought to another. Indeed, as Hichem Djait has explained, throughout this transition there was an intermingling of the two perspectives, where "Orientalism used first Christianity and then secular humanism as a stick to beat Islam." But it would be through this transition that Europe and its intellectuals would finally converge on the idea of progress and "of a civilizing or liberating mission."[9] In this sense, rather than viewing a Christian religious worldview being overtaken by a secular one, it is more accurate to describe it as a transition in which religious discourse was redeployed in a more secular framework, where "anyone who studied the Orient a secular vocabulary in keeping with these frameworks was required."[10]

The discursive power of this change should not be underestimated, because it allowed Eurocentric theorists to assign Europe an exemplary status relative to other civilizations, thereby locking Islam into a temporal cage from which Europeans had freed themselves and marched out of many centuries past.[11] Immanuel Wallerstein captures well the ideological utility this intellectual change offered the West:

> The core of the explanation that was developed was remarkably simple. Only European "civilization," which had its roots in the Greco-Roman world of Antiquity (and for some in the world of the Old Testament as well) could have produced "modernity"—a catchall term for a pastiche of customs, norms, and practices that flourished in the capitalist world-economy.... There must be, there must always have been, something in the non-European high civilizations that was incompatible with the human march toward modernity and true universalism. Unlike European civilization, which was asserted to be inherently progressive, the other high civilizations must have been somehow frozen in their trajectories, incapable therefore of transforming themselves into some version of modernity without the intrusion of outside (that is, European) forces.[12]

Such intellectual changes were already visible by 1697 with one of the pioneers of the Enlightenment, Peter Bayle (1647–1706), whose monumental *Dictionnaire historique et critique* (Historical and Critical Dictionary 1697) influenced French encyclopedists like Diderot and other rationalist philosophers of the eighteenth century. Indeed, his *Dictionnaire,* which many called the "arsenal of the Enlightenment," marks a turning point from which to evaluate the emergence of a new civilizational discourse.[13] But it was not until Orientalists in the late eighteenth and early nineteenth centuries—like Volney, Montesquieu, Hegel, and Renan—focused on comparing Islam to Europe, that we can say this discourse became the dominant way of understanding the "difference" between Islam and the West. Because it was not until then that such differences were pinpointed, so as to indicate a kind of typology of social types that accused Islam of cultural deficiencies in its distorted path to achieving modernity. It is in this intellectual context that the idea emerges that the "underdeveloped" nature of Islamic societies was not simply a product of political and economic factors, but something much "deeper." In the words of our contemporary Orientalist Bernard Lewis, it was the product of a "classical Islamic view."[14]

Constantin Volney (1757–1820), whose multivolume encyclopedia *Description del Egypte* (1809–1822) came out of the Napoleonic Expedition of Egypt, provides a clear illustration of this new temporal ideology. In his detailed description of the Egyptians, he denounces Islam for its crudity and anti-scientism, "bearing the mark of the barbarism it grew out of."[15] In his *Travels in Egypt and Syria,* for instance, he uses a discourse that will become a staple of Orientalist thought toward Islam, a discourse that will have a great effect not only on European thinkers but Muslims like Kemal Ataturk and other Middle Easterners as well. Volney's description of Islam, in the passage below, effectively uses the temporal script that will shape many intellectual and political thinkers to come:

> So far from helping to remedy the abuses of government, the spirit of Islamism, one might say, is their original source. To be convinced of this, simply examine the book which is the repository of that spirit.... Anyone who reads the Koran will be forced to admit that it has no idea either of man's duties in society or of the formation of the body politic or the principles of the art of governance.... If amidst the babel of this perpetual delirium any grand design or coherent meaning ever breaks through, it speaks with the voice of an obstinate, impassioned fanaticism.... The inevitable consequence of all this is to set up the most absolute despotism in the person of the ruler through the blindest self-sacrifice on the part of his followers. And this indeed was Muhammad's goal. He wanted, not to enlighten but to reign. He sought, not disciples but subjects. Of all the men who have dared to give laws to nations none, assuredly, was ever more ignorant than Muhammad. Of all the absurd creations of the human mind none is more wretched than his book.... *It would be easy to prove that the troubles of the State and the ignorance of the people in that part of the world are more or less directly traceable to the Koran and its morality.*[16]

Even before the example of Volney, the French Philosopher Voltaire would write a play with the title *Fanatism, or Muhammad the Prophet,* depicting Muhammad as a theocratic tyrant, "who uses the sentiments and beliefs of human beings in order to serve his 'affreux desseins'."[17] Likewise, for the great German philosopher, Hegel, Islamic civilization was of use only insofar as it had the historic task "to hand on Greco-Roman civilization to modern Europe" where "the Spirit had moved from Islam to modern Europe, whose historical mission was to absorb the antithesis into a synthesis, and nothing was left in the Muslim world except sensual enjoyment and oriental repose."[18] Interesting enough, in his *Lectures on the Philosophy of History*, although Hegel praises Islam as serving an important function in the East by introducing the abstract One into that part of the world, thereby "transcending the negativity of the Oriental mind," he still ends up finding it lacking, in that, unlike the concrete manifestation of the Spirit in Europe, its version of universalism was too abstract, causing the Spirit to lose its energy, thereby eliminating Islam "from the stage of history."[19]

As we can see here, Islam was no longer viewed in the Medieval sense as a monotheistic sect led by a false prophet, but as a civilization in and of itself that had played a role in the evolution of man, but somehow, owing to its internal makeup, ceased to evolve. For Ernest Renan (1832–1892), this was expressed as a natural course of development, where "different peoples have different abilities to move along this path.... There is a hierarchy of peoples, languages and cultures.... The Semitic spirit and Islam have conquered the world, but it can produce nothing else."[20] In his now very famous lecture of 1883, entitled "Islam and Science," which he delivered at the Sorbonne, he came to the conclusion that "Islam was the characteristic product of the Semitic mentality. It was a religion which prevented the use of reason and growth of science.... There had never been, there could not be, such a thing as a Muslim scientist: science had indeed existed and been tolerated inside Islamic society, but the scientists and philosophers were not really Muslims."[21] So that even when there were individuals within the Islamic world who passed on a philosophical legacy, like Avicenna, they were not, in Renan's mind, really Muslims or Arabs, for science came to them only as "fossilized remnants of the ancient Hellenic world."[22] This denial is in keeping with Renan's view of the development of mankind, where Muslim philosophy is considered to be an oxymoron, for which *falsafa* (Arab philosophy) evolved from an outside, non-Islamic, source. In Renan's own words, "the Muslim is in the profoundest contempt of education, science, [and] *everything that constitutes the European spirit.*"[23] All one has to do to see this truth, says Renan, is visit the East or Africa, where he will be "struck by the hidebound spirit of the true believer, by this kind of iron circle which surrounds his head, rendering him absolutely closed to science, incapable of learning anything or of opening himself to a new idea."[24] The contempt he has for Islam, and the Semitic race from which it arose, is spelled out explicitly:

> One sees that in all things the Semitic race appears to us to be an incomplete race, by virtue of its simplicity. This race—if I dare use the analogy—is to the Indo-European family what a pencil sketch is to painting; it lacks that variety, that amplitude, that abundance of life which is the condition of perfectibility. Like those individuals who possess so little fecundity that, after a gracious childhood, they attain only the most mediocre virility, the Semitic nations experienced their fullest flowering in their first age and have never been able to achieve true maturity.[25]

In keeping with this new temporal discourse, Renan's denunciation of Islam is tied to a "stage in human development through which Europe itself has passed . . . and from which it has won deliverance."[26]

As we can see here, the nineteenth century represents a period in which the ideas of *development, progress, evolution, social forces,* and other similar historicist terms were becoming the reigning tools for explaining civilizational, cultural, and religious differences. Dissimilarity between societies and civilizations were now viewed through the lens of a historicist narrative with its views that all that exists rests on some historical man-made force that is self-evolving, continuous, and changes in accordance to particular meetings of social and cultural forces that become altered by the internal dynamics of its constituent parts. Hence, each civilization, whether it is a religious or cultural force or the act of spirit, classes, status groups, or racial characteristics, contains within itself a developmental seed that rises in accordance to its particular type. In Albert Hourani's fine précis of this intellectual change, "history as such assumed a new importance: it was the working out of the nature and destiny of the universe, and the study of history was the attempt to define the laws by which the working out took place."[27]

Thus Islam itself became a phase in the historical development of civilizations, one of many in the world, each having its own essential time and space. This new system of thought can be characterized as a Toynbee-like-archive list of civilizations, each of which can be narrated, by a gifted historian or social scientist equipped with the proper conceptual tools, from its origins on, as though one were describing a biological organism from its simplest one-cell structure to a more complex multicell unit. Where and at what point of development each and every unit is to be classified is a decision that needs to be made by a competent individual who has mastered the skills to evaluate the temporal point or historical stage it now resides in.

This point of view affected both intellectuals and statesmen alike, as is the classic examples of the sociologist Max Weber and the British Prime Minister Lord Cromer. In the case of Cromer, whose book *Modern Egypt* would gather together many facets of this new historical narrative into a simple system any literate person can comprehend (and one that will remain with us from his time to our very own, as the case with Thomas Friedman, Nail Ferguson, and others today suggests), the occupation of Egypt, he argues, is being used by the British out of an act of kindness toward the less-developed Egyptian and Islamic peoples of the Middle East. Cromer's reasoning for this is quite clear: Islam, even though it is a "noble monotheism," is a failure as a social system. The list that he provides of why it is a failure would become the script that many after him would plagiarize in their attempt to rationalize either the hostile bombardment of that part of the world (as in the case today with the U.S. bombing of Iraq), as would "indigenous" Muslim elites charged with "developing" their society (as we will see with the case of Kemal Ataturk). As a religion, Islam is patriarchal and oppresses its women; it does not separate mosque and state; it is intolerant to minorities and other faiths; it permits slavery and forced bondage; and, straight from Renan and Volney before Ataturk, it discourages science and reason. Therefore, it is no surprise he holds the belief that "Muslims can scarcely hope to rule themselves or reform their societies."[28]

In more academic circles like that of Max Weber, the perception was that, if development, rationality, science, and capitalism developed in Europe first and not elsewhere, then part of the explanation for its success might lie in Christianity itself, especially its Protestant variant, leading Weber to a massive historical comparative analysis of many world religions with that of Christianity, including Islam. Though Max Weber was quite critical of the dehumanizing characteristic of modern forms of rationality, his search for the uniqueness of the "Western" mode led him to rely on Orientalistic representations of Islam. To no surprise, he found the answer he was looking for on what distinguishes "Western" civilization from Others: Islam resembles the "pure type" of what he calls a "prophetic book-religion," which it shares with the Jewish and Christian traditions, but unlike the latter two Islam's "ethic is 'feudal,' oriented—even in its mystical form—towards 'world conquest' and not towards 'world renunciation' as in Christianity."[29] Because of this difference in its ethics and ascetic orientation toward the world, he concludes that it must be internal features in Islam that caused it to fail in developing the type of formal rationality it needed to produce modernity. Those reasons are, "the obviously unquestioned acceptance of slavery, serfdom, and polygamy; the disesteem for and subjugation of women; the essentially ritualistic character of religious obligations; and finally, the great simplicity of the modest ethical requirements."[30] Because of the combined effects of its particular "feudal" nature, mixed with a particular form of rationality not congruent with modernity, Islam—as a world religion—does not have the proper characteristics to develop a modern society like that found in the West.

Of course, as we have already pointed out, the emerging expansion of colonization throughout the world by the rising power of Western states, gave this new intellectual system vibrancy. There was a void left over by this European expansionary thrust into the global South to explain why one sector of the world ruled and produced more wealth, machinery, finished goods, bigger bridges, steamships, and militaries than any other sector of the world. In the case of the Muslim world and, in particular, the Ottoman Empire, the fact that there was outright colonization from the Napoleonic period on, especially with the occupation in 1881 of both Tunisia and Egypt, added a deep sense that something about that part of the world had led to its decline and subordination to Western powers. Thus emerged the idea that Islam, like other "traditional" religious or cultural systems, must contain some type of barrier that does not permit it to progress along the same lines as the West. It is as though there is a genetic defect that has dwarfed Islam's development into a mature, fully functioning specimen.

Kemal Ataturk: Islam as an Obstacle to Producing the New Turk

> We shall adopt hats along with all other works of Western civilization.
>
> —*Kemal Ataturk*

This persistent nineteenth-century, Eurocentric discourse condemning everything Muslim penetrated deep into the center of the old Islamic Ottoman

Empire, reaching the political elites of Istanbul. Indeed, the so-called founding father of modern Turkey, Mustafa Kemal (hereafter referred to as Ataturk), was to become the man who would put into practice what colonizer's like Cromer were unable to do themselves: to force upon their subjects a strict dose of Eurocentric political, economic, and, most significantly for us here, cultural reforms. Moreover, Ataturk was known to be an admirer of precisely those Western intellectuals who looked with deep contempt upon Islam, namely Montesquieu, Voltaire, Rousseau, and positivists like Comte, "whose books are still on display in the presidential villa in Ankara."[31] As Kemal Ataturk's biography seems to indicate, one has to be impressed by the deep influence and successes of Orientalism in its power to provide a vocabulary and a set of ideas that even the elites of the colonized, in their effort to take state power, could use politically for their own will to power.

As we saw with some key European Jews like Theodor Herzl in the last chapter, I argue here that many of the Turkish elites were similarly affected by this inferiority complex and, as a way to deal with this tension, created for themselves the task of remaking their identities in the image of those more powerful. Kemal Ataturk and the others who followed him sketched a detailed account of what they imagined to be "the West" and proceeded to adopt it, all while they strategically attempted to overturn anything that smelled, tasted, or looked Islamic or Ottoman, transforming everything from the state, urban planning, the uses of public space, and historical memory down to the more intimate details like "proper" attire and headwear, veiling, and even the type and use of utensils during family meals. Ataturk, through the new-found ideology of modernization, instituted national changes, with the intention of producing the new Turkish and Occidentalized Self in both the public and private realms.

The Shattering of the Ottoman Empire

But, although the underlying issue that shaped and produced this anxiety was the deep-felt desire in the colonized world to "catch up" to their colonial masters, the despairing nature in which the colonial encounter left the global South's polities and economies in shatters would cause the new emerging political and intellectual elites to search for a new paradigm to base their new societies on. The centrifugal forces that were undermining the Ottoman Empire created increasing competition on how best to deal with this new reality.

To make things worse, the problem that the Turks had to face, like others of the global South, was the new reality that their part of the world, which was once part of the core of the ancient world system—with the Muslim world at its center—by the mid-nineteenth century, found itself at the losing end, swallowed up whole and relegated to the margins of a Western-centric world, with the "Muslim world" generally, and the Ottoman Empire more specifically, now residing at the losing end of this system, subordinated to European and, later American power, whereas previously it had stood far ahead.

The effects of this new world order on the social structure of the Middle East in the nineteenth century would be profound, evolving in qualitatively new ways that mark it off from all hitherto historical systems. As a result, the Islamic *umma* (community) in the nineteenth century disintegrated both materially and politically as it entered the global political economy, causing a dramatic change in the structure and identity of the non-Muslim millets (ethnic groups). Modernity, in a sense, restructured every aspect of the Muslim world, from its class makeup and trade patterns to its formal political structure. Religious, gender, and ethnic identities were especially impacted by this new reality. The Greek revolt of 1821 would signal the beginning of this process. Arab nationalism, beginning later in the nineteenth century and reaching maturity only after World War I, would eventually add momentum toward complete fragmentation. Dar al-Islam was slowly and surely being hacked to pieces, and in its place we begin to see the rise of Greek, Arab, Turkish, Kurdish, Armenian, Jewish, and other nationalist movements.

All these changes would ultimately dismantle the prior symbiotic world of the Ottoman Empire by destroying the linkages local elites needed to maintain their alliances with the old imperial center (Istanbul). In the process, even after a concerted effort by Istanbul to negate this fragmentation in the *Tanzimat* reforms of the mid-nineteenth century, local notables were increasingly freed from their ties to the center. Whereas before this great transformation Muslims and non-Muslims were integrated across space by Istanbul's influential political and economic power to pull the multiple religious and linguistic groups together, to form symbiotic relationships, this was no longer the case by the end of the nineteenth century.

The incorporation of the Ottoman Empire into the capitalist and colonial world system had similar effects on the economic side as well. In many provinces of the Ottoman Empire, by the late nineteenth century, "the move from locally manufactured goods to purchases of food and raw materials in exchange for European manufactured goods altered" the balance of power between Muslims and Christians, Greeks and Turks, and so on.[32] As more and more trade of the Middle East was redirected from a coherent regional system to one that was linked to Europe and the West, Christians, Greeks, and Armenians benefited directly as a result of foreign protection agreements that were set up to benefit these religious confessional groups. The increase in trade with Europe provided new-found strength to these merchant classes against the Islamic center, adding yet more wealth to the non-Muslim populations who now had special cultural and religious privileges granted to them by the European powers, linking them more densely with Europe.

But more profound for us here was the ideological repercussions that this new hierarchy created between the crumbling Ottoman Empire and the "West." This new imbalance of political and economic power would have a significant political and psychological effect on the multiple national identities that would eventually emerge out of the rubble left behind by this colonial encounter. The lens through which all actors of this new world order came to understand their world was becoming ever more *racially* tainted, leading to an interpretation of a world where religion, language, ethnicity, and nation were reinterpreted in light of this new hierarchy, producing the belief that one group or another possesses some unique trait that legitimates its superior or unique characteristics above the rest. In the judgment of the new masters of the globe, Muslims fell quickly to the bottom and were designated as racially and culturally inferior to the West.

Faced with this new political and economic conquest by European colonial regimes, which eventually would cause structural problems of political and economic underdevelopment in the Middle East region, Ataturk and others came to measure their standing in the new global order by comparing themselves to the West, which was believed to have acquired refined qualities that they, the weak Muslims, now needed to emulate. In this sense, the incorporation of the Middle East into the capitalist world system had major racial and national implications that informed the ideological lens through which the colonized produced their new societies. These movements had to literally produce new national identities that they believed would allow them to respond effectively to the hegemonic power of the global North, and in the process grabbed on to those circulating in the minds of the colonizer.

Struggling to free themselves from colonial rule and create in its place a new society, Kemal Ataturk, and the movement he represents, responded by consuming the Orientalist script in its entirety.

Turkey Attempts to Cross the Bridge

It is against this political, economic, and intellectual background that we can understand the intervention of people like Kemal Ataturk. Ever since the humiliating destruction of the Ottoman Empire and its eventual death after World War I, Turkey has been dealing with the outsider's insistence on labeling it as a "bridge between East and West," marking it as a "gateway" to the Orient. In this bridge metaphor, Turkey becomes the actual site not only to spatially enter the East, but the location through which one is transported through time, from the land of progress and modernity to the land of backwardness and the Middle Ages. Therefore, Turkey's elites, headed by Ataturk, had "been trying to cross the bridge between the East and the West for more than a hundred years now, with a self-conscious anxiety that it is arrested in time and space by the bridge itself."[33] Indeed, the present debate on whether or not to allow Turkey membership into the European Union continues to refer to the markers of East and West, indicating "that the Occidentalist fantasy is still at the heart of the hegemonic imaginary."[34]

As we will see, the elites of Turkey have been so thoroughly immersed into this fantasy that they delved deeply into its Orientalist representations, doing everything in their power to pull Turkey from the imagined East side of the bridge to the other Western side. Resat Kasaba captures well how this makeover penetrated into everyday life: "What the people wore, how they lived, what kind of music they listened to, and even what they ate"[35] all formed the basis for a nationalist project to transform the "Oriental" self into a modern, civilized, and "Occidentalized" self. For these Kemalist leaders, "formal elements of change, such as the outward appearance of people, the cleanliness of the streets ... became synonymous with modernization and consumed an inordinate amount of their time and energy."[36] As Bryan Turner also observed, "The mimetic quality of Turkish secularization had to be carried out in detail at the personal level, in terms of dress, writing and habit."[37] Kemalists even made a "fuss about introducing ballroom dancing, replacing traditional Turkish music with opera, and so on."[38]

Photo 3.1 The image of Kemal Ataturk in his tuxedo and Western attire can be found everywhere in Turkey.

The actual objective of these changes was first and foremost to destroy all the Islamic symbols of the Ottoman Empire. It initially began in November 1922, with the elimination of the Caliphate, a political institution that goes back to the death of the prophet Muhammad in 632 ACE. But the reforms became ever more forceful immediately after the proclamation of the Turkish Republic when Ataturk closed down all religious courts and Islamic schools, the office of the chief *mufti*, as well as many other Islamic and religious institutions.[39] Soon after these initial reforms, more focused efforts were introduced by Ataturk, including the adoption of the Gregorian Calendar (1926), the shutting down of convents and sacred tombs, and the abandonment of the Ottoman Arabic script for that of the Latin alphabet and Western numerals. He also forbid Muslims to take their religiously prescribed pilgrimages to Mecca. The famous Hat Law of 1925 would be one of his symbolic highlights in which he prohibited all civil servants from wearing the fez. In 1935, the traditional Friday Muslim day of rest and prayer was officially abandoned in favor of Sunday.[40]

By enacting these reforms, Ataturk accepted the Eurocentric discourse and believed that such interventions were necessary for building a modern and new society, and that in order to cross the bridge one had to institute dramatic changes, one that involved a sharp rupture from past Ottoman ways. In so doing, he not only accepted the views of people like Volney, Renan, Cromer, and Weber, but he went so far as to insist on using Islam as the symbolic marker from which Turkey must distance itself. Turkey had to travel temporally and spatially *away* from Islam, in order to become a new and modern nation. In this sense, he followed many nationalist elites of his time, who demanded a change in the character of the nation so that it could be recreated to fit the paradigmatic figure of the modern, superior West. By carefully overhauling the nation's history, tradition, and culture, and by making the nation less "primitive" and more "modern," Kemal Ataturk, like Third World nationalist elites elsewhere, believed that through such reforms he was not only en route to creating a modern civilization in the image of the West, but also producing subjects who were exact replicas of the European. He was totally obsessed with the idea of development that promised to magically transform, within one generation, the "underdeveloped, primitive, and traditional" Turkey he knew into one that resembled the "progressive" civilization of the West.

Thus a new, nationalist project emerged in the twentieth century. Long gone was the colonizer's idea that required a racial and evolutionary period of waiting for a match to occur between biology and civilizational development. Rather, the nationalist had produced a new discourse that permitted him the power to do something very different. *Instead of waiting for the hand of evolution to signal his destination, he now had to become an activist with the will to make the non-modern perform to the capacity achieved by his Western counterpart.* What the nation needed to demonstrate to the European world was that it, too, could be like the West: dynamic, productive, secular, civilized, and rational. This was indeed perceived to be a new era in the life of the nation, an era in which "static" and "unchanging" traditions would finally come to an end. For the colonized, such a project would have seemed ludicrous before the twentieth century, when the question of remaking "ourselves" in "their" image was subdued by the reality of direct colonialism. The spreading of liberal ideals to include non-Western peoples could only have become a reality with the success of national liberation movements taking state power.

But unlike many of his contemporary nationalist elites in other regions of the decolonizing world, distancing the self from the past meant for Ataturk a complete rupture with that very past. In Ataturk's own words,

> There are a variety of countries, but there is only one civilization. In order for a nation to advance, it is necessary that it joins this civilization. If our bodies are in the East, our mentality is oriented toward the West. We want to modernize our country. All our efforts are directed toward the building of a modern, therefore Western, state in Turkey. What nation is there that desires to become a part of civilization, but does not tend toward the West?[41]

Ataturk was highly influenced by the ideas of Ziya Gokalp (1876–1924), a man Ataturk referred to as the "intellectual father of the new Republic," whose influential pamphlet, *The Principles of Turkism*, warned of the cultural threat that Turkey faced by the emerging powers of the West and recommended the following: "There is only one way to escape these dangers, which is to emulate the progress of the Europeans in science, industry and military and legal organization, in other words to equal them in civilization. And the only way to do this is to enter European civilization completely."[42]

By heeding Gokalp's warnings, Ataturk saw himself as a Turkish man, who, having already acquired the proper traits of a civilized man, was well equipped to lead the country across the bridge to modernity. At times this self-aggrandizing image of himself took on narcissistic qualities, as the following example, which he wrote in his 1918 diary, illustrates:

> If I obtain great authority and power, I think I will bring about by a coup—suddenly in one moment—the desired revolution in our social life. Because, unlike others, I don't believe that this deed can be achieved by raising the intelligence of others slowly to the level of my own. My soul rebels against such a course. Why, after my years of education, after studying civilization and the socialization processes, after spending my life and my time to gain pleasure from freedom, should I descend to the level of common people? I will make them rise to my level. Let me not resemble them: they should resemble me.[43]

His preference here for language like refusing to "descend" to the level of common people, who instead need to be "raised" to a "higher" level, demonstrates clearly his internalization of the colonizer's temporal template. Fearing that "progress" might bypass Turkey, he comforted himself with the idea that, with the guidance of elites like himself, who are properly educated in highbrow Western culture, there was hope that the common people could be lured to a new world out of the old. He could raise the masses from their deep sleep so as to become one with the "speed and movement that define our century." In this way he agreed with Ziya Gokalp, who also loved the time machine idea of development: "We shall skip five hundred years and not stand still."[44]

The role of the developmental state was thus seen as an instrument of change that had the capacity to turn the new nations from passive to active agents of modernity. Although this didn't occur until after World War II, when articles and books appeared with titles like, "The Modernization of Man," "The Impulse to Modernization," "The Modernization of Religious Beliefs," *Modernization of the Arab World, Modernizing the Middle East,* and *Becoming More Civilized* began pouring out.[45] Ataturk had already envisioned the turn toward "modernizing" and "speeding up history," years before any of these books hit the bookstores. The details by which he proposed to see such changes reached down to every sector of society, as , for instance, in a speech he gave in 1925 where he proposed that what "the country needs was to train waiters to provide table service in a manner suited to civilized people."[46]

To get to that highest stage of modernity, Ataturk spoke out strongly against what he believed to be Islam's sanction against certain forms of artistic and scientific expression that he viewed as essential to his modernization project: "A nation which does not make pictures, a nation which does not make statues, a nation which does not practice science, such a nation, one must admit, has no place on the highroad of civilization."[47] Decades before Daniel Lerner published *The Passing of Traditional Society* (1958), Ataturk preached what would eventually become dogma: To develop and modernize, reforming the state and economy, was not enough; the nation must also transform its interior self by creating new cultural practices that were on a par with the West. His insistence on such cultural reforms was loud and clear: "We will become civilized.... We will march forward." At times he even used metaphors that sounded as if they were pulled straight from Koranic texts: "Civilization is a fearful fire which consumes those who ignore it."[48]

It was to this modernizationist discourse that Kemal Ataturk responded favorably. By claiming the "modern" as his own preferred subject matter, Ataturk sought to remove from the nation's body all those behaviors, cultural traits, and systems of thought that he perceived as forming the stumbling block to producing a new Turkey. Ataturk focused his mind on eradicating Islamic and Middle Eastern elements from the Turkish nation, as the following remark makes clear: "In the face of knowledge, science, and of the whole extent of radiant civilization, I cannot accept the presence in Turkey's civilized community of people primitive enough to seek material and spiritual benefits in the guidance of sheikhs. The Turkish republic cannot be a country of sheikhs, dervishes and disciples. The best, the truest order is the order of civilization."[49]

Like his colonialist predecessors, Ataturk shared the idea that people of the non-Western world were of a different cultural type than those of the West. But Ataturk passionately believed that *these differences could be overcome,* that the Turkish nation, with the proper mind-set of visionary modernizers, could transcend its present condition and be remade in the image of the West. To that end, he would search for those characteristics that are peculiar to modern Western societies and transplant them into Turkey, just as a gardener would select his favorite plants from a neighboring garden and replant them in his own backyard. Only through this radical makeover would Turkey overcome its archaic predicament. Ataturk believed that he could literally pluck those irritating Islamic roots out of the soil of Turkey, just as a landscaper plucks weeds out of a well-manicured lawn. "The fez sat on the heads of our nation," he complained, "as an emblem of ignorance, negligence, and fanaticism and hatred of progress and civilization."[50] It, too, along with many other Islamic and Oriental characteristics, must be removed from the new Turkey forever, for it is only by this route that "our thinking and our mentality will . . . become civilized."[51]

Westernizing the nation's cuisine fit into this plan as well. Already by the late nineteenth century, one of Turkey's earliest cookbooks declared that "because of the changes in lifestyles, the old dishes were no longer satisfactory, and that the '[Turks] need to adopt a new cuisine from the West that goes better with our new conditions'."[52] Decades later, this would become dogma, when even something as trivial as the production of a soda beverage was influenced by this discourse, as in the case of Cola Turka, whose Turkish producer would claim that the company "prides itself in producing a soda that looks and tastes exactly like its American counterparts."[53] It is apparent that this radical turning away from anything that smacks of the old and turning toward all that is Western is a destructive discourse that compelled Kemalists "to assert their Western identity by denying and repressing the oriental within themselves."[54]

Even the music had to be "updated," especially anything that sounded like it originated from an Arab source or was influenced by "folk" traditions. As Meral Ozbek has argued, "Any Turkish music that did not fit into the officially sanctioned categories of Turkish art music, Turkish folk music, Turkish light (pop) music, or polyphonic (Western) music was assumed to be Arabesk music and therefore subject to censorship.... Turkish classical and folk musicians condemned Arabesk for polluting the 'pure' traditions with Arab influences."[55] As in the establishment of the prestigious Turkish AKM (Ataturk Cultural Center) concert hall in Istanbul, this was especially true with highbrow culture, in which consuming Western classical music and opera was now considered to be "cultured" in civilized (read Western) ways. Indeed, this huge concert hall, standing proudly at the center of Taksim Square, which is one of the most visited locations in Istanbul, functions as a multipurpose performance center and includes a number of concert halls and theaters as well as houses Turkey's premier symphony orchestra, opera, and ballet company. In the words of Alev Cinar, "with its repertoire devoted to Western classical music and ballet, its modern architecture, and its name derived from the iconic founder, Ataturk, AKM stands as a monument of official Turkish modernity that recognizes and adopts the standards of European high culture as the universal norm of civilization."[56]

This obsessive, even quite crude, desire to force a makeover upon the Turkish subject was most evident in reforms involving public dress. The 1925 Hat Law forbids civil servants from wearing not only the fez, but also the turban and the robe. It officially discouraged the wearing of the veil. These were all considered by Ataturk and his followers as symbols of Islam and premodernity and were thus seen as in opposition to the creation of a modern Turkey. Ataturk often referred negatively to all of these, giving special attention to the veil, which he considered to be a "barbarous posture" and an "object of ridicule." In other words, true modernity could not be realized unless the mark of Islam was removed from the body of the Turk. Such authoritarian interventions demonstrate how far Ataturk and his followers were willing to go in wiping out symbols of Islam and the Ottoman period, which they now, under the colonizer's gaze, considered to be backward and a sign of civilizational degradation. This was especially true in the case of the veil, where "women in Turkey had started to take up Westernized forms of dress [and] making themselves up according to an image of the proper Turkish woman."[57]

Interestingly enough, although many scholars today highlight the veil as the most contested clothing symbol in many Islamic societies, Ataturk held special contempt for men's clothing, because he recognized its strategic function between himself and other male opponents, challenging him for power in the early formation of the republic. The large number of references he made to men's clothing and body indicates that he was especially focused on eradicating the symbols of Islam from the bureaucratic leadership of the new Turkish state. Because men filled most of the positions of the state, with women only making slight gains in access to public institutions, he made it a high priority of his administration to target any public officials who remained in positions of power from the "old regime." Indeed, when he passed the Hat Law of 1925—which he considered a "revolutionary step" in the direction of producing a civilized society—he justified it on the grounds that it was necessary in Turkey's journey toward joining Western civilization:

> The issue of headgear, which is completely unimportant in and of itself, is of special value for Turkey, which wants to become a member of the family of modern nations. We propose to abolish the hat worn currently, which has become a mark of difference between Turkey and other modern nations, and replace it with the hat that is the common headgear of all modern civilized nations.[58]

He himself became part of the performance, and he took special care to acquire the most luxurious Western wardrobe available, becoming famous for his tuxedos, silk pajamas, and brimmed hats, presenting himself in a sort of iconic way to look like a male model. In his very first meeting with Parliament in October 1927, for instance, he proceeded to give a six-day talk, in which he highlighted his attacks on Ottoman and Islamic attire. Dressed in his elegant Western attire, which included a black suit with a white tie and a top hat, he presented himself as the embodiment of the new and modern Turkey, and proceeded to ridicule any male in the audience who wore the symbols of Islam as markers of shame and backwardness. While giving his six-day talk, he stopped abruptly in the middle of his presentation, pointed at a man in the crowd, and denounced him in front of all in attendance for the type of dress he was wearing: "He has a fez on his head, and a green turban round the fez, a traditional waistcoat on his back, and on top of it a jacket like mine. I can't see what's below. Now I ask you, would a civilized man wear such peculiar clothes and invite people's laughter?"[59] In this sense he used his body as an instrument to measure the "distance between the republic and the Ottoman state, which was projected as barbaric, incompetent, and despotic," compared with the modern and civilized Turkey, which, under his paternal guidance, was now in the making:[60]

> Gentlemen,... I tell you as your own brother, as your friend, as your father, that the people of Turkish Republic, who claim to be civilized, must show and prove that they are civilized, by their ideas and their mentality, by their family life and their way of living. In a word, the truly civilized people of Turkey ... must prove in fact that they are civilized and advanced persons also in outward aspect.... The grotesque mixture of styles [of our dress] is neither national nor international.... My friends, international dress is worthy and appropriate for our nation, and we will wear it. Boots or shoes on our feet, trousers on our legs, shirts and tie, jacket and waistcoat—and, of course, to complete these, a cover with a brim on our heads.[61]

The use of attire in this fashion was intended to erase the distance between the "West" and Turkey. It was a sort of uniform that Turks would have to adopt as they travel "upward" and "rise to the level" of other civilized peoples of the world. Seen this way, clothing became one of the prerequisites of launching Turkey into the modern age, serving the function a space uniform has for an astronaut's launch into space. It is because of this obsession to remake themselves in the image of the powerful that we can say with confidence that these Kemalists not only accepted the colonizer's discourse of European supremacy, but also attempted to forcefully reproduce, in the most paternalistic and intimate ways, all their Turkish subjects into the new Turk. The appearance of Ataturk and his family at public functions, in which they presented themselves as hyper-Westernized, was consciously counterposed to the now caricatured Muslim other, dressed in the traditional turban and robe, "with his veiled wife following forty paces behind him," and he riding his donkey as she followed behind him on foot.[62] In the words of the Turkish feminist Deniz Kandiyoti, this equating of the traditional male with the Ottoman and Islamic past, which included such images as the untamed, masculinized, traditional Muslim patriarchal male—with his tribalistic and backward proclivities to oppress women—were now interpreted in terms of the temporal gaze, as a "deficit in civilization." By beating the symbols of Islam over the head with these types of progressive sounding discourses, "the civilizing mission [of Kemalists] ... was portrayed as the struggle of science and enlightenment against ignorance and obscurantism."[63] Toward this objective of Westernization, Ataturk not only used his body, but also his wife and stepdaughter as well as his predisposition to consume classical music, European philosophy, opera, and alcohol. All of these came to be symbols of where Turkey needed to go and what it should become.[64]

Even private details like the type of furniture or the kind of utensils households used and the way they ate meals were deeply affected by this colonizer's gaze. Eating with one's hands, for example, and dipping into a meal with bread instead of "proper utensils" now served as markers of distinction between the old Oriental and backward ways of the past and the civilized and modern Turkey of the future. These new etiquettes, as Pierre Bourdieu has explored in other contexts, "implied not simply a refashioning of tastes but also a hierarchy of worth whereby former habits ... could be redefined as unhygienic or even repulsive and older patterns of deference could be deemed uncivilized." In short, they provided cultural markers used to "refashion habit among social groups seeking to shape new subjects."[65] The appropriation of Westernized clothing, music, art, philosophy, food, and furniture was seen as the method through which the new Turkey could be produced and help it successfully cross the bridge to the other side.

Marginalizing Ottoman Istanbul and Islamic History

A key feature of this Kemalist tendency to distance modern Turkey from its Ottoman past included both the marginalization of Ottoman Istanbul in favor of Ankara and Taksim Square and narrating a historical link away from Mecca and toward forging new links elsewhere. Both of these efforts were intended to produce a Turkish identity "untainted" by the Ottoman and Islamic period. Kemalists, as we will see here, followed a similar path that Zionists had preferred in their effort to create a rupture with Jerusalem, Arab Palestinians, and Arab Jews, by creating the new cities of Tel-Aviv and West Jerusalem as well as by occidentalizing the Jewish subject.

Like their Zionist predecessors, who viewed old Jerusalem with suspicion, Kemalists looked upon old Ottoman Istanbul with disdain. It was an urban center saturated with Islamic history, palaces, mosques, and other symbols of a civilization they wanted to leave behind. As was the case of Tel-Aviv for the Zionists, Kemalists in 1923 chose the city of Ankara as the new capital of Turkey, precisely because it could be built from scratch with urban and architectural features that were more in line with Western and modern societies, producing "boxes of glasses and concrete." This was in keeping with the modernist discourse of "rational planning" and urban design and not unlike that of Brazilia in the mind of the French architect Le Corbusier, whose love of "straight lines" and airy arteries uncontaminated by the "Porcupine-like" urban centers of the past, set the tone for these hyper modernists.[66] Ankara was a prime location in which to develop a new capital, precisely because, unlike Ottoman Istanbul, it did "not bear any significant marks of Islam and had not played an important role in either Ottoman or Islamic history." Bearing no visible marks of the past, it was a perfect demonstration of the Kemalist elites' effort to dissociate itself "from Islam and Ottoman times."[67]

To hide or marginalize the Islamic past in Ottoman Istanbul, on the other hand, would have been impossible. Too many vestiges of the past littered the landscape, with its multiple historical sites, like Hagia-Sophia and the Blue Mosque. The fact that the Topkapi Palace, representing the center of Ottoman power, remained standing only added, for the Islamophobic Kemalists, to the complication. In their view, given that Istanbul remained a major economic and political hub, they had to devise a strategy for producing a "new Istanbul" that would counteract the old Istanbul. Toward this end, they relocated the center to a place that was seen as neutral and less tainted, choosing a site on the hill overlooking the Ottoman city and the Sultanahmet complex, and marking Taksim Square as the new central location of "modern Istanbul." They chose Taksim Square, precisely because "there were no significant marks of Islam or Ottoman political power in the area." It also had the benefits of housing many of the non-Muslim populations, whose synagogues and churches were more visible than mosques, all of which convinced Kemalist nationalists that it was a prime location to create a city center that would foster their efforts to distance themselves from "the Ottoman-Islamic center both in geographic terms and in cultural terms."[68]

These efforts worked quite well, and even today, after a revival of Islamic identity, the Sultanahmet region of Ottoman Istanbul remains a tourist haven, with its mosques and palaces functioning as a museum, denying its contemporary inhabitants the living reality of its historical vastness. In Alev Cinar's words:

> The old city center, Sultanahmet Square, gradually became a tourism enclave, which was neatly packaged and presented for the tourist gaze as part of the old and distant past as if to deny its existence outside of this enclave. The Hagia-Sophia Church/Mosque was turned into a museum, together with the Topkapi Palace and several other structures in the area, where once the imperial power of the Ottoman dynasty had reigned.... What had been the center of a vast empire for five centuries was suddenly designated an adjacent district that no longer bore any political viability or national significance for the newly forming secular republic.[69]

The attempt to completely suspend the Islamic-Ottoman cultural landscape from the living reality of contemporary Turkey was especially evident in the new historical narration of Turkish identity. With the establishment of the Turkish Historical Society (1931) and the Turkish Linguistic Society (1932), under the leadership of Kemal Ataturk himself, emerged a nationalist historical narrative that would project a Turkish origin that minimized the Muslim period from its historical memory. The task of these "historical societies" was to craft a historical narrative that would break the identity of Turks from the Ottoman and Muslim period, with the hope of producing a clean slate on which the nationalists could create the new Turkish subject. A new "Turkish Historical Thesis" was developed and distributed through the public Turkish school system, whose claim that the Turks originated from Central Asia and Migrated to Anatolia was in keeping with the objective of creating a rupture and a temporal distancing from the Middle East environment in which Turkey was historically a central part of. They also "invented the so-called 'Sun Language Theory' [which] proposed that 'pure Turkish,' as an ancient language uninfluenced by Middle Eastern cultures, had been the foundation stone for the development of many, If not all, other languages." All of these drastic measures of breaking with the Muslim and Arab Middle

Photo 3.2 A bridge connects "New" and "Old" Istanbul. One cannot help but be reminded of Epcot's bridge when reading how Kemalists articulated their plans for building Ankara and Taksim Square in Istanbul.

East, especially in terms of both language and history, served to disconnect "future Turkish generations from the written Ottoman cultural heritage,"[70] which unsurprisingly was the Kemalist objective all along.

The Ministry of Education produced school textbooks in which they historically revised the narrative so as to create a more direct association between Turkey and the West, taking special care to deemphasize the contributions and linkages of the Arab and North African provinces to modern Turkey. Indeed, it was not until 1995, with the success of the Islamic Welfare Party, that "affinity between Turkish and Arab cultures of the Middle East was allowed in official accounts of geography and history."[71] Moreover, in the initial publication of the massive text, *The Outline of Turkish History*, these Kemalist not only date the origin of the Turkish state to begin 9000 BCE, but also limit the history of the Ottoman Islamic period to a meager 26 out of 467 pages.[72]

Thus, the creation of the Turkish nation would be crafted by these new official historians as having little in common with the Arab world and would break radically with the old narrative of time and space embodied by the *umma*. It produced a historical narrative in which the centrality of Mecca was avoided. Whereas in the old Ottoman imperial conception it was a high priority for the Sultan to temporally link Istanbul with Mecca, in this new narration Mecca was nowhere to be seen. This new historical script would shatter the Ottoman time-space historical paradigm by going on a quest for a new "golden age" that would dislodge Turkey from its old anchor, and in the process, carefully reframe social perceptions of time and space that would make it possible to construct a more Occidentilized Turkish subject.

Conclusion

In this chapter, it is apparent that Kemal Ataturk and his colleagues envisioned a nationalist project whose intention was to remove those elements that were perceived to be dangerous to the production of a healthy "modern" and "civilized" Turkish nation. In this way, Kemal Ataturk and other Turkish nationalists attempted radically to transform the Turk by contrasting the future modern nation of Turkey with that of the past Turkish-Muslim self. As time went by and this construct started to produce a Turkey that envisioned itself as a transformed being, many Turks began to contrast themselves with the Arabs, Iranians, and so on, at every opportune moment. This self-transformation, therefore, helped to define for generations what the "new Turk" was made of, everything that "they" (read Arab and Iranian) were not. Ataturk's vision was a powerful contribution in this revisionism, as in the following statement: "Alas, the Western lands have become the daysprings of knowledge. Nothing remains of the fame of... the Arab, of Egypt. The time is the time of progress, the world is a world of science. Is the survival of societies compatible with ignorance?"[73]

These Kemalists accepted wholeheartedly the colonizer's gaze and wanted to display a new Turkey, with the aim of demonstrating that it was no longer contaminated by the Oriental and Islamic world. They followed the Orientalist script to the extreme, Occidentalizing not only public institutions of governance and public administration, but intervening in very private realms so as to inscribe both a new body and new personal aesthetics. Such changes were intended to both spatially disconnect Turks from the Orient in general and Islam in particular and to temporally "elevate" them above all others in the region, especially the Iranians and the Arabs. All of this came about with the hope that they would no longer be judged unfit to cross the bridge to modernity and that finally the colonizer's gaze would no longer stare with contempt upon their bodies and culture.

But there is one outstanding difference between these Kemalists and the colonizer: In the Kemalist's world, as it was for Israeli nationalists, whereas they chose to pursue the colonizer's Orientalist and racist discourse, they reinvented the colonizer's ideology in innovative and destructive ways. It was as if the Turkish nationalist saw eye to eye with the colonizer and then revised it a bit so as to give themselves the power to rule over the territory they now called Turkey. Although the Kemalists might have felt outsmarted and defeated by the victors of the modern world and believed in the Western judgment that their own nation was primitive, backward, and underdeveloped, and continued to use the same dichotomies of "developed" and "underdeveloped," "modern" and "primitive," they nonetheless differed from their Eurocentric predecessors in that they were able to take the colonizer's discourse one step farther. They *exaggerated* the colonizer's version of reality by including an additional step in the modern/non-modern dichotomy: *They were not inherently born to remain underdeveloped or primitive.* Rather, with a little help from the new vanguardist state, the primitive, backward self could aspire to become modern by following the criteria established by the West. They believed that success could be theirs if they followed a step-by-step guide to modernity. Thus, what essentially changed hands from the colonizer to the Kemalists was that the latter believed they could rule and administer their own people more efficiently and could provide a more disciplined regime of governance with the capacity to produce a more productive and civilized nation than what the colonizer had previously offered. Here, as in the Israeli case, anything that is suggestive of the Orient is something to be removed—Koran, fez, veil, and all—unless, of course, it advances the tourist industry in which the Muslim is ornamentalized or the "primitive" Arab is given a license to entertain "modern" Turks and Western guests for a night of tea and belly dancing, with a camel at times included in the package.

Chapter 4

Arab Time Travelers and Cultural Schizophrenia

> We need to emulate as much as possible the rational life of the West; but I have come to disagree with them about the spiritual life and have come to see that what there is of it in the West is not good to emulate. For our spiritual history is different from the history of the West and our spiritual culture is different from its culture.
>
> —*Muhammad Husayn Haykal*[1]

> We Muslims have the one, true faith, but Allah gave you the iron which is inanimate, amoral, neither prohibited nor mentioned in the Qur'an. We will use your iron, but leave our faith alone.
>
> —*King Abdal-Aziz*[2]

IN 1965 NAZIK AL-MALAIKA, an Iraqi poet, in a speech entitled "Literature and Mental Invasion," addressed the Fifth Arab Writers' Congress. Unhappy with the Westernizing tendencies of her Arab brethren, she complained that "We let them teach us their social customs, their behavior, their way of dealing with people ... and we started wearing their clothes and eating their type of food. We started discarding what was essential in our culture," she continued, "including those traits which made us superior to the West, and took cheap and harmful wares in their place."

> Open an Arabic periodical and you will find one article on Arthur Miller, followed by another on Marcel Ayme, a third on Bruno Walter and yet another on Voltaire. What is more, the writers and critics who produce these articles

> write them not from an Arab point of view but from a purely Western one, so that if you translate the whole periodical into a European language the Western reader will find nothing novel or interesting in it.

What troubled al-Malaika most was not "the merits of these Western men of letters," which she admired, but the fact that her own Arab culture, which has "its own literature, its own religion, and its distinctive culture" was being marginalized and replaced by this Western intrusion: "To admire all their writings unquestionably means nothing less than that we have lost our identity and abdicated our intellects." She warns, in an apocalyptical fashion, that if we Arabs continue to adopt the Western culture in place of our own, we will "destroy ourselves."[3]

Nazik al-Malaika's view, as we will investigate in this chapter, represents a stark break with the Kemalist strain. Many Arab intellectuals reconsidered the Kemalist strategy of all-out assimilation of Western modernity and especially rejected the notion that modernization equals Westernization. Inspired by the Japanese model, these intellectuals searched for an "authentic" past culture that they could identify as their own, with the hopes of excavating, both figuratively and literally, a collective personality that would be distinctive to their own "heritage." Arab nationalists placed great significance in the idea that modernity came in multiple colors, and that their cultural and spiritual side had much to offer in their quest to advance into the modern world. Although they accepted the Western judgment of their *present* cultural and religious practices as "backward-looking," they believed that they once had—before they fell into a deep sleep—a spiritual and cultural side that is quite appropriate for the modern world. What was needed, in their estimation, was not the total discarding of their tradition, but a careful and precise evaluation of what is good and progressive in their original culture and religion versus what is harmful and obscurantist that they can now discard, and once they find and "rediscover" their "true" self they will again be "awakened" and march forward to the other side of the bridge.

So in order to challenge the colonizer's judgment of the time of the Arab and Muslim as being "premodern"—as represented in the Social Darwinist narrative—Arab nationalists coalesced around a project to reinvent the time machine. Although they accepted the fact that the type of vehicle manufactured for this time travel had to follow some of the elements found in the model developed by their Western counterparts, namely the nation-state, they opted for a new brand that was distinctive to them. As we will see in this chapter, although the raw material used for this manufacturing was far from set, they knew, so they thought, that somewhere, deep in their collective personality, lay a heritage that they could claim as their own. With the proper guidance of indigenous professionals and intellectuals, furthermore, they could recover the proper material to be used to build a time machine that finally could propel them into modernity.

Thus, unlike the Kemalists and Arab Westernizers before them, these Arab nationalists refused to blame Islam wholesale for their backwardness. Instead, they chose a selective path, blaming *present* Muslims, especially the clergy, whom they accused of practicing irrational methods of imitation, for their *umma*'s backwardness. With the ghost of Hegel whispering in their ears, they dreamt of a glorious past, where reason reigned, but because of the coming of a dark age, reason left the Muslim lands and traveled West. It was their duty, they argued, to return the original spirit of the Arabs to its rightful place. By doing so, the malaise could be turned around, if, and only if, an elite cadre of intelligentsia, both religious and secular, could rediscover the "true" and untainted essence of a long-lost self. As we will see, sometimes this "rediscovering" came in the form of linking "our" self to an ancient civilization (who were dug up by the colonizer), and at other times it was tied to an adolescent Arab symbolized by the Bedouin (who initially were highlighted by army generals, such as the British John Glubb, and Orientalist painters and photographers, who turned the Bedouin into symbols of the Arab). At other times rediscovering meant tracing the true self back to the activities of the Prophet and the original pious Muslim community of 7th-century Medina (expounded by indigenous Muslim scholars). The indigenous Muslim scholars, who are typically referred to as Islamic modernists, would turn out to be the most effective proponents of the three discourses, by arguing that "if Islam would shed its recent superstitious additions and root itself in the very reason that had given it its power, it could act as the foundation for a Middle Eastern scientific and industrial revolution."[4] Even though, in their estimation, Islam was outdistanced by the West, it possessed, deep in its religious roots, elements of truth and reason that could lead to a revival of strength "capable of catching up with Europe."[5] They made great effort to demonstrate that the weakness comes not from their true and original religion, "but rather the result of an ignorance of the true Islam. The cure . . . lay in a return to the genuine religion."[6]

But, given the fact that the engineers empowered to produce this time-traveling vehicle were infatuated with the Western model (hence, "catching up with Europe"), what they ended up manufacturing was invariably saturated with reused Western gadgets. The Arab and Muslim intellectual and political elites we cover here, in their refusal of the Kemalist path, asked their archaeologists, historians, Islamic scholars, poets, musicians, and others to dig deep into the Arab and Muslim cultural and archaeological landscape, so as to find material appropriate to manufacturing an "authentic" vehicle. The only problem, as Frantz Fanon warned us decades ago, was the fact that "the colonized intellectual, at the very moment when he undertakes a work of art, fails to realize he is using techniques and a language borrowed from the occupier."[7] In other words, the pieces these engineers selected—be they Phoenician, Pharaonic, Bedouin, or Islamic—were pulled straight out of the colonizer's storage houses, which Arab nationalists "discovered" lingering in such discrete places as European museums, British army manuals, or the books of Orientalist scholars.

In this sense, although the Western colonizer was recognized as the political enemy, he remained the teacher, keeping the Arab nationalist in the tight grip of the ontological gaze of the West. Indeed, we can say that the Arab nationalist internalized the insults and judgments of enlightened Europeans toward his own subjects as he tried to awaken them from their slumber. In Hamid Dabashi's summation, "Muslims, believing or otherwise, were beholden to the power and mystique of 'the West,' more a figment of their own captured imagination than a reality *sui generis,* and no matter what they did, opposed or embraced it, they ended up corroborating and further ossifying the ontological veracity of that thing they kept calling 'the West'."[8] The power of the gaze was so deep that it constantly informed the elites' entire artistic and political arsenal used to "free" the indigenous population from its colonial condition. In Fanonian terminology we can say that "the colonized are caught in the tightly knit web of colonialism."[9]

The perceived backwardness of the Muslim people when compared with the West, mixed with the feeling of being humiliated by an occupying foreign force, made it all that much more necessary to claim a sphere that they could use to inspire their scarred dignity. We will follow the lead of

Partha Chatterjee's analysis of Indian nationalism to explore the more typical response of nationalist anticolonial movements. Although Chatterjee's creative scholarly intervention did not aid us much in analyzing Kemalism and Zionism (nor, as we will see in the next chapter, Islamism), his work, as we can clearly deduce from our discussion of his monumental contribution in the introduction to this book, is highly applicable to Arab nationalism. Given the fact that Arab nationalists were deeply in awe of the power of the West, they devised a way to reproduce the colonizer's cultural and temporal script by acknowledging the latter's scientific and technological superiority and proceeded to emulate those things that they understood as universal items of modernity, things like statecraft, economy, and science. However, emulating this exterior material domain produced in them a desire to create a spiritual interior domain that they could call all their own, a unique and distinct Arab personality. But as we will see, this interior domain, which they identified as their true personality, required quite a bit of invention, which their colonial predecessors had already unearthed and manufactured generations earlier. The irony of this is that the most creative aspect of such nationalism, whose intention is "to fashion a 'modern' national culture that is nevertheless not Western,"[10] was in fact first launched by the colonizers. It was they who created a discourse of colonial difference so as to mark, both culturally and racially, the Other as temporally and spatially distant, creating in effect a narrative script, which Arab nationalist would only slightly revise.

What is most significant about Chatterjee's insight here, is that, in the process of insisting on their difference from the colonizer in the interior domain, they selectively uprooted historical and cultural artifacts in the attempt to *dress* their alleged nations with symbols of authenticity. In Joseph Massad's understanding, "The new cultural norms are modern inventions dressed up in traditional garb to satisfy nationalism's claim of a national culture for which it stands. This new culture, however, is not so much *traditional* as it is *traditionalized*."[11] With the power to employ symbols of tradition by using modern communication—such as print media, radio, museums, archaeology, historical writings, a legal system, tourist sites, and so forth—nationalist movements, in the process of usurping control from the colonizer, would mobilize an inventory of discourses through which they would construct their "authenticity."

It was in this nationalist context that Arab political and intellectual elites strung together a narrative whose purpose was to subvert the colonizer's insistence on placing Arabs and Muslims on the lower temporal scale of civilizations, insisting that they, too, had a past self that they can rediscover to set them on a fast track to modernity and progress. Like other anticolonial nationalist movements elsewhere, therefore, we can characterize Arab nationalists as possessing, to use a psychological term, a *split personality*: the interior and exterior. The interior is the "real" and "authentic" self, where one's true identity is located and thus must be protected from any external contaminants. In terms of national or civilizational identity, things like traditions, heritage, customs, and religions are essential parts of the self, and, as such, cannot be discarded at will in the effort of becoming modern. But there is this exterior level that can be adopted from the colonizer with little damage to "our personality." Things like governance, reason, science, education, and public administration, being free of any particular culture and universal in nature, are understood as having little to do with the essential self and thus can be appropriated with little fear of losing one's true identity.

As we saw in the first chapter, in our discussion of how Epcot Center, being a typical site for the reproduction of a Eurocentric discourse, posits the world in binary terms, where one side, represented by "folk" cultures, mosques, and handcrafts, is less developed/evolved than the Future World side of science and industry. Arab nationalists, being confronted with the colonizing and judgmental regimes of the West, proceeded to reproduce the temporal script embedded in this Epcot narration by likewise splitting their identity in two, one with a mature, urban, civilized, and modern Arab self and the other a temporalized childlike past, those being the Bedouin, Phoenician, Pharaonic, or Hittite eras and the like. Even Islam, because it contains revelations or truths that cannot be temporalized, can be scrutinized, they maintained, by the instruments of reason so as to be "more in line" with "modern circumstances." Yet in all cases, these secular Arab nationalists, being confronted by colonial Darwinism, searched for ways to align this temporal gaze so as to show a past child that has now come of age and matured into adulthood.[12] In the remainder of the chapter we will explore how Arab nationalist mobilized all of these discourses so as to build an effective time-traveling machine with the means to launch Arabs into adult modernity.

The Arab Kemalist

Not all Arab nationalists followed this split-personality identity. Indeed, there were many, especially in the 1920s and earlier, who were staunch supporters of a Kemalist-like orientation to remove the Orient and adopt Eurocentrism with little filtering. Like the Kemalist before them, a substantial number of Arab intellectuals looked to the example of the colonizer as a source of inspiration to radically alter their people. As did the Kemalists up north in Turkey, these Arab intellectuals wanted to transform the Arab not only in the material domain but in the cultural and spiritual as well. They were especially inspired by the way the Kemalist regime successfully reoriented its civilizational identity and were particularly intrigued by the manner in which it proceeded to break free from Ottoman/Islamic affiliations. In that sense, Kemalist Turkey, for these Arab thinkers, demonstrated that the most effective way to move forward into the age of modernity and progress was, in their minds, not to "regress" into an Eastern orientation, but rather to set their sails West and never look back. Looking West, they argued, was the only way they could awaken their people from their deep sleep. To achieve enlightenment, to join civilized humanity in its forward march to a better age—all of this could be done only by removing the shackles of Eastern traditions.

Muhammad Husayn Haykal, one of the most prominent twentieth-century Egyptian intellectuals, who was known to have swayed a few times between this Western and Eastern orientation, in his short visit to Turkey in 1927 praised Kemal Ataturk, in an unqualified manner, for bringing to his people "the Turkish renaissance" and introducing radical reforms that the rest of the Eastern world ought to emulate. For him, Kemal Ataturk was "tearing down the old wall of tradition which separated the peoples of the Ottoman Empire from progress and civilization for innumerable generations," and he predicted that "the demolition of this dividing line will open the way to the flow of civilization from West to East."[13] Ismail Mazhar, another Egyptian intellectual, in a paper that was published around the same time as Haykal's, would also acknowledge with favor the Western orientation of Turkey, indeed placing its historical significance for world humanity parallel to that of the Bolshevik Revolution in Russia. What he found most inspiring about the Turkish example was the manner by which it articulated a "progressive" and "modern worldview" that will surely, in his estimation, free Asiatic people from the subjugation of a "backward mentality," one that will finally "be superseded by the modern European mentality."[14]

Internalizing this colonizer's temporal gaze, therefore, had led many Arab nationalists to believe that Europe's success in the material domain was the result of historical change predicted in the Darwinian theory of the survival of the fittest, and that if the Middle East wanted to be one of the winners, it had better accept all of the colonizer's template, both material and spiritual. Indeed, many of these Arab intellectuals were thoroughly influenced by Spencer and Comte and the whole Positivists' system of thought. As Charles Smith points out, by placing Islam in the Positivist framework of historical development, "religion in general and Islam in particular were considered unsuitable to the demands of the modern age."[15]

But arguably the most influential and significant of all the Arab intellectuals to take hold of this Kemalist orientation was Taha Husayn, whose 1938 book, *Mustaqba al-Thaqafa fi Misr* (*The Future of Culture in Egypt*, 1938), would be regarded as the symbolic piece of work to argue for a thorough Occidentalizing approach. Taha Husayn was a blind man born in 1889 in an Egyptian small town in Upper Egypt.[16] In *The Future of Culture in Egypt*, he placed himself in direct opposition to other Arab nationalists who were in support of what he called the "Eastern orientation." His main argument was that Egypt has historically been part of a Mediterranean civilization and only recently "corrupted" by the East. He argued vehemently against those who posited Egypt as part of the East, complaining that such intellectuals were being "totally illogical" and making a "deplorable mistake": "this talk of a spiritual East," he argued, was "no good" and indeed was "dangerous" in that it deceived many Egyptians to identify with an Eastern civilization, which historically they had little contact with:[17] "[Some] Egyptians have deduced the weird and illogical conclusion that they are Easterners not merely in the geographical sense of the term, but in mentality and culture. They regard themselves as being closer to the Hindus, Chinese, and Japanese than to the Greeks, Italians, and Frenchman. I have never been able to understand or accept this shocking misconception."[18] For him, Egypt has always been oriented toward the North and West, and any other affiliation is understood as devious to its true nature: "whether we like it or not, we are connected with the civilized nations of the West."[19]

Thus, modernity, for Taha Husayn, in complete contrast to other Arab nationalists that we will soon discuss, does not come in multiple colors and flavors. There is only one way of being modern, and it is European. For Egypt to be modern, "independent Egypt must become part of Europe, for that is the only way to become part of the modern world":[20]

> Believe me, dear reader, our real national duty, once we have obtained our independence and established democracy in Egypt, is to spend all we have and more, in the way of strength and effort, of time and money, to make Egyptians feel, individually and collectively, that God has created them for glory not ignominy strength and not weakness, sovereignty and not submission, renown and not obscurity, and to remove from their hearts the hideous and criminal illusion that they are created from some other clay than Europeans, formed in some other way, and endowed with an intelligence other than theirs.[21]

To make his point as clear as possible, he cites a famous Western poem and asks his Egyptian readers not to confuse which side of the binary they belong: "We Egyptians must not assume the existence of intellectual differences, weak or strong, between the Europeans and ourselves or infer that the East mentioned by Kipling in his famous verse 'East is East and West is West, and never the twain shall meet' applies to us or our country.... Our country has always been part of Europe as far as intellectual and cultural life is concerned, in all its forms and branches."[22] Like his Kemalist counterparts, his appeal for Occidentalizing the Arab runs quite deep, to all branches of life, including the most intimate things like clothing and culinary practices: "We learned from Europe to sit at the table with a knife and fork. We wear the same kind of clothes." He continues, with much approval, that Egyptians did all this "without discrimination, without examination to know what is actually bad versus what is unsuitable for us. So [deep] has the European ideal become our ideal that we now measure the material progress of all individuals and groups by the amount of borrowing from Europe."[23]

Taha Husayn is unapologetic for his Occidentalizing tendencies and argued with much passion for Egypt to "follow the path of the Europeans so as to be their equals and partners in civilizations, in its good and evil, its sweetness and bitterness, what can be loved or hated, what can be praised or blamed'."[24] In the first few pages of his treatise he heeds a few words of caution: "I am worried because we are now burdened with truly immense responsibilities toward ourselves and the civilized world which we may not fully appreciate." He goes so far as to be concerned that if we fail to affiliate ourselves completely with the West, not only will we fail to progress but even further lose Western respect: "We may fail to make the progress we should, either through sheer neglect or insufficient determination. Such failure will be counted against us by Europeans in general and by our friends the English in particular."[25]

Tawfiq al-Hakim, in a 1933 open letter to Taha Husayn, was the most blunt about his approval of this Westernizing discourse, even at times traversing Arab self-hatred, as when he asked Egyptians to disavow any "alien, non-Egyptian components," especially of the Arab variety, which he described as a "strange amalgam" that "distracted us from the reality of our own spirit." If Egyptians are to progress, there needs to be a "total and uncompromising liberation" of its culture. In his letter to Taha Husayn, he asked his friend to take the lead in freeing Egypt from any "Alien Arab elements": "your first duty towards us is to separate one element from the other."[26] This desire to separate and free Egypt from its Arab orientation was also stated clearly by Hasan Arif in the same year as Hakim's letter to Husayn:

> Whether or not Egyptians intermixed with Arabs [in the past], the present people of Egypt are radically different from the Arabs in every way. The Egyptian is Arab neither in his [external] form, his mentality, his grasp of moral values and social life, his temperament nor his customs. The Egyptian nation possesses a self-contained personality which springs from its own environment and long history, which predates Arab history by thousands of years. The Egyptian nation's existence is independent of the Arabs, the Muslims, the Christians, and the entire world.[27]

This was indeed similar to the case of some Maronite Christians of Lebanon, a large number of whom identified their identity deeply with French culture and proceeded to produce a nationalist project whose intention was for the Lebanese to emulate the French, "not only in the material domain," argues Asher Kaufman, "but in the spiritual" as well. These Lebanese nationalists "based their demand on the assertion that they were part of Western civilization, that they were in fact the French of the Levant and that there were no cultural and political ties between them and their Arab neighbors."[28] Indeed, to bring this point home, they constantly referred to Lebanon as "the Paris of the Middle East." In the words of Nissim Rejwan, "Far from averting their gaze from the possibilities of the new world of Europe and regarding it as a hostile force to be resisted and repulsed Westernizers tried to revive their society in such a way as to make its way of life and thought approximate, or even correspond, to those of Western societies."[29]

The Discourse of "Arab Heritage": Or, the Reproduction of Epcot in Arab Nationalism

But the failure of Arab political actors to end British and French colonization in the first quarter of the twentieth century would eventually delegitimize the ideological stand of these Occidentalizers, leaving the political field open to new ideological orientations. This is because the most Western-oriented political and intellectual elites, succumbing to the status quo of occupation, at times even colluding with the colonizer by serving in the colonizer's bureaucracy, put to shame any credibility in a Kemalist path of Western assimilation in the Arab world. The fact that, in the first half of the twentieth century, the Arab Middle East remained under British and French colonial rule convinced many Arab nationalists to respond quite differently than their Turkish counterparts to the north—who successfully removed the colonizer.[30] By the 1930s and definitely by the 1940s, a new generation of Arab nationalists emerged, one that would adopt a more cultural schizophrenic approach, creating the split personality complex we discussed previously. Even though they, too, shared with Taha Husayn and his Occidentalizing supporters the goal of bringing forth a new social order that, they believed, could supersede the nonviable "old order," with the hope of a new nation emerging on the ruins of the old, they differed from these Kemalists in that they passionately believed that there is an interior self that, with diligence and hard work, can be revived so as to serve and offer the nation the best route toward the road to progress.

It is this belief of a true authentic self that is different from the colonial regime's culture that drove these nationalists to embark upon "reviving heritage." But what part of that heritage one should revive is not so self-evident. History offers an infinite variety of narratives that one can use to construct a "nation" or a "culture," and the idea that there is an objective historical artifact waiting to be unearthed that will once and for all define a people is a narrative that has fooled many in our times, not only those who are emotionally tied to a nationalist project, but also academics, intellectuals, archaeologists, historians, novelists, museum curators, and others. Indeed, this search for a self to revive can be viewed, in a Foucauldian sense, as a "will to power" by an elite group that, in its search for an "authentic culture," produces a logic in the infinite texture of history by unearthing a representation in which *it* stands as the embodiment of a long lost self, which *it alone can bring back to life.*

To simplify things, we will explore three "heritage" items that Arab nationalists decided to place special emphasis on in their effort to revive the soul of the nation or *umma*: classical ancient civilizations, Bedouins, and the pious activities of the Prophet and his "true," uncorrupted message of "rational Islam." Moreover, choosing one of these, as we will soon discover, was itself contested and had much to do with conflicting discourses over issues like secularism, the place of religion, the extent of the nation's border (territorial or the entire Islamic *umma*?) and whom the nation includes and excludes. But from our point of view, the most significant aspect of these discourses is the variety of ways the temporal template is activated to make these narratives produce a self. As we will see, the underwriter of this temporal script, if not the official author, is the colonial interlocutor who, while often hidden in the narrative, is nonetheless constantly in the minds of the indigenous "heritage" producers as they are constructing "their past," be it a Bedouin, a Pharaoh, or a Muhammad and the Koran.

Bedouins in the Colonial and the Arab Nationalist Imagination

As was discussed in the first chapter, colonial regimes' insistence on essentializing the difference between themselves and the Other was based on a temporalized script, a script whose intention was to distantiate the Arab and Muslim spatially and temporally from their Western self. Colonial difference, therefore, legitimized the subordination of the global South to colonial rule by positing the colonized—sometimes in a biological and other times in a cultural evolutionary framework—as too immature for self rule. Representing the Other as living in tents, herding goats, riding camels, and living in a nomadic and Bedouin "premodern" lifestyle was part and parcel of placing the Arab into a time narrative that made him or her appear belong to an earlier age of man. Of course, some of these constructs were of a romantic sort, where Western Orientalists, feeling entrapped in ugly industrialized urban zones of polluted areas like that of late-nineteenth-century Manchester, England, dreamt of the "noble savage," who lived free and in the wild.[31] Yet no matter what the intentions were, romantic or strictly utilitarian in nature, the effect in either case created a temporal trope around which the Arab's culture and civilization were understood. Moreover, the *effects* were exceptionally productive in that, by positing this difference, the colonized would likewise insist on maintaining this script, but only after removing the colonizer and replacing him with the modern (male) nationalist who himself has matured from his childlike Bedouin past.[32] This is the same template that organizes Epcot Center, which we explored in chapter 1, only this time it is the "modern" Arab nationalist sitting in Future World while placing his childlike, folkloric Bedouin culture on the *Other* side of the bridge and in another time.

Lets first explore how the Bedouin image came to signify the Arab under colonial rule. Nineteenth-century Europe, with the inception of mass tourism and print media, was flooded with the publication of travel accounts of people discovering the different cultures of the world. In these travel accounts, the Arab was one of the staples of these narratives, usually placed, along with African nomads, as living outside of history, trapped in a state of childhood, and immune from any real change. Such travel accounts, moreover, provided Europeans with a cognitive map of the world that made the world appear as naturally unequal, with them being the mature, civilized race who was in a position to rule over the youthful children of the Orient.[33]

Photography was a major arsenal in this endeavor. Ronald Hawker notes that without major foreign photographic documentarians like Wilfred Thesiger, Ronald Codrai, and Ramesh Shukla, who created a massive inventory of images of the Emirati society—what Hawker describes as a "bank of historic images"—today's indigenous Emiratis nationalists would probably have identified a different symbol for their nation than the Bedouin and the Falcon, the two images that now have come to represent the Emirates and their nation. Indeed, it was the photography of foreign residents, who carefully selected "pristine" images of the desert and the Bedouin, that would inspire local Arab elites to place special emphasis on Bedouin life and to create a "heritage" discourse and assemble artifacts in museums as well as to run annual "camel races" and create shopping malls fully decorated with "authentic" Bedouin imagery.[34]

Another colonial form of representation that had a significant impact on producing an Arab in the image of a Bedouin who is both spatially and temporally distant from the modern Western self, was the very influential field of nineteenth-century biblical commentaries. Johann David Michaelis, the influential, late-eighteenth-century German writer we met in our discussion of the debate over whether or not European Jews were assimilable into European culture, indeed thought of his contemporary Arabs as the best *living* representatives of the ancient Jews at the time of the great biblical prophets. For Michaelis, the Arabs, who were unable to mature into adulthood and thus lived frozen in time, became a sort of window through which to view life as it existed in the days of the great Jewish patriarchs. They were the living laboratory of a long-lost age, thus representing Europe and Christianity's Oriental childhood: "One will hardly find a people that has kept its customs the same for so long as the Arabs.... Everything we know about these customs coincides so exactly with the most ancient customs of the Israelites and thus gives the richest and most beautiful elucidations of the Bible."[35] For him, the customs of the ancient prophets "have been preserved in these people, who have been cut off from the world." Indeed, so thoroughly have they been preserved that "when reading a description of the nomadic Arabs one believes oneself to be in Abraham's hut."[36] Carsten Niebuhr (1733–1815), a German contemporary of Michaelis, was in large measure in agreement with this notion of a preserved tribal Arab. In his highly influential book, *Description of Arabia* (1772), he repeats Michaelis's thesis almost word for word:

> Coming among them [the Arabs], one can hardly help fancying one's self suddenly carried backwards to the ages which succeeded immediately after the flood. We are tempted to imagine ourselves among the old patriarchs, with those adventures we have been so much amused in our infant days. The language, which has been spoken for time immemorial, and which so nearly resembles that which we have been accustomed to regard as of the most distant antiquity completes the illusion which the analogy of manners began.... Arabia has scarcely known any changes, but those produced by the hand of nature.[37]

These biblical commentaries would produce in the colonizer the image of the Arab as a tribal man living in the desert with his camel and goats and would become the trope through which Christian Europe would see all Arabs.

But arguably the most influential individual in this genre was not a cultural producer or biblical commentator but a British colonial officer by the name of John Glubb, who was only second in command in the Arab Legion of Transjordan in the 1930s. In Joseph Massad's thorough analysis of the man, we come to know him as the most productive creator of the Bedouin as signifying Arab, where in fact, Glubb acts, in Massad's words, as a colonial judge who has the "authority in defining the cultural landscape of Jordan," which included everything from "what one eats, what sports and music one plays, what one wears, how one speaks, and how one moves became all-important rituals suffused with specific significations." In this sense, John Glubb was quite transformative in that he produced what later Jordanian nationalists would consider to be major symbols of their nation. Everything "from a flag to military dress," in Massad's words, "became part of this process of nationalizing not only the Bedouins but also everyone living in Jordan":

> Glubb's investment in a certain Bedouinization of what became Jordan will ... have played a crucial role in *identifying* the country nationally, literally of conjuring up national cultural borders and a national personality, which is always already ... imbricated in racialized and classed imperial notions of comportment and aesthetics.... [He] was meticulous in his plans for the production of new species of Bedouins, nay, a new species of Arabs, albeit a species that came to be known as Jordanian.... Glubb's project entailed molding the Bedouin's body and mind into something new. The new Bedouin came to possess a new epistemology.... This new [Bedouinized Arab] was to become the icon and the symbol of the emergent Jordanian nation. His body was to become the national body.[38]

But Massad's analysis is even more nuanced than this, and he warns against viewing Jordanian nationalists as accepting this trope unchallenged. *Jordanian nationalists were extremely careful to reposition this colonial temporalized script so as to place themselves in the driver's seat of their newly manufactured time machine.* Indeed, Jordanian nationalists performed a creative stunt with this colonial trope. If the colonizer understood the Arab as a Bedouin tribal Other living in premodernity so as to place his Western self as temporally and spatially modern, the Jordanian nationalist removed the colonizer from the driver's seat and placed himself as the modern, urban Jordanian who has outgrown his immature Bedouin days of living in the desert with camels and goats.

In this way, as Massad's argument suggests, the Jordanian nationalists allowed the Bedouin trope to remain as long as it was understood that such creatures, even though they live alongside present-day Jordanians, nonetheless are temporally and spatially distant from "modern" elements of the Jordanian

Photo 4.1 The Museum of King Hussein in Amman displays a Bedouin tent and one of the king's many automobiles, creating a temporal narrative of Bedouins as the past of "modern" Jordan.

nation. Although their "primitive customs" remain an "authentic" part of the Jordanian self, the fact that they are spatially and temporally distant from modern Jordanians allowed these nationalists to feel that they have escaped the colonizer's insult of placing them low on the scale of civilizational and cultural development. But the fact that they remained under the racial epistemology of the colonizer's script, one could just as easily argue that their entire reframing of the colonizer's template remained deeply committed to it as well.

This is what we mean by our argument that the Arab nationalists, even when they seek to create a distinctive time-traveling vehicle, tend to reproduce it with recycled Western gadgets. What they in actuality did was to place the tent-dwelling desert Bedouin "as living in a *past* time, a traditional time, an *allachronic* time" that is spatially and temporally distant from modern urban Jordanians. The implied understanding, in their stunning reproduction of the colonizer's template, is that in the evolutionary schema of time, "at some point *all those* who are today identified and who identify themselves as Jordanians must have lived like the Bedouins in their evolutionary childhood before they became modern urban adults."[39]

Nowhere is this more clear than the way the Jordanian Ministry of Tourism carefully packages Jordan to the world. In major tourist sites like Wadi Rum, Jerash, or Petra, they carefully note, in all of their travel brochures, hotels, and other media sources where "heritage" information can be found, that the Bedouin in the sites are simultaneously juxtaposed to "real" Jordanians, taking special care as to display all of the modern attributes of the nation.

In my own travels to Jordan, I have seen King Hussain dressed in one picture with Bedouin symbolisms, eating *mansef* (the Jordanian culinary dish) with his hands, where he is shown to be sitting in tents, sharing his time with Bedouins. At other times, he is shown to be dressed in the most Western of all clothing, standing next to European and American leaders, or in the driver's seat of one of his hundreds of most expensive and up-to-date European and American racing cars, appearing more Occidental than James Bond himself.

This is very different than the pictures I see in Istanbul of Kemal Ataturk, where he is never presented in his "traditional" apparel, with Turkish elites. Rather he is very careful to always present himself in tuxedos, brim hats, and silk pajamas. This is a stunning reminder of the differences in cultural representations of the nations in the Middle East. Unlike the Turkish case, but similar to other nationalist methods of representations that Chatterjee and others have analyzed, Arab nationalists have a more schizophrenic personality. Representations of a major political figure participating in "old world" traditions would be hard to find in Turkey, with the possible exception of a few marginal images that the new government has been permitting in the past few years. This is not the case in states in which Arab nationalism is the reigning ideology, as I have learned in my recent visits to other Arab nations like Morocco, where Muhammad V and his two sons, Hasan II and Muhammad VI, like Jordan's King Hussain, are sometimes dressed in "traditional" garb and at other times in "modern" clothing.

Similarly, in the United Arab Emirates, the boom in the oil industry has led to massive investments in producing a glittering urban landscape, littered with high towers set beside a number of sites and institutions that symbolize and represent heritage and tradition, "including," as Ronald Hawker explains,

Photo 4.2 King Hussein is often shown in his "Bedouin" dress in tourist sites and elsewhere, but he is more often shown in his "modern" dress.

"seasonal camel racing, Bedouin-like hospitality tents, museums and architectural restoration projects."[40] All of this is intended to stage authenticity but with the characteristics we find in Jordan, where all heritage sites are displayed in quite impressive and expensive "modern" sites, like shopping malls, or stored in the extensive museum halls.

This tampering with the colonizer's temporal script, however slight, is what makes it possible for Jordanian and other Arab nationalists to present themselves as the agents of change. Thus, the proliferation of restaurants, museums, and hotels serving tourists who seek the Arab that they have imagined when gazing through Orientalist films and photography, or when elderly Germans visit Dubai to get a glimpse of "Arab lifestyles"[41] or, in the Jordanian case, tourist visiting hotels like Taybat Zaman, which assures its guests "that their 'village' will transport [them] to a past time of long ago."[42] Here, the intentional contextualizing of "modern" symbolism lurks in the background, may it be the "seven star" hotel itself or the English-speaking and highly educated (and "cosmopolitan") tour guides. The colonizer's temporal script remains, but its agents have been altered. The driver of the time machine is an Arab, and the vehicle itself has been altered so as to make it appear authentic to this "new Arab man" in control of the wheel.

Ancient Civilizations in Colonial and Nationalist Discourses

But there was one difficulty with this image of a Bedouin for the Western colonizers: Many of the regions that they conquered not only included nomads and tribes, but also world empires, possessing both a large bureaucratic structure and evidence of "ancient civilizations." The existence of both of these could threaten the Eurocentric discourse concerning the distinctiveness of their own civilization, which they defined as having its origins in the Greco-Roman world of antiquity.[43] These Other civilizations, particularly in Asia and the Middle East, could not be easily incorporated into the linear story of progress that these colonizer's had used in their earlier assessment of the people they colonized before the mid-nineteenth century. How can you maintain that the reasons the West marched forward in history, while others stagnated, are products of your unique history, beginning with Ancient Greece, if the other regions you are now colonizing also have had similar types of civilizations? The only way to do this is to devise a new classification system so as to maintain a discourse of Western distinctiveness that would permit the West to retain its myth of its special character, explaining why it alone evolved to a higher stage than these other ancient civilizations. To do this, the rhetorical and ideological "tools of empire" would have to be sharpened a bit more.

Edward Said captured well the tools at work in the restructuring of this discourse in the age of imperialism. Modern imperialist, in their effort to conquer the global South, came equipped, not only with a mighty military machine, but also a large number of Orientalist scholars who would study in detail all aspects of the territory they now occupied. Having power, in this modern sense, also meant that you have the means to produce representations of the Other. Museums, archaeology, and the unearthing of the colonized territory provided the means and power to narrate a story that places you as the legitimate authority over the people and their resources. In Egypt, Syria, Lebanon, Iraq, and Palestine, from Napoleon's invasion of Egypt in 1798 to General Allenby's colonial escapade in Palestine at the end of World War I, Europeans played key roles in the founding of major museums and archaeological digs, whose sole intentions were to "rediscover" Mesopotamia, Babylonia, Phoenicia, and, most importantly, the Ancient Egypt of the Pharaohs.

The interesting thing here is that these colonial representations of ancient civilizations work quite differently than the mother colonies' own "ancient histories," where the narrative is particularized and nationalized as belonging to its own Western civilization, their "own" specific "cultural heritage." But when it comes to the ancient civilizations of the colonized, like that of Egypt or Babylonia, they are treated as "universal" in nature, not belonging to any "particular" people but to humanity in its entirety. Although these archaeologists and others did provide historical and archaeological information about the places they excavated and included such information in their sources, the information claimed those ancient civilizations possessed universal qualities of man's general progress toward civilization. In her analysis of the Metropolitan Museum's curators, for instance, Melanie McAlister discusses how museum curators, upon their retrieval of Egyptian archaeological material, spoke about "the 'delicate, superb craftsmanship,' the 'graceful' and 'realistic' quality of the pieces, whose 'style' and 'perfection' were 'incredible'." She cites a *New York Times* art critic who is quick to note that "it is an exhibition of art, not history, that 'Tutankhamun' captivates the mind and bedazzles the senses." McAlister's description of this tendency of Western museum curators to turn a historical piece found in the global South into a universal item is telling: "The history was the frame for the art, rather than the art serving as illustration or evidence for the history."[44]

A good example of this at work is a letter dated 1922, in which Western Egyptologists argued strongly against the pressure by Egyptian nationalists to "give up" Tutankhamun's tomb to the Egyptian government: "The unique discovery, with its wealth of historical and archaeological facts belongs not to Egypt alone but to the entire world."[45] Notice that the narrative, by constructing Tut's tomb as "universal" whose "common heritage is to mankind," in effect makes its Western Egyptologists not only its discoverers and its protectors but those who know that the treasure is "something too ennobling and too precious (too 'human') to belong to any one people (Arabs) or any one nation (Egypt)."[46]

Yet a more efficient method at the colonizer's disposal is to marginalize the link of these Middle Eastern ancient civilizations to any living traditions and histories in the region. As Malcolm Reid suggests, in his *Whose Pharaohs?*, a large number of images and descriptions of ancient Egypt by Westerners, even when describing *current* issues, would significantly marginalize any evidence of Egypt being tainted by Islamic or Arab modern inhabitants, best exemplified in the famous frontispiece of the Napoleanic expedition's *Description de l'Egypte.*[47] "This usage slights Islamic and modern Egypt and seems to imply that somehow 'Egypt ceases to be Egypt when it ceases to be ancient'."[48]

This is what Arab nationalists were up against as they were seeking to remove Western regimes from their territory. As we will see, if Western imperialists possessed the tools of empire, then there was nothing keeping Arab nationalists from wresting control of these tools and using them for their own political objectives. Just as Western Orientalists could manifest a narrative that places them as the legitimate rulers of the world, leading the Other less-civilized inhabitants toward progress, so, too, can indigenous nationalist elites tamper with the narrative so as to subvert the story just enough so that they become the leading agents of change over their own people. Indeed, with the weakening of the British and French colonial regimes and the rise of Arab independence movements after World War I, there arose among Arab elites the understanding of the political utility of nationalizing the Pharoanic, Phoenician, and the other ancient empires. To do so they would have to restructure the colonizer's insistence of delinking these ancient civilizations from their Arab context by situating their movements as the sole agents of recovering their long-lost selves.

In this way some Arab nationalists proved to be unimpressed with the Western claim that the ancient civilizations of the Middle East were "universal" in nature and contested the colonizer's insistence on delinking these civilizations from the history of Arabs and Muslims. These nationalist maintained the *Egyptianness* or *Arabness* of Egypt, and proceeded to challenge and subvert the colonizer's narrative by claiming the ancient civilizations as a treasure of their own that *they* had offered to the world. Present day Arabs, when no longer alienated from their true self, could once again become the beacon of light in the world just as it did many centuries earlier when it brought humanity the first glimpse of enlightenment and civilization.

Major intellectual and political elites from al-Tahtawi to Nasser began to revise the colonizer's temporal script of ancient civilizations, by articulating a vision of time in which the Arab and his nation take possession of the vehicle, whose components consist of parts as far back as Pharoanic and Phoenician times, that will carry them forward into modernity and progress. They insisted that it was through the Arabs, in the guise of flourishing civilizations of the Nile Valley, Mesopotamia, Phoenicia, Babylonia, the Levant, and the Maghrib, that world humanity had first experienced true civilization, in effect negating the colonizer's claim to be the originators and discoverers of civility and progress.

But in making this argument they had to accept a large chunk of the colonizer's discourse, including the notion that their present condition was a result of their society's fall to barbarism and stagnation. The only way they could "recover" and "reawaken" from their "sleep" and move forward in time was to eradicate their present society from all of the diseases that weaken it and keep it from evolving and crossing to the other (modern) side of the bridge. To do this, some suggested the ancient civilizations could be the remedy, the push toward this healthful recovery. A good example of this is Ahmad Husayn, an Egyptian Lawyer who in 1933 founded Misr al-Fatat (Young Egypt). In his search for "resurrecting the glory of ancient Egypt, he complained that "Egyptians have cut their ties to their ancestors." Fearing the accomplishments of the ancient Egyptians would be lost to his fellow Egyptian Arabs, he warned them that if they failed to reconnect to their true genius, misery and stagnation would await them, creating true obstacles to their nation's development and progress: "'Nothing distinguishes us [as a nation] so much as one thing. This is what keeps us underdeveloped. It keeps us in a wretched condition, tortures us, leads us off the right path. This thing is ignorance, ignorance of our country, ignorance of our history, ignorance of ourselves and our potential'."[49] His belief in this genius of ancient Egypt is so powerful that he has moments, as in his visit to the Luxor Temple with nationalist friends, when he was so awestruck by this experience as to be reborn:

> Everything that surrounded us filled our souls with enchantment.... Suddenly, powerful feelings overcame me and I launched into some songs from *The Glory of Ramses*. ... My blood was burning in my veins from the anthems we had been singing. My heart was beating on account of my passing into this solemn monument that I had heard about for so long. I wanted to swallow everything around me. I wanted to carry it with me and hide it in the folds of my soul.... I stood while my companions marveled at the extraordinary expertise which had raised these walls and which had righted these cloud-scraping columns.

> We stood next to these columns, when suddenly the place engulfed us and we almost lost consciousness of our own existence.... I was reborn, a new creature.... I had been resurrected.... I now saw the columns of Karnak and its monuments, not as ruins, but as if they were a living thing that spoke.... I stood there as if I were receiving orders and instructions.[50]

Being in the presence of these ancient sites made him feel like he had discovered a part of himself he had not known he had. This is why, for him, Egypt "should be resurrected anew and returned to her original path. We need to shake off the dust of indifference and sloth. We need to fill ourselves with faith and determination. We need to gird ourselves with inner strength. We need to labor until Egypt is reborn with her strength, with all her sublimity and greatness.[51]

Many of these Arab nationalist admirers of ancient civilization, however, kept firmly in their mind the Orientalist judgments of the religious traditions of the Arabs, especially Islam. Some internalized an Islamophobic tendency to see Islam as the central reason for the descent of the Arabs and Egyptians into barbarism and stagnation. In Albert Hourani's wonderful summation of the psychology of this desire to reach back to ancient civilizations, he locates it in "the belief of many Arab thinkers that the superior strength and stability of Western society is due to the limitations which have been imposed upon the action and influence of religion."[52] In other words, these Arab nationalists found the ancients of interest, simply because it allowed them to latch on to an identity that is not corrupted by any present-day religion, particularly Islam, which they labeled, in agreement with the colonizer's judgment of them, as a defective vehicle for traveling through time. Phoenicianism, Pharaonism, and so on were all pre-Islamic and thus "espoused by men who promoted European culture and who saw the [ancient] past as the source" of Arab renaissance.[53]

This was, of course, not unlike what we observed in Kemalist Turkey, where they, too, desired to break from the Ottoman Islamic past so as to build a society on a new foundation, uncorrupted by its religious and Islamic past. Similarly, these secular Arabs, who swallowed completely the colonizer's discourse of the backwardness of Islam, jumped over the period of Muhammad and all that followed him, and instead turned to the symbols of the Pharaohs, the Phoenicians, the Hittites, and all the others they could relinquish from their Western archaeologists. It's important, of course, to keep in mind here that the intentions of these Arab nationalist varied quite significantly from those of the colonizer. The colonizer's intention for digging up Middle Eastern ancient civilizations was to make sure that the local indigenous inhabitants did not equate their symbolic value to their Arabness, by making it universal and unattached from its regional affiliations. Indeed, as we saw, Western archaeologists, under both colonial and postcolonial rule, did all they could to delink ancient civilizations from local cultural attachment by making them universal symbols of world humanity. Arab nationalists attempted to specify the civilizations as Arab or Egyptian, so as to ensure that they would be credited with the mark of genius, claiming that it was they, the Arabs, who created a treasure that they could now share with the world. Notice here that in making such claims, the Arab nationalists' temporal script intersected with that of their colonizers' in that they both believed that the glories and genius of their region of the world lay not in the traditions the locals are *now* practicing, but rather in those of pre-Islamic, ancient civilizations.

The Centrality of "Modernizing Muslims" in Colonial and Nationalist Thought

Arab Nationalists Deny Ancient Civilizations as Origins of Renaissance

Arab proponents of the ancient civilization route soon would be on the defensive, as other Arab nationalists accused them of collaborating with the colonizer. In the words of Ali Sami al-Nashshar, a professor of philosophy at the University of Alexandria, "The British were behind all this." In order to destroy the unity of the Arabs, he argued, it was in the colonizer's best interest to make them believe they have multiple and distinct ancient civilizations. For al-Nashshar and others, it was a form of a divide-and-rule strategy, whereby the colonizer would promote "Pharaonic, Assyrian, and Babylonian nationalisms" with the intention of making the Arabs believe "that they are not Arabs."[54] Others, like Abd al-Rahman Azzam, would likewise deny the notion that a nation like Egypt was the "continuation" of its Pharaonic past and argued instead that the more appropriate link would be to its "Arab religion, customs, language, and culture."[55] For the majority of Arab nationalists, therefore, a Pan-Arab and Pan-Islamic identity would soon take hold as a more preferable and unifying alternative than the separatist, territorialist formulation found in the discourse of a return to the ancients.

There was good reason for fearing the colonizer's intention to divide and rule. This trend to locate a pre-Islamic past, after all, had its origins in colonial policy, where colonial regimes at times would narrate myths about particular groups' origins, so as to create conflicting identities over the territories they ruled. For instance, in Morocco and Algeria, the French were strong advocates of producing a Berber identity, by claiming that they were racially and culturally Indo-European, thereby implying that they were different from the Other Arabs and Muslims around them. In the words of Kaufman, "with the right guidance, the French believed, it would be possible to strengthen their [Berber] distinct identity and to stop the process of their assimilation into the Arab-Muslim society.... Already in Algeria the colonizers encountered Berbers and begun developing a strong romantic view towards them, considering them perfect candidates for gallicization."[56]

This colonial policy of divide and rule was extensively used and had some successes. But it usually emphasized the production of ethnic and religious separatist identities rather than ancient civilizational formulations. The reason the British and French chose to groom Jewish, Berber, Christian, Druze, and other ethnic and religious identities over the Pharaonic or Phoenician types is beyond the concerns of this book, but suffice it to say that to pursue the latter would have contradicted their Eurocentric civilizational discourse of progress and genius that we discussed previously. Instead, these colonial regimes opted for placing special emphasis on dramatizing the other forms of divisive identities, such as that of Maronite Christians in Lebanon, Berbers of North Africa, and the Jews scattered throughout the Middle East, particularly those of Morocco, Algeria, and Palestine. Sometimes the divide and rule would be implicit, as in the case of the mid-nineteenth-century trade capitulation agreements, whereby Europeans gave special trading privileges to Jews, Greeks, and the Christians of the Arab world. Other times it was more explicit, when the colonizer would give colonial citizenship rights to one or more "minorities," as was the case, upon the insistence of powerful French Jewish groups like that of the Alliance Israelite Universelle, whose Jews of Algeria eventually were granted French citizenship.[57] This did, of course, vary in different contexts, where, in some cases, the British preferred to unite behind a pan-Arab movement, as in the case of the Hijaz during

World War I, when they were seeking the assistance of the Arabs to defeat the Ottoman Empire and its pan-Islamic ideology.[58] But in all of these cases the dominant trend was to emphasize ethnic and religious separatist identities, where the colonizer would decree special privileges for Jews, Berbers, Copts, Druze, Maronites, and others, so as to weaken pan-Arab and pan-Islamic movements.[59]

The Arab resistance to this divide-and-rule policy did, however, create enough controversy among Arab nationalists, that the proponents of equating the nation's personality as having origins in pre-Islamic ancient civilizations found themselves on the margins of Arab nationalist movements by the 1940s. As a consequence, the most significant remaining identity was that of an Islamic nature, where Arab nationalists returned, in a selective fashion, to the age of the rightly guided Caliphs (Muhammad and the three leaders of the Islamic community after his death), seeking to use this period to mobilize the larger Muslim world in their effort to remove the colonizer and create the new societies they so eagerly wanted.

Indeed, within Islamic teachings, ancient civilizations were characterized by most Muslims as "the age of ignorance" (commonly known as the *Jahiliyya* period), before the coming of the revelations of truth by Muhammad, and were traditionally seen as sinful periods guided by polytheist figures of Pharaohs, sun Gods, and other polytheist symbols. They were largely disconnected from what would come later, when the archangel Gabriel revealed the message of God to Muhammad. The origin of the self, for the Muslim-dominated region, which would later become the Middle East, was seen by many as more genuinely linked to this period than to ancient civilizations. Indeed, growing up as a child in Jordan, upon my many visits to my mother's hometown of Jerash, I always felt that the preserved ancient Roman ruins always seemed disconnected from my relatives' and the other locals' history, with the tourists strangely obsessed with an area we as children used as prime locations to play hide and seek. Indeed, as Elliott Colla has suggested, a major theme in many Islamic texts is "that throughout history God has periodically revealed his truth to peoples who have rejected or remained indifferent toward it. For such peoples, there is special punishment: destruction. The ruins of the ancient civilizations stand as concrete proof of this.... Ruins confirm a central tenet of Islam, namely, God's transcendence over the created world. In this light, the physical remains of Pharaoh's destruction ... signify (negatively) as warning to those who would reject God's message and (positively) as encouragement to the faith of believers."[60]

In Defense of Islam, or Islam Is Our Path to Progress

But by far the most significant reason that Muslims over the past two centuries preferred to link their identity to the early period of Islam and not to other affiliations was directly related to the colonizer's insistence on insulting Muslims for their Islamic beliefs. In that sense, the desire to return to an authentic Islam was in a constant conversation with the colonizer's obsession with proving that Islam was an obstacle to progress, creating the desire among Muslim elites to find ways to save face by pleading with the colonizer that their religion, once cleansed of its present-day irrational practices, could be made to adapt to modern conditions. These nationalists would come to be known as Islamic modernists, whose main objective was to build Islamic ideas and institutions that were also "compatible" with the modern age. They were persistent in their belief that a golden age in Islam existed at the time of its founding, but owing to the corrupt practices of later generations of misguided Muslims, it was now in dire need of reform. Hence, through the efforts of right-minded and highly trained elite Muslim scholars like themselves, Islam's great contributions to reason and development could be once again exposed to the world, allowing Muslims to get back into their own time-traveling vehicle and continue on the road to progress and modernity.

For these Islamic modernists, the Arab nations must prove to both Europe and themselves that they, too, could effectively, upon their liberation from the colonizer's grip, evolve without giving up their "traditions," "culture," and "religion." Though Muslims are temporally behind the West, they are nonetheless capable of "catching up" if they selectively and carefully borrowed from the advanced nations, while retaining some essential traditions of their own. Otherwise, they argued, Muslims of the Arab world will lose themselves and come "to resemble the crow who wanted to imitate the peacock's strut but failed, and eventually forgot his own original way of walking," thereby becoming "the object of derision of both crows and peacocks"[61]

The big question for these nationalists, therefore, was how to respond to the colonizer's insistence of placing them and their religion on the lower end of the civilizational scale. Their answer to this question, as we will see shortly, with intellectuals like Sayyid Jamal al-Afghani and Muhammad Abduh, was simple: the cure to their backwardness was to be found in the original truths of their religion as conceived in the early days of its founding. Although Muslims and Arabs could emulate certain useful arts of Europe, particularly those universal qualities like science and governance, fundamental issues of morality and tradition were too essential to the well-being of the populace to be left behind as they traversed a route into modernity. Indeed, if anything, those traditions, once cleansed of their present corruptions by poor practitioners of the faith, would be essential for the flight into progress.

As one member of these Islamic modernists argued against those who accepted the Western judgment that Islam is doomed to barbarism, "Does he not understand that religion is our path to civilization and progress?" He called on his fellow Muslims "to safeguard the empire's Islamic character and to shun foreign influences that could only lead to its weakening."[62] In making these statements, Islamic modernists believed that Islam "was the one true, complete, and perfect religion, which could satisfy all the desires of the human spirit.... He wished to show ... Islam was in harmony with the principles discovered by scientific reason, [and Islam was] indeed the religion demanded by reason.... Islam, being neither irrational nor intolerant, could save" the colonized Muslim world from its present backwardness and deep sleep.[63]

The key idea in the thinking of many Islamic modernists was that, in their defense of Islam, there are essential features of the religion that are not possible to change (key revelations from God to the faithful), whereas other features are open to change "without damage" (such as practices that were applicable to earlier times but now are outdated and irrelevant).[64] These practices were seen as "stagnant" remains practiced by the orthodox establishment, whose only interests were to conserve and adhere to traditions that had served a period marked by the medieval-like era of the Ottoman Empire. Their greatest objective was "to rescue Islam from the hands of reactionary orthodoxy, presenting [themselves] as a flexible creed capable of resolving the problem of the modern world."[65] Being equipped with the proper mind-set of a modern man, they understood themselves to be the vanguards of Islam, who knew well how to resuscitate their ill brethrens by offering new ideas that could serve to awaken them for the journey ahead. Hence, by challenging the Islamophobia of their Western critics, they insisted that the social ills of the *umma* "had its source not in Islam itself, but in the Muslims" of today, who, if brought back to the "straight path" could once again join the West in its triumphant march into the utopian future of modernity.[66]

Even Muhammad Husayn Haykal, who we met earlier as being a proponent of Kemalism, would by the 1930s change his position to fall in line with the Islamic modernist wave, by becoming quite disappointed with his earlier views: "'I had tried [to transmit] to those who shared my language the intellectual culture of the West and its spiritual life, so that we might adopt them both as models and as guides. However, after all my labors, I realized that I had planted seeds in barren soil. Even when the earth accepted them, it produced nothing for them'."[67] For him, this failed strategy of emulating all of what the West had to offer, caused much humiliation and divisiveness between the elites and the masses, and his only solution was to return to an authentic tradition:

> A nation whose present is not connected with its past is bound to lose its way.... Hence, the chasm has kept widening between the masses of the people of the East and those calling for the ignoring our past and turning with all our might in the Western direction; and hence the revulsion of the masses at adopting the ideological life of the West while yet insisting on emulating its science and industry. But since ideological life is the foundation of existence for both individuals and for peoples, there was no escape from going back to our history in search of foundation for our ideological life so that we may emerge from our humiliating stagnation.[68]

The Druze Arab Lebanese nationalist, Shakib Arslan (1869–1946) would push—in his *Why Are the Muslims Backward While Others Are Advanced?*—this line of reasoning even further, by claiming that Arab Kemalists of his day were colonial agents who

> seek to Europeanize the Muslims and other Easterners and to make them disown their distinctive characteristics and their historical traditions so that they will become, in the manner of a chemical compound, dissolved and transformed into a different substance. Only the mean and low-minded can entertain the idea that man should disown his heritage.... They act in contravention of the inherent instincts manifested by every nation in its desire to preserve its special characteristics in matters of language, faith, customs, architectural style, and cuisine.[69]

He continued to denounce all Kemalist and their Arab proponents as directing a "ruthless attack on Islam," whose only intention was "the destruction of the spirit of Islam" and all other Eastern traditions.[70]

Afghani and Abduh

But the two most significant Islamic modernist thinkers are arguably Sayyid Jamal al-Afghani and Muhammad Abduh. Afghani (1838–1897) was one of the original Islamic modernists to argue that Islam contains within it the "proper" elements the Arabs and other Muslims will need in confronting the challenge of the West. In Afghani's estimation, Islam in its golden age had all the features of a great civilization, everything from a strong foundation of reason to solidarity and political unity. If Muslims "returned" to accepting the truths of the original message, there is nothing that they have to fear about accepting the fruits of reason, for the two are not in contradiction. His main objective, therefore, was to show to Muslims and Europeans that Islam, far from being the source of their problem, was in fact the key to progress. In Hourani's fine summation of Afghani's central idea: "What had once been achieved could be achieved again: on the one hand by accepting the fruits of reason, the sciences of modern Europe, but also, and more fundamentally, by restoring the unity of the *umma.*"[71] In Afghani's own words, Islam can have a healthy political function to play in the *umma*'s attempt "to unite Muslims and arouse them from their slumber and acquaint them with the dangers threatening them and guide them to the way of meeting those dangers."[72]

Indeed, central to Afghani's system of thought was that the problem Muslims are experiencing today, relative to the West, is the loss of reason and truth that was given to them in the original message. The decay of the *umma* was the eventual tampering of its true essence, and thus the revival of the community is tied to rediscovering Islam's truth. This was, in his view, the best way to confront the true enemy of the *umma*: imperialism.[73] Applying the original principles of Islam, therefore, is the duty of his fellow Muslims and is the best route to defeat the imperialist powers. Though the West would like the world to believe that it was their civilization who invented rationality, for Afghani the argument that rationality belonged to Western civilization and only later was diffused to the rest of the world was a farce, because it was first introduced to the world by Allah and his messenger Muhammad, and from there passed on to others. Strangely enough the *umma,* who were rationalism's original benefactors, were those who now sought to take it back from the other usurpers, the West itself. In Roxanne Euben's words, "although rationalism is currently associated with Western culture, Afghani insists that Islam has contributed substantially to the evolution of human rationality and that, in addition, the very universality of rational methods and the truths they produce belies constructions of Islam as inherently incompatible with rationalism."[74]

Muhammad Abduh (1849–1905) became the prime disciple of Afghani and contributed a great deal to Islamic modernism. Abduh met with Afghani in Paris in 1884 and together organized a pan-Islamic organization, whose intentions were to reform Islam and meet the challenge of the West. While there, he became fluent in French and read widely the most influential writers of Europe, including Ernest Renan, Rousseau, and the Social Darwinist Spencer. Not only was he well read in European literature, but he had penned letters to Tolstoy and visited Spencer in his home in Brighton and was known to be in good standing with the British imperialist Lord Cromer. In all of these encounters, he was quite friendly to the idea of progress, as developed by Herbert Spencer, and proceeded, like Afghani before him, to show that Islam, before it was distorted by future Muslims, had hidden deep within it all of the traditions of reason and science needed for Muslims to set it on the path of evolutionary development.[75] Indeed, there was no contradiction between science and revelation.

In his autobiography near the end of his life, Abduh claimed that the major objective of his life was to "free the Muslim mind from the shackles of indiscriminate obedience to tradition—*taqlid*—, so that they could understand Islam as their forefathers had conceived and understood it."[76] In his words,

> I strove to learn and teach the true faith and morals of Islam from the original sources. I tried to demonstrate that the religion was given to man as a guiding light against aberrations of reason. Reason, maintained, is qualified to test the truths of religion. In fact it must do so, but there must come a point in the process when reason should accept the dogmas of religion. Reason thus employed fulfills the will of God in preserving order in the world, and can be considered as an ally of religion, teaching men to respect truth, which is the basis of noble and good action.[77]

A good part of his activism was to lay the institutional and intellectual foundations of a proper way of studying Islam so that its treasures could once again be available to the *umma.* By creating a well-versed group of modern Muslim scholars who were equipped with a proper method of evaluating the original sources of the tradition, Islam would be guarded against medievalists who bring down present-day Muslims by replacing them with an elite cadre of trained *ulama.* This elite community of scholars would comprise individuals who "understand religion as it was understood by the elders of the community before dissension appeared." These scholars, moreover, would be able "to return, in the acquisition of religious knowledge, to its first sources, and to weigh them in the scales of human reason, which God has created in order to prevent excess or adulteration in religion, so that God's wisdom may be fulfilled and the order of the human world preserved; and to prove that, seen in this light, religion must be accounted a friend to science, pushing man to investigate the secrets of existence, summoning him to respect established truths, and to depend on them in his moral life and conduct.[78]

In the desire of these two Islamic modernists, we can see how liberal Muslims of their persuasion proceeded to fortify a particular reading of Islam that they believed would negate the Eurocentric judgment of their religion. But by doing so, in the words of Hamid Dabashi, they altered a diverse religion "into a singular site of ideological resistance to European colonialism."[79] Infatuated with the glittering wealth and power of their colonizer, they turned to their religion with the aim of reproducing the world of their colonial masters, not just materially and politically, but ideologically as well. Dressing this up with an Islamic flavor did not hide the fact that they accepted the temporal judgment of their masters as they proceeded to alter facts on the ground so as to "prepare" the *umma* for a renaissance like the one they were obsessed with in the West. They became the elite Muslim agents who were "instrumental in robbing themselves of their own intellectual heritage as they aggressively transformed their religion into a singular site of combatant conversation with and revolutionary uprising against colonial modernity."[80]

Conclusion

Arab nationalists, whether using the trope of the Bedouin, the Pharaoh, or the Prophet, were thus complicit in appropriating the colonizer's Eurocentric temporal template and only superficially dressed their time machine so as to present it as authentically Arab or Muslim. Moreover, Arab nationalists, in line with Orientalist discourse of the decline of the Muslim Ottoman Empire, in accepting the colonizer's insistence that "Islam" and the Arab world are in a decadent state, projected themselves as the indigenous civilizing agents that would transform the nation "from stagnation and medieval slumber into awakening and modernity."[81] Positioning themselves as the surgeons who would send a shock into the weak heart of the Arabs and Muslims, moreover, allowed them to place themselves as the legitimate rulers over "their" land and people, a very familiar anticolonial nationalist narrative.

Indeed, one can easily argue that rather than freeing themselves from their colonial masters, these Arab nationalists, in all these disguises, marched directly into a Eurocentric understanding of historical development and forced all other voices to the margins with the intention of creating a hegemonic project that forbade all other possible dissenting voices. The multiple and creative nature of the response of the colonized does not take away from the fact that they collectively were far from exiting a revised cultural Darwinist evolutionary template and proceeded, like their colonial masters, to judge the present multitude as behind, childlike, backward, and all in need of an enlightened elite to lead them into a new stage of history, progress, and modernity. In Massad's useful summation of these nationalists, in the Arab nationalists obsession with appeasing the civilizational discourse of the West, most of their thinking "is based on a revivalist impulse underwritten by an evolutionary narrative," which seems to be unable to resist reinforcing it.[82] By internalizing this civilizational discourse, they accepted the Western judgment that Arabs and Muslims are far "behind" Western civilization and thereby acknowledged the supremacy of Western civilization.

In our next chapter we will see that it is precisely this obsession to placate Western civilizational judgment of Islam that Islamists objected to and proceeded instead to turn the lens on the West as being a poor measuring rod of progress. But in their puritanical response, they, too, confirmed the epistemological and ideological foundation of Eurocentrism and proceeded also to divest the multitude's diversity by projecting a singular reading of "proper Islam."

Chapter 5

The Islamist Time Machine and the Rebellion Against the Colonizer's Civilizational Insult

Islamism and the Legitimacy Crisis of the Colonizer's Civilizational Discourse

The Sheikh and Me in Mecca

After an extremely exhausting, yet spiritually rewarding day of completing a Hajj ritual in Mecca in January 2004, my mother and I went outside the great mosque in search of our American group of Hajjis. Upon finding them, I took the first available seat to rest, with my mother finding an empty seat beside me. At that moment our senior American sheikh from New Jersey got up and insisted that my mother ought to remove herself from the company of men to sit in the "women's area." After a number of days of experiencing similar scenarios, I was no longer able to keep silent, deciding to confront the sheikh in front of many other Hajjis. I insisted that my mother and I were exhausted and she would remain here with me, telling the sheikh that "I did not appreciate your policing of rigid gender segregation." He responded just as forcefully, claiming that "since we are in Mecca, we have to practice our religion in its proper form, not what suits us at the time."

After it became obvious to him that my mother was not about to move, he looked toward me and became quite disturbed and added, "you are obviously Westernized. The problem with much of your young generation is that you have lost your true religion and have imitated the culture of the West by losing sight of proper Islam." Insulted by being branded as some kind of colonial surrogate of the "West" and not wanting to be outdone, I returned fire, "It is you who has been Westernized, for the prophet Muhammad did not invent these gender divisions. It was only much later in history, indeed in our modern era, first originating in the West and then accepted by men like yourself, that such rigid and dichotomous understandings of gender came into being." We continued this debate for some thirty minutes, with the sheikh trying to demonstrate to me and the other men around us the textual evidence for this gender division, while I, likewise, attempted to provide a completely different interpretation of those same texts.

We will discuss the Islamist and other gendered discourses in our next chapter. This example, however, provides us with clues of how deeply dependent Islamist discourse is on this thing we have come to call the West. What became obvious to me, throughout this encounter, was the feeling that this debate was not simply about hermeneutics, or who had the most persuasive argument. Instead, what troubled the sheikh most was that he interpreted this challenge to be between two men, representing two radically antithetical "civilizations." The fact is that he thought of himself as representing authentic Islam, while I, on the other hand, was nothing more than a spokesperson for the West, regurgitating something exterior to the true religion, in a sense belonging to a secular culture somewhere "West" of Islam.

Given the history of our modern racially stratified world, including the activities of many of its secular social movements we have already discussed, the sheikh's view of me is not all that surprising. The constant and never-ending judgment by Western and indigenous secular elites had left this sheikh with a scarred identity that he wishes to express through a religious discourse that *seems* to be in direct opposition to the West. Indeed, browsing the shelves of any bookstore or watching mainstream American television, it is clear that many contemporary scholars and commentators make the assertion that Islam is the main culprit of the current world disorder, with Islam representing a sort of a return to the Dark Middle Ages.[1] The linear model of history that these "experts" and reporters use lends itself to the notion that "modern" and secular Western identities, being of a higher civilized social order, ought to replace obsolete and dangerous religious systems that belong to a "pre-modern" (read Islamic) world.

The sheikh's criticism of me had to do with this humiliating context, a feeling of defeat at the hands of the West, which many Muslims feel daily. In the case of the sheikh, connecting me to Western political voices fueled his anger against me. He interpreted my remarks as another judgmental intervention by the West, where the latter placed itself at the center of world history, demanding that the rest of the world bow before the shrine of progress that it best represented. But for the sheikh to bow to this shrine would be a painful insult to his own God, acting as hidden injuries of civilizational discourse,[2] to use an analogy coined by Richard Sennett and Jonathan Cobb, when discussing the humiliating impact of a superordinate's discourse of self-worth over the subaltern Others.

As in Sennett's and Cobb's discussion of the psychological damage upper-class discourses of merit had on the poor and working classes, similar psychological scars occur globally when one civilization, the West, is highlighted as

Photo 5.1 A New Jersey–based Hajj guide to Mecca. He and I had many interesting debates about "modernity" and "tradition" and what "Islam" has to say about women.

the most superior, forcing all Other civilizational identities to pay respect to a small sector of the world population in the most humiliating and degrading manner.

But as we will see, rather than simply being victims of modernity, Islamists invented new versions of modernity that challenged the norms of Western notions of progress. That is, Islamists preferred to create alternative symbols, in which they dressed themselves with competing badges of dignity. Their alternative versions of modernity in the form of Islamic cultural performances were informed by their knowledge of a world-system hierarchy of civilizations. In other words, by being fed a version of modernity that was ultimately racist, Islamists felt the pressure to reject Western-sanctioned notions of proper modernity in favor of that of a perceived authentic Islamic religion.

Islamists as Radical Time Travelers

As we discussed in the previous chapters, Jewish nationalists, Kemalists, and Arab nationalists all bowed to their colonial and anti-Semitic masters. They attempted to create a "new," more up-to-date version of the Arab, Jewish, and Turkish national subjects. In all three cases, they wanted to distantiate the modern national subject from the East and what they perceived as their archaic, former childlike self. Indeed, this distancing between the modern and non-modern Arab, Jew, and Turk became a measuring rod for how far their nations had evolved in comparison to the stagnant child that they *once were.* This temporal view of the world became the dominant worldview of Arab, Jewish, and Turkish elites, from the 1870s to the 1970s, and informed their major political and intellectual projects well into our own time. Muslim modernists like Afghani and Abduh did try to provide a less-humiliating response to the colonizer's gaze, by trying to defend Islam as a religion that is compatible with modernity. But they, too, as we saw in the preceding chapter, created "an apologist discourse" that sought to reinterpret the religion, in a defensive manner, so as to make it compatible with "modernity."

In contrast, the Islamists we cover in this chapter dropped the defensive nature of the response and partially turned away from the colonizer's temporal script by decentering Eurocentrism and placing *Islam as the real measuring rod of progress.* Islamist intellectuals like Sayyid Qutb and Islamist political elites like Khomeini, in contrast to past nationalists, would turn to *Islam as the only true civilization that has the proper elements to push humanity forward.* Hence, while they rejected the apologetic nature of past anticolonial movements, they heavily clung to the time-machine aspect of the original colonizer's temporal template. Where they differ from their predecessors is that they decided to pull on a different lever than the one chosen by Arab, Zionist, and Kemalist time travelers, all the while accepting that they, too, could launch the faithful to a future utopia that they envision that Allah originally prescribed to them.

Our reading of the Islamist movement is quite different from that offered by many scholars of Islam. Best exemplified by Gilles Kepel, Emmanuel Sivan, Benny Morris, and other Orientalists, these scholars represent Islamists as people outside of modernity who have "turned back the clock." It is as if these Islamists were placed into a time machine that erroneously sent them into the wrong period of time. In this image of Islamists as out of touch with their actual time, the time machine itself is thought to have some kind of dysfunction, causing it to send people to incorrect time-space coordinates.

In my judgment, this is a drastic misreading of the Islamist movement. Rather than dismissing Islamist movements as "trends out of time," I prefer Bobby Sayyid's proposition that it might be more useful to see them as "swimming in the broad currents of modernity."[3] Mainstream scholars of Islamist movements tend to reify and naturalize the colonizer's temporal dichotomy between the "modern" and the "traditional," placing Islamists in the latter category. For these scholars such temporal categories are assumed to be based on a natural difference between "traditionalist" Islamists and the "modernist" West, thus presenting each as containing their own time-space coordinates. The problem with this perspective is that such figures like Qutb and Khomeini make sense only in the context of colonial modernity. Such Islamists, in the words of Bobby Sayyid, represent "a modern political trend and not some atavistic revival of traditional belief."[4]

This type of analysis allows us to see that Islamists are not only reproducing the discourse of colonial modernity but are in effect proposing a *more radical* reading of the script than their predecessors, by asking us to accept a strategy in which modernity is dressed *unapologetically* in Islamist clothing. In this sense, Islamists, far from representing characters "out of time" are, indeed, very much in tune with the ideological precepts of colonial modernity. But in their call to transform their community into a futuristic utopia, they are asking their Islamist intellectuals, archaeologists, novelists, film producers, historians, and other producers of cultural media to unearth a modernist script that is in *every detail informed by Islamic symbols.* For them, reorienting the *umma* to return to the uncontaminated message of the original Truth is the only way to secure true progress and to fulfill the destiny of man. In this sense, Islamists are Social Darwinists from the global South, dressed in Islamic attire and proposing a new age of enlightenment, which decenters the West and praises the Islamic message as the true measure of man's perfection. In Elliott Colla's provocative reading of the Islamist movement, they "represent the emergence of powerful counter-tradition of dissident Islamist thought, modernist in outlook, though opposed to the Western and secular character of the elite's expressive culture."[5]

The decentering of the West does not mean that Islamists have liberated themselves from the shackles of colonial modernity. Indeed, if anything, the discourse that they have appropriated is itself deeply committed and constrained by the binary structures the colonizer put into place in the nineteenth century. The hegemonic nature of the colonizer's script of positioning Islam and the West as different human species has become *the episteme* through which Islamists think, write, and speak about the world. As we discussed in previous chapters, the global binary of this colonizer's script is highly *productive*, in that it constructs and frames the lens through which Third World elites rebel against Western Social Darwinist thought. In this sense, Islamists are not simply appropriating a religious ethos from a time-immemorial authentic Islamic source but, rather, are themselves using a binary script whose original authors are the colonial masters of the past. It is this Orientalist script that makes Islamists appear to be performing a tradition belonging to a real foundational moment called Islamic tradition, when in fact what makes it possible is the actual way Islam was inscribed into the binaries of colonial modernity. In the words of Bobby Sayyid, "The political role of Islam was not the natural product of an 'Islamic' culture but, rather, was a consequence of the way in which Islam was inscribed within [colonial modernity] itself."[6]

The Legitimacy Crisis of Kemalism and Arab Nationalism in the Middle East

The Short-Lived Success of Kemalism and Arab Nationalism

It is with the rise of Islamism that the foundation of global Eurocentrism was finally shaken. Before that period, Kemalism and Arab nationalism, as the two leading hegemonic forces up until the 1970s, were so infatuated with Eurocentric definitions of modernity that they did all they could to appease the Western judgment of their civilization and religion. This would change with the rise of the Islamist movement, whose central task was to heal the scars that remained from the colonial encounter and wished instead to replace the injured dignity with new badges of self-worth. With the rise of this counter-project of modernity, whose "intellectual, spiritual, and political alternative to the *Nahda* vision"[7] would put to shame the ancien régime, which shamefully bowed to colonial Eurocentrism. This retreat of Eurocentrism included all of the local Arab and Kemalist surrogates, who were themselves soon put on the defensive.

By the 1970s, there arose a legitimacy crisis in the old anticolonial movements that revolved around the success of their original promise to "raise" the Arab, Iranian, and Turkish world to a "higher level" of development, holding out the promise of remaking the people of the global periphery so as to be able to reach for the sky and become wealthy, prosperous, strong, and fully functioning and respectable citizens of the civilized world. By the 1970s this promise no longer seemed to hold much merit, as the periphery witnessed the rise of huge shantytowns, high unemployment rates, and alienation from stable family and community life, especially in the 1980s and 1990s, when *infitah* (free trade agreements) and the free trade ideology penetrated all aspects of the region. Instead of adulthood and independence, the scene looked more like a child begging the colonial master for handouts. Instead of the futuristic utopia that was promised to them by the Kemalist and Arab nationalists, they sensed that they were now living in a world of utter submission and humiliation.

The Kemalist and Arab nationalist regimes that came into place after World War II were thus based on the promise of transforming their part of the world into something better, more progressive, and egalitarian than what they had been forced to live under during the humiliating years of colonial rule. They were an oppressed people because of both "external" (imperialism) and "internal" (traditionalism) reasons, and they concluded that in order to successfully launch their societies into progressive modernity, they would need to reject both outside control and the tight grip of archaic traditions and feudal-like institutions.[8] Many of these political and intellectual elites accepted the colonizer's judgment that Arab and Islamic culture and religion was in dire need of "updating" and change, with the assumption that in order to be modern and civilized, one had to remove religion from the public sphere and place it, at best, in the hidden domain of the private. Many anticolonial Third World regimes accepted this premise and saw religion and traditions as obstacles to modernizing and developing their societies. To join modern civilization, they believed one had to speed up the process of evolution by allowing an elite intelligentsia to force change on the ignorant and religious masses. In the words of Mark Juergensmeyer, "The secular nationalism of the day was defined also by what it was not: it was not one of the old ethnic and religious identities that had made nations parochial and quarrelsome in the past."[9] They wanted to build a "new society" in which they could manufacture a new kind of human being who was temporally and spatially distant from what they had been like in the past. To do this these anticolonial movements sought a two-stage process, first to replace the colonizer by an indigenous progressive-minded group and then to enact a local cultural and intellectual revival (which Arab nationalist called the *Nahda*), with the hope that, at the end of this process of struggle, they would be rewarded with a prosperous society that has overcome its past feudal-like state.

Much of the criticism of the old nationalist movement revolves around this loss of faith in the promise these movements made, that they would bring about global equality, political freedoms, economic prosperity, and social justice. This legitimacy crisis was not only widespread among the poor, its least benefactors, but also the professional and middle classes who were once the greatest source of supporters of Kemalism and Arab nationalism, but had "been propelled toward religious nationalism after trying to live as secular nationalists and feeling betrayed, or at least unfulfilled."[10]

Indeed, it is this class of men and women who now use their organizational and intellectual skills to narrate an Islamist challenge against their once-prominent friends and political parties. What changed all of this was the realization that the twin promises of the old anticolonial movements proved to be a big deception: First, the intervention of the West into the Middle East (especially the United States) not only failed to go away, as was originally promised, but in actuality became more pervasive, and second, those anticolonial movements, rather than serving as an oppositional force to this Western intervention seemed to be actively in collusion with the West. What was once seen as a revolutionary movement acted more in line with a traditional comprador-like project in complete collusion with the hegemonic

West. From there it was easy to conclude that if the people of the Middle East and Islamic world were to finally liberate themselves from external oppression, then not only would they have to continue to struggle against Western domination, they would also need to remove those very Kemalist and Arab nationalist regimes that serve the interests of external powers.[11]

Islamism Came into Being Because of the Constitutive Nature of Colonial Modernity and Eurocentrism

This is also where we have to be careful not to assume, as Bobby Sayyed reminds us, that it was a self-evident fact that Islamists would be leading this charge. Many who analyze this legitimacy crisis directly link the failure of the old movements to the rise of Islamism, and consider it simply a natural process. This is based on a very essentialist claim that there was an Islam lying around in the region, and then it just rose into action because secular movements failed. These scholars of the Islamist movement assumed that Islamism came into being simply because Islam was already part of the culture and identity of the people in the region. And then, only after the fact, when modernist and secular regimes failed to deliver their promises, a number of devious actors came along and grabbed it and used it for their own political end, as though it was just there naturally waiting to be used as a symbol of resistance.

But the reasons that Islamism came into being are more related to the way Eurocentrism and colonial modernity inscribed Islam as their inassimilable Other. Having swallowed whole the entire edifice of Eurocentrism, Kemalist and Arab nationalists delegitimized themselves when colonial modernity came to its tragic unraveling in the 1970s. The radical arsenal of these past anticolonial movements no longer had much appeal, when they participated, like their past colonial masters, in oppressing the people and unequally distributing the wealth of their countries. Given the fact that Islam was placed as the devious Other under these regimes, they in fact guaranteed that the symbols of resistance to their regimes and to colonial modernity would be those same Islamic symbols it tried to keep outside of "respectable" politics. Thus the rise of Islamism as the voice of the discontented should not be seen strictly as the natural alternative to the policies of Kemalism and Arab nationalism, which failed to provide employment and services. It can also be seen as the product of secular regimes, whose infatuation with racist colonial modernity constituted Islam as its rebellious Other. Islamism, in other words, was in the womb of colonial modernity waiting for its birth. The fact that colonial modernity was intent on making Islam a religion in need of therapeutic recovery or a complete makeover, belonging to a past age no longer in keeping with progressive modernity, ensured that Islam, as such, became the dominant sign of resistance. This is why Islam rather than liberalism or socialism came to signify the most radical of all anticolonial movements. Liberalism and socialism, in their overdependence on Eurocentrism and the insulting civilizational discourses it had come to represent, was made impotent with the legitimation crisis of colonial modernity.[12]

The Examples of Qutb and Khomeini

We can see this at work among the two leading figures of Islamism: The Egyptian Islamist intellectual Sayyid Qutb and the Iranian Political Islamist Ayatollah Khomeini. We will discuss them and their biographies in more detail in the next two sections of this chapter, but for now, we are interested in how they articulated their Islamist project to colonial modernity and its regional surrogates. Indeed, their denunciation of their local regimes was based on the fact that secular Arab nationalists, far from liberating their countries from the grips of the colonizer, were totally dependent on their Western masters. Rather than bringing true development and uplifting the region, Islamists accused these regimes as the agents of a downward spiral, where the masses are left both demoralized and hungry. Both Qutb and Khomeini were able to clearly articulate a dissident voice, because they understood the magnitude of the grand failure of the old anticolonial movements to bring real change to the region. In a precise and concise manner, they put to shame the small circle of elites who benefitted from the plundering of their countries' resources, leaving meager resources and wealth for the remainder of the population. Sayyid Qutb captured this very powerfully:

> Who will dare to claim that those million of hungry, naked, barefoot peasants whose intestines are devoured by worms, whose eyes are bitten by flies and whose blood is sucked by insects are humans who enjoy human dignity and human rights? ... Who will dare to claim that the hundreds of thousands of disabled beggars, who search for crumbs in garbage boxes, who are naked, barefoot,

> with faces crusted with dirt? . . . Who will dare to say that they are the source of authority in the nation, based on democratic election?[13]

He accuses Arab nationalists of rendering their nations as slaves "not only to our resident masters, but to any authority that may hover from the West [Capitalist bloc] or the East [Communist bloc] thousands of miles away."[14] Similarly, in one of Khomeini's more articulate moments, in a 1979 speech, he, too, was able to enunciate clearly the stark failure of the Shah regime to uplift the Iranian masses: "An enlightened heart cannot stand by silently and watch while traditions and honor are trampled upon. An enlightened heart cannot see its people being drawn towards baseness of spirit or watch in silence while individuals around Tehran live in slums."[15]

But it was in their skillful ability to comprehend that to effectively resist the existing Kemalist-like regimes, they could no longer rely on a liberal or socialist strategy, because they seemed as shallow as the existing regimes, in that they, too, accepted much of the racial schemes of the colonial masters. Instead, they skillfully grabbed onto the most radical Other that was already contained in the insult itself and used it as a dagger to puncture the heart of the existing modernist regimes. By being placed as the most distant outsider of all the possible discourses of resistance, people like Qutb and Khomeini were clever enough to know that Islam was the most powerful symbol of resistance to colonial modernity. Sayyid Qutb said it best when he claimed that

> Islam is a complete social system which differs, in its nature, conception of life, and means of application, from any Western or applied system in today's world. Surely, Islam has not participated in creating the existing problems in today's societies. These problems have arisen as a result of the faulty nature of the applied systems in the modern world, and as a result of banishing Islam from the real context of life.[16]

Qutb's clear denunciation of the collusion-like behavior of these old anticolonial movements was eloquent and to the point: "All of these nationalistic and chauvinistic ideologies that have appeared in modern times, and all the movements and theories derived from, have also lost their vitality. In short, all man-made theories, both individualistic and collectivist, have proved to be failures."[17] Let us now turn to a detailed analysis of Sayyid Qutb, to see how effective some Islamists were in appropriating the most distant Other of colonial modernity.

Sayyid Qutb and the Orientalizing of the Self

> "What a shame! Those Muslims, who emulate the orientalists, pass on as the high brow intellectuals and masters of Islamic thought, while at the same time they are produced according to the models provided by Zionists and crudsaders."
>
> —*Sayyid Qutb*

The West as Diseased: The Koran as the Measure of Progress

If Zionists and Kemalists preferred to remove the Orient in constructing an Occidentalized national identity, Islamists aggressively moved in the very opposite direction, removing the Occident in constructing an Orientalized identity. In this section, we will explore the biography of one of the most significant Islamist intellectuals, the Egyptian Sayyid Qutb (1906–1966), to see how this change took root. Born in a rural town of Musha in 1906 in the Asyut Province, some two hundred miles south of Cairo,[18] Qutb would witness firsthand "the failures of both Egyptian liberal and socialist regimes—in later years from behind the bars of Nasser's prisons,"[19] where he would be executed in Cairo in 1966, on the accusation that he plotted to assassinate the Egyptian President Gamal ʿabd al-Nasser in 1964. In these seven decades of his life, he was transformed from a fairly secular and successful literary figure to a radical Islamist. It is largely his later career that we are interested in here, because it is his writings of 1949 and after that he would be most known for. His intellectual influence on the Islamist movement, as Samir Amin noted, remains unparalleled: "The recordings of Ayatollah Khomeini, the long educational talks that the Arab television stations, from Morocco to the Gulf, offer their viewers, the religious education propagated by the militants, the endless range of books and pamphlets shelved in the bookshops under the Islamiyat label, have added nothing to the master's thinking."[20]

As we will discover, Sayyid Qutb, in his later life, viewed Kemalism, Zionism, and Arab nationalism with much disdain, all of which represented to him a very serious and dangerous assault on the Muslim world.[21] Indeed, he labels them as all in a state of *jahiliya*, a Koranic term used to describe pre-Islamic pagan societies in "the age of ignorance." For Qutb, as is the case for Islamists generally, Kemalism, Zionism, and Arab nationalism, far from representing human progress, have lowered mankind to a beast-like existence. Instead of Islam being the obstacle to progress, he turns the Kemalist and Arab nationalist logic on its head by arguing the contrary: "From the point of view of 'human' progress, [*jahili*] societies are not civilized but are backward.... Only Islamic values and morals, and Islamic teachings and safeguards, are worthy of mankind. These provide a permanent and true measure of human progress. Islam is the real civilization and Islamic society a truly civilized community."[22] The *Jahili* regimes of the Kemalist and Nasserite variety "have dissociated themselves completely from the religion of God." They have rejected Him "totally, and they do not refer, in matters of their legislation, economy, socialization, ethics, and mores, to the book of God."[23]

Whereas Kemalists and Arab nationalists rationalized Westernization as an important step in the direction of modernizing the nation, Sayyid Qutb provided a different reading of such discourses. As Abu-Rabi paraphrases Sayyid Qutb's understanding of modernizing discourses, "the white man exploits us to the fullest, and any mention of modernization by the colonizer and his numerous 'intellectual slaves' is a travesty of justice."[24] Far from moving humanity forward, such projects have brought us to the brink of disaster: "Mankind today is on the brink of a precipice, not because of the danger of complete annihilation which is hanging over its head—this being just a symptom and not the real disease—but because humanity is devoid of those vital values for its healthy development and real progress."[25] "Even Western scholars," Qutb reminds us, "realize that their civilization is unable to present healthy values for the guidance of mankind and does not possess anything to satisfy its own conscience or justify its existence."[26] The only system that can possibly create meaningful progress is the *din* of Islam, for "Islam is the only system that possesses these values and this way of life."[27]

He is especially repulsed by elites who purport to represent the Muslim world and talk of "reforming" Islam to meet the requirements of the modern world:

> We find some people who, when talking about Islam, present it to the people as if it were a culprit in need of defense against its accusers. Among their defenses, one goes like this: "It is said that modern systems have done such and such,

> while Islam did not do anything comparable. But listen! It did all this some fourteen hundred years before modern civilizations!" Woe to those who resort to such a defense! Shame on them! Indeed, Islam does not take its justifications from the *jahili* system and its evil derivatives. And these "civilizations," which have dazzled many and have broken their spirits, are nothing but a *jahili* system at heart, and this system is erroneous, hollow, and worthless in comparison with Islam.[28]

Indeed, the call for a return to a rightly guided Islamic way of life offers Mankind a more superior life than that offered by Arab nationalists and Kemalists. For Islam "has come to change *jahiliyyah,* not to continue it, to elevate mankind from its depravity, and not to bless its manifestations masked under the euphemism of 'civilization.' ... We reject all [*jahili* systems], as indeed they are retrogressive and in opposition to the direction toward which Islam is leading."[29] To borrow and emulate such Western—*jahili*—models "without thought or assessment," Qutb continues, is understood by animals like "monkeys who emulate everything they see."[30]

The historical remnants of Western colonialism and Western penetration, for Qutb, have outlived direct colonialism insofar as "the West still maintains collaborationist agencies in the colonies in Asia and Africa, and has created new conditions in the so-called independent states in order to replace Islam with secular creeds and doctrines which negate the Unseen on the basis of its scientificity." The postcolonial regimes found throughout the Muslim world have joined hands with the West in developing a "morality so that [postcolonial society] becomes like that of animals."[31]

We can already see major differences here between Sayyid Qutb and modernizers like Kemal Ataturk. This becomes especially clear when we look at how these two different projects measured and evaluated "progressive change." As we discussed earlier with Kemal Ataturk, the standard was clearly the West, with the Koran and Islam viewed as obstacles to be overcome in the development of civilization. Indeed, when the issue of Islam and the Koran were discussed at all, they were evaluated critically in light of "modern times." In other words, Kemalists and Arab nationalists applied their construct of the West to critically evaluate the Koran, with the latter usually viewed as best left to the private arena. This was especially the case for modernizers like Sayyid Jamal al-Afghani and Muhammad Abduh, who used the West as a measuring rod to evaluate the Koran, searching the Holy Book to look for anything in it that they could demonstrate, to paraphrase, that "we Arabs and Muslims have traditions and a past civilization that can be useful (admittedly with some slight revisions to our culture and religion) in our efforts to modernize like you—the modern West."

Sayyid Qutb and other Islamists, on the other hand, applied the Koran *to deconstruct the West.* Here, the measurement of progress is not based on a standard produced by the West, but one that is judged by the Koran itself. The major question for Islamists is: "Have these Arab, Turkish, Iranian and, for that matter, the imperialist states of the Western world lived up to the standards provided by Allah?" This is a fundamentally different question than that asked by the Occidentalizing and modernizing elites. Because, whereas the modernizing elites use the West as the standard for measuring progress, Sayyid Qutb transforms the debate in such a manner that the Koran becomes the judge of all things good and just. Thus, whereas Islamic liberals and Kemalists ask, "Can the Koran meet the challenge of the *West*?" Sayyid Qutb and other Islamists prefer to ask whether or not the West and their Muslim collaborators can meet the challenge of the *Koran.* Thus for Qutb, the West was viewed as an obstacle to be overcome in the development of mankind. As Ali Mirsepassi has argued in his *Intellectual Discourse and the Politics of Modernization,* "The most striking factor behind the rise and popularity of Islamic politics was that it articulated an alternative discourse to overcome Western-centric projects of modernization."[32] It is the Koran instead of "Western sources of knowledge [that] becomes the criterion."[33]

Challenging Western-centric assumptions can be viewed as a strategic move by Qutb to dismantle the logic in what he believed to be remnants of the colonial era, what he identifies as cultural colonialism. According to him, the colonization of the mind is much more dangerous than economic and political colonialism, which can be easily removed by force. It is the colonization of the soul, mind, and body that poses the most serious threat to the existence of the Muslim world—indeed, mankind as a whole. Colonialism, even after its withdrawal from Muslim lands, has penetrated into the very heart and fabric of postcolonial Muslim societies. Nowhere is this more apparent for Qutb than in the defeatist mentality he finds in Muslim intellectuals in charge of "reforming" the educational system:

> In our schools and colleges, we study, in a specific manner, distorted Islamic history and blown-up European history. This error is not unintentional; it is rather a reflection of a hidden desire on the side of imperialism that does not want us to be proud of our history. Instead, it wants us to consider Europe as

> the only prime mover of human history. Once we have given up on our past showing appreciation of the European role in history and giving allegiance to the White Man, our control by imperialism would be made easy.[34]

But this questioning of Eurocentricism came late in Sayyid Qutb's life. As Ibrahim Abu-Rabi has argued, in the early phase of his work Sayyid Qutb, "considered Islam and the Arabic language as foreign to the Egyptian mentality."[35] Indeed, in his earlier writings Qutb shared some of these Eurocentric ideas. According to Abu-Rabi, early in his career as a literary critic, Qutb goes so far as to argue "that the state should control and direct the religious education of the Azhar for the achievement of national goals, and that the Azhar should be barred from proliferating the types of ideas that are incompatible with the demands of the modern age."[36] He even critically comments on the practitioners of folk religion, ridiculing the practices of a shaikh he knew in his childhood village, who "rarely takes a shower."[37] In his last publication, *Milestones,* he reflected critically on his earlier assumptions:

> Until then, I had not rid myself completely of the cultural influences that had affected my thinking in spite of my Islamic attitude and inclination. The sources of these influences were foreign—alien to my Islamic consciousness—yet these influences had clouded my intuition and concepts. The Western concept of civilization was my criterion, and it prevented me from seeing clearly.[38]

This shortly would all change. If there is one life-altering event that we could point to as Qutb's moment of "conversion" to an Islamist vision, it would be his trip to the United States in the early 1950s, when he stayed at a college in Denver, Colorado. During his time there he was surprised at the number of churches and how often Americans attended them: "Nobody goes to churches as often as Americans do."[39] But he was disappointed to learn that church attendance did not necessarily signal piety, for "no one is as distant as they are from the spiritual aspects of religion." The example he provides is a posting of a church event he found in a college dormitory, advertising an *entertainment* function: "Sunday October 1, 6:00 PM Light Dinner; Magic Show; Puzzles; Contests; Entertainment." Even more shocking to Qutb is what he observed after deciding to attend the event: "The dancing intensified.... The hall swarmed with legs.... Arms circled arms, lips met lips, chests met chests, and the atmosphere was full of love." The most disturbing moment for

Qutb was when he witnessed the pastor dim the lights to create a "romantic dreamy effect" with music in the background playing the famous song "Baby, Its Cold Outside."[40] After this visit to the United States and upon his return to Egypt, Qutb later said, "I was born in 1951."[41]

It was this experience in the heart of the Occident that Qutb saw clearly, in his mind, the magnitude of the tragedy the "West" had brought to the world. From there it was a short exercise to conclude, as he did, that the West had no basis for judging Islam. Insofar as the West persistently points to Islam as the cause for the lack of economic, scientific, and technological development of much of the Muslim world, Qutb, after his experience in the United States, was moved more than at any other time in his life to forcefully respond to this unjustified accusation. Instead of accepting the West as victorious over the Muslim world, as do the Kemalists and many Arab modernizers and reformers, he goes on the offensive and aggressively launches an attack on this Eurocentric way of thinking:

> Look at this capitalism with its monopolies. Its usury, and so many other injustices in it. Behold this individual freedom, devoid of human sympathy and responsibility for relatives except under the force of law; this materialistic attitude which deadens the spirit; this behavior, like animals, which you call "free mixing of the sexes"; this vulgarity which you call "emancipation of women"; these unfair and cumbersome laws of marriage and divorce, which are contrary to the demands of practical life; and this evil and fanatic racial discrimination.[42]

Here he is ridiculing those Muslims he accuses of being struck by *Westitis* and he wants to invite them to see that if they looked at Islam objectively, removed their colonizer-stained lenses, what they would find in Islam is a *din* "with its logic, beauty, humanity, and happiness, which reaches the horizons to which man strives but does not attain." Unlike what you find in Occidentalized ways of living, Islam provides "a practical way of life and its solutions are based on the foundation of the wholesome nature of man." But unfortunately cultural colonialism has seeped so far into the conscience of many Muslim elites that they are beyond his reach. Indeed, these Occidentalized elites "are defeated before this filth in which *jahiliyyah* is steeped, even to the extent that they search for resemblances to Islam among this rubbish heap of the West."[43]

It is at this point in his life that he begins to use the language of disease that becomes a staple of Islamist discourse in the 1970s and after. He claims "It is essential for mankind to have new leadership!" for the West is now on the decline "not because Western culture has become poor materially or because its economic and military power has become weak," but rather because "it has lost those life-giving values that enabled it to be the leader of mankind."[44]

The Removal of the Occident and the Islamization of the Self

So what needs to be done to change this sad state of affairs? The confidence and exuberance with which Qutb addresses this question is at this point in his life as solid as it could possibly be. He argues, in a discursively compelling way, that "we need not rationalize Islam to [those infected by Westitis], nor appease their desires and distorted concepts." Instead, Muslims need to put behind them defeatist mentalities of this sort and respond to the West and Westernizing Muslim elites by confidently informing them that "the ignorance in which you are living makes you impure, and Allah wants to purify you; the life you are living makes you impure, and Allah wants to cleanse you; the life you are living is low, and Allah wants to uplift you; and the condition you are in, is troublesome, depressing, and base, and Allah wants to give you ease, mercy, and goodness." Remove this disease from your midst and allow Islam to enter your life and "change your concepts, your modes of living, and your values," and understand that it is Islam that "will raise you to another life so that you will look upon the life you are now living with disgust [and allow Islam to] introduce you to values so sublime that you will look upon all other values in the world with disdain."[45]

For Qutb, therefore, it is the insertion of this colonial mentality into the Muslim World and its eradication that the Islamist movement must address, for "Holy war against colonialism today necessitates the emancipation of the conscience of nations from spiritual and intellectual colonialism, and the destruction of those systems that drug out the senses." The Islamist movement must be "cautious of any tongue, pen, society, and group that conclude a truce with those colonialist camps which are bound by common interests and principles."[46]

His use of the term *jahili* is meant to illustrate how far these Westernizing regimes of the Muslim world have strayed from the Islamic path. Indeed, he seems to indicate that the contemporary situation of Muslims is even graver than that of the original *jahili* society of the seventh century:

> We are today immersed in *Jahiliyya* like that of early Islam, but perhaps deeper, darker. Everything around us expresses *jahiliyya*: people's ideas, their beliefs, habits, traditions, culture, art, literature, rules and laws. Even all that we have come to consider Islamic culture, Islamic sources, philosophy and thought are *jahili* constructs. This is why Islamic values have not taken root in our souls, why the Islamic worldview remains obscured in our minds. Why no generation has arisen among us equal to the caliber of the first Islamic generation.[47]

This *jahili* contamination includes "philosophy, history, psychology (except the experimental branch), ethics, comparative religion, sociology (except statistics)," insofar as they all contain within them an "implicit or explicit enmity to the general religious understanding of life and in a specific way to the Islamic worldview."[48]

Qutb wants to be clear that there is no such thing as "an adaptation of Islam to modern social needs of life." This accommodationist position infuriated him terribly, because it reduced Islam to the margins of modern life, allowing *jahili* ideologies to dress themselves in Islamic attire while in fact destroying the foundations of a just religion. "Islam never said to people that it would not touch their modes of living, their concepts, and their values except perhaps slightly." Nor did it "propose similarities with their system or manners to humor them, as some do today when they present Islam to the people under the names of 'Islamic Democracy' or 'Islamic Socialism'." And it surely is unacceptable to claim that "current economic or political or legal systems in the world need not be changed except a little to be acceptable Islamically."[49]

> The purpose of all this rationalization is to appease people's desires! Indeed, the case is very different! The change from this *jahiliyyah*, which has encompassed the earth, to Islam is vast and far-reaching, and the Islamic life is the opposite of all modes of *jahili* life, whether ancient or modern. The miserable state of mankind is not alleviated by a few minor changes in current systems and modes. Mankind will never come out of it without this vast and far-reaching change—the change from the ways of the created to the ways of the Creator, from the systems of men to the system of the Lord of men, and from the commands of servants to the commands of the Lord of the servants.[50]

Notice here that Qutb is asking for a complete eradication of "foreign" influences and the reimplementation of the Islamic order. The need to remove the disease of the Occident with a healthy dose of Islam, however, does not come easy. For Qutb, "we, who are the callers to Islam" need to first "provide a certain style of thinking or paradigm of thought, purified from all the *jahili* styles and ways of thinking that are current in the world and have poisoned our culture by depriving us of our own mind." In this effort to reintroduce the righteous and just *din*, those who are called to Islam must be cautious not to allow their enemies, or themselves for that matter, to "try to change this *din* in a way alien to its nature and borrowed from the ways of the predominant *jahiliyyah*." If the latter occurs "we will deprive [our *din*] of its ordained function for humanity, and we will deprive ourselves of the opportunity to remove the yoke of the popular *jahili* ways that dominate our minds."[51] Islam is a self-sufficient system that needs to emulate no other model. It "is intended to penetrate into the veins and arteries of a society and to form a concrete organized movement designed to transform it into a vibrant dynamic community."[52]

Like many Islamists that would come after him, Sayyid Qutb vehemently opposes the idea of removing Islam from the public arena. For him, to allow it to dwell only in the private sphere is a sure way to ensure the success of the enemies of Islam, creating the framework for the complete negation of God's sovereignty and the enslavement of men to other men. "Islam is a unity that is indivisible," he proclaims, and "any one who divides it into two sections is outside this unity, in other words, he is outside this religion."[53]

> There is no ruler save God, no legislator, no organizer of human life and of human relationships to the world, to living things or human beings save God. From him alone is received all guidance and legislation, all systems of life, norms governing relationships and the measure of values.[54]

The so-called Modernizers, with their well-intentioned "reforms," who strenuously exert themselves "to confine Islam to the emotional and ritual circles, and to bar it from participating in the activity of life," are working against Islam's "complete predominance over every human secular activity, a pre-eminence it earns by the virtue of its nature and function."[55] Islam was introduced to the world "in order to change the reality of humanity as a whole." The idea that it should be hidden away in some dark corner and removed from the public square is a sure way to change this *din* from an active agent of mankind to one that belongs to theory only, to ornamentalize it as though it were just another display in some sophisticated museum. These self-proclaimed Modernizers of the religion "who attempt to alter this vision either under the name of renewal, reform or progress, or under the guise of eradicating the remnants of the Medieval age or under any other slogan are our real enemies. They are the enemies of humankind."[56]

For Qutb it is essential that sovereignty is returned to its rightful owner. The total Islamization of society, where Islam is free to roam the streets, the schools, the courts, indeed every place at all times, is the goal of the Islamic movement. As he stated so clearly, to declare God's sovereignty means the comprehensive revolution against human governance in all its perceptions, forms, systems, and conditions and the total defiance against every condition on earth in which humans are sovereign. "All systems ruled by man-made institutions, in which the source of power is human ... making some the masters of others with disregard to God," are all *jahili* systems. All of this is the unjust "extraction of God's usurped sovereignty and its restoration to Him."[57]

Here, Sayyid Qutb is speaking directly to Kemalists and Arab Modernizers. "All of these nationalistic and chauvinistic ideologies that have appeared in modern times," he argues, "have also lost their vitality" for they are "all man-made theories" and have now "proved to be failures."[58] As usual, his message is clear and crisp: "In the world there is only one party of Allah; all others are parties of Satan and rebellion.... For human life, there is only one true system, and that is Islam. All other systems are *jahiliyyah*."[59]

Islamists after Qutb

Many Islamists after Qutb would accept his criticism with little revision. For instance, Ali Shariati, John Voll correctly argues, "rejected the separation of various realms of human life as exploitative and opposed to Islam."[60]

> The very structure of tawhid [the One-ness of Allah] cannot accept contradiction or disharmony in the world.... Contradictions between nature and metanature ... science and religion, metaphysics and nature, working for men and working for God, politics and religion ... all these forms of contradiction are reconcilable only with the worldview of shirk—dualism, trinitarianism or polytheism—but not with tawhid—monotheism.

On the question of imitating the insulting Eurocentric discourse, there was already in place the clear denunciation of Iranian intellectual and political elites by Jalal Ale-Ahmad, who accused them of accepting the Westernizing insult and becoming in the process like the colonial masters of the past. Indeed, Jalal Ale-Ahmad coined a catchy word that captured the collusion in a clear and picturesque way: *Occidentosis.* Interestingly enough it was Ali Shariati who popularized this term, when he used it in a 1970s speech he gave, addressing the writings of Fanon and Sartre.[61]

> I speak of "Occidentosis" [Gharbzadegi] as of tuberculosis. But perhaps it more closely resembles an infestation of weevils. Have you seen how they attack wheat? From inside. The bran remains intact, but it is just a shell, like a cocoon left behind on a tree. At any rate, I am speaking of a disease: an accident from without, spreading in an environment rendered susceptible to it.[62]

But it would not be until Khomeini that Qutb's polemical strength would finally come to fruition as a successful movement. In a 1979 speech, Khomeini captured well the ideological collusion the Iranian regime of the Shah had with Eurocentric colonial modernity:

> [O]ur problems and miseries are caused by losing ourselves. In Iran until something has a Western name it is not accepted.... The material woven into our factories must have something in the Latin script in its sleeve edges.... Our writers and intellectuals are also "Westoxicated" and so are we.... We forget our own phrases and the word itself. Easterners have completely forgotten their honor.... As long as you do not put aside these imitations, you cannot be a human being and independent.[63]

Such a discourse would even become appealing to individuals and groups active in the Palestinian resistance to Israeli occupation. A pamphlet from an anonymous writer, claiming to represent *Islamic Jihad* in Palestine in the late 1960s:

> The Jew in Israel is an integral part of a modern, materialistic culture, or rather, he is its true essence, who possesses its tools, its way of life, its values, and methods, and who supports it totally.... On the other side stands a human being whose [political] regimes divested him of his true, historical and doctrinal identity, and divested him of 13 centuries of history and culture, and

> gave him 50 years or less of intellectual distortion, anxiety, and a contradictory and alien sense of belonging. On this side stands the individual of the Islamic homeland, on whose face they tried to put the mask of the Western culture, without being able to fit the mask around the original features. The [Islamic] nation did not turn out for battle with the tools of the Western culture, and its approach and methods.[64]

Islamists Re-Orient the Colonizer's Temporal Template

When it comes to the creation of a historical narrative, the difference in constructing a link with the past so as to narrate the future utopia between the modernist regimes of Kemalism and Arab nationalism with that of Islamists is very telling. Kemalists, as we discussed in an earlier chapter, sought in essence to negate and marginalize the Islamic and Ottoman past, with the belief that to be modern was understood to be as leaving "behind" archaic cultural and religious baggage. For Arab nationalists, on the other hand, such a drastic castration of the past was frowned upon and viewed as too drastic a break. Instead these Arab nationalists chose a more schizophrenic approach by permitting a link to the "golden age" of Islam in which they searched the scriptures and early period for signs of possible fragments that they could take with them as they ascended into the modern age. But in both cases, the underlying idea they shared was the belief that in order to create the future utopia and to evolve into a modern people, the Islamic religion had to be either removed entirely from the historical narrative (Kemalism) or revised, scrutinized, and modernized, so as to make it "relevant" to the project of progress, development, and science (Arab nationalism and Islamic modernists). In the case of Kemalism, they would appropriate the 5,000-year-old "Turk" (the period before the time of the Muslim) as the appropriate material to be used in their time-travel, whereas for the Arab nationalists, some elements of the pre-Islamic period were appropriate for the flight. They were also open to the idea of taking along some of the remains of the original Islamic period, but to do so required that the remains be filtered and reinterpreted in light of Reason and progress. Both of these movements, therefore, were under the spell of their prior colonial master and believed that in order to evolve like their superior, they needed to create an identity with past historical epics that was unencumbered by the undesirable remnants of that past. Islamists would also search for the golden age of Islam, but they would make sure that all of the remains that they collected were authentically Islamic and untainted by elements of any other historical periods that either preceded or followed the original message. For Islamists, to time travel into the future utopia meant the complete eradication of any historical substance tainted by non-Islamic elements, which they identified, as we discussed with Qutb, as belonging to the *jahilliya* period and thus unworthy of the future community that they wanted to build.

To make their version of time travel possible, these Islamists appropriated the same space-time tactics as their Kemalist and Arab nationalist predecessors. In order to represent the kind of future utopia they imagined, they strategically used spatial and temporal markers to signify and mark their desired trajectory. They deliberately created Islamists theme parks and selected certain urban spaces, parks, and restaurants, architectural designs and styles, and pursued what they identified as Islamic developmental and economic practices, all of which would be used as part of the building material needed to manufacture the proper time-traveling device.

In the case of Kemalist Turkey, Ankara and Taksim Square were used as urban spaces representing modernity, while marginalizing Ottoman Istanbul as a tourist zone. Arab nationalists also used the spatial element as they spatially marked the Bedouin as temporally distant from the new and improved modern Arab, living in urban metropolises. Islamists had to reappropriate these spatial and temporal techniques, as they, too, searched to mark their futuristic projects. But instead of making the Islamic distant and in need of developing, they turned their focus on the "golden age of Islam" as marking the only straight path to utopia.

Islamists in Turkey, for instance, refused to use either Ankara or 1923 as the marking point of the modern nation and proceeded instead to excavate Islamic Ottoman Istanbul and 1453 as their spatial and temporal coordinates. In order to provide an alternative to Kemalism, these Turkish Islamists aggressively promoted an urban policy that "reflected a desire to insert Islam into national space—both the nationalized space in Taksim Square and the conceptual space of the nation wherein the national identity was formulated."[65] The choice to use 1453 instead of 1923 as the commemoration year for the establishment of the Turkish nation also served the same function, namely, to destabilize the modernist ethos of their Kemalist contenders. Thus Islamists also created a bipolarized notion of modernization, but they preferred to turn the polarities in the opposite direction, thereby activating the space-time of Islam.

In the Arab world, Islamists would overturn the Arab nationalist version, which selected classical "world-heritage" sites like the Pharaonic and Babylonian period as markers of the *Nahda,* or national awakening, thereby identifying strongly with pre-Islamic civilizations, treating those civilizations of the distant past "as a vital source of self expression."[66] This would radically change with the onset of Islamism in the Arab world, where they promoted an alternative version that challenged the official historical narrative found in Arab nationalism. Instead of swallowing the Eurocentric version, "which took West-oriented modernity and secularism as a constitutional basis" of their Arab nationalist and Kemalist competitors, they used temporal and spatial markers that exaggerated the Eastern, Oriental, and Islamic past.[67]

Islamists Destabilize Eurocentric Time and Space

Islamists are excellent readers of scriptures, and it is easy to see how they were able to take key references about pre-Islamic civilizations from the Koran and other sources so as to dislodge the historical narratives of their predecessors. As Elliott Colla has eloquently argued, the Koran contains a large number of references to the pharaohs and the many struggles past prophets have had with key pre-Islamic rulers. Islamists like Hassan al-Banna and Sayyid Qutb would use these references by *making the past pharaohs the living examples of present-day rulers of the Arab world.* They come to signify, in Islamist ideology, the contemporary Western colonial regimes and all of their local and Arab and Turkish surrogates, thereby making the Islamists equivalent to the original *umma,* struggling for its existence against the *jahilliya* tribes of pagans. As such, al-Banna and Qutb were able to designate the present ruling regimes as "inseparable from a general state of apostasy and ignorance, *al-Jahiliyya,*"[68] a phase of mankind that needs to be set straight, so as to move toward emancipation.

In the pre-Nahda period, before the rise of Pharaonism and Phonecianism, the "ancient civilizations" were from a distant past and disconnected from the present self. The ingenious maneuver by the Islamists was to resignify the distant past and project it onto the present. If there is anything to be learned from the ancients, it was that those who disobeyed the revelations of God or remained indifferent toward them would be doomed: "for such peoples, there is a special punishment: destruction." The ruins of ancient civilizations stood as concrete proofs of this.[69] Notice that like their Kemalist and Arab nationalist challengers, these Islamists also kept the pre-Islamic period alive in the present, but unlike the nationalists, they used the ancients as symbols of a corrupt and archaic present that needs to be removed before the umma can move forward like it did in the original seventh-century Islamic Medina period. "In this discourse, ancient Egypt is associated with what is wrong with modern secular culture, with the moral foundations of the nation-state, and with the tyranny of Egypt's rulers whether of the ancient past or modern present."[70]

Notice here that these Islamists are using the same temporal template as those found in all the other modernists nationalist projects, only they decided to pull on the opposite side of the binary that Eurocentric modernity crafted for them in the nineteenth century. As Alev Cinar has argued for the case of Islamists in Turkey, they "were similarly modernizationist in producing a discourse that defamed the present conditions of the nation and established the Islamist party as the agent of modernity that sought to liberate and transform the nation and guide it to its rightful place in the future."[71] Pharaohs, Hittites, Phoenicians, or the Turks were all designated as part of the inauthentic present that needs to be replaced and quarantined in a massive makeover, in which new mosques, shrines, and theme parks were seen as the desired cultural objects of renewal, for the creation of the "true self."

Cinar provides a good example of this in one of the official Web sites of the Refah Party in 1997, which attempted to depict Istanbul as deeply anchored in the Ottoman-Islamic past that has been contaminated by the Occidentalizing policies of 1923 and the Kemalist state:

> With the onset of the Republic, Istanbul has lost its status as the capital city of an empire. What was once the capital of three empires in a row, became just another big city of a nation-state. Again with the Republic, Istanbul lost its status as the center of the caliphate of the Islamic World. With the closure of *tekkes* and *zaviyes* [dervish lodges] the riches mystical spheres in history moved out of daily life of Istanbul. All these destroyed Istanbul and its identities, which were the products of hundreds of years of experience. Istanbul, which is primarily a city of history, has been torn away from its history and its historical riches (cultural, religious, social, architectural, folkloric).... One of

> our priorities is to open up Istanbul's cultural riches to our people. As a result of the cultural crisis that we have been living for two centuries [with the onset of Westernization] our people have been torn away from these cultural riches. [Under these conditions] cultural life has become alien to its own people and history, and cultural activities have become a means to undermine our own cultural roots.[72]

Such reinterpretations of Istanbul were intended to demonstrate that Kemalists, far from creating a future utopia, allowed the Ottoman-Islamic city to be morally and historically corrupted by Westernizing urban trends and designs, which they now hoped to correct by restoring its true Ottoman-Islamic essence.

Thus, rather than using the ancient civilizations for their renewal projects of the present, these Islamists narrated an Islamic past to challenge the Eurocentric claims of their predecessors, thereby making the modernist regimes the pharaohs of the present, with the Islamists as its savior. The local modernist regimes were cast as being ruled by a *jahilliya*-like group that danced to the tune of its colonial masters whereas they, representing genuine Muslims, were here to bring back the true and authentic community, which could now be placed in the driver's seat of the time-traveling vehicle.

Nowhere is this clearer than in the writings of the two Egyptian Islamists Hassan al-Banna and Sayyid Qutb. Hassan al-Banna, like Qutb after him, loved to read and think about the Pharaonic period of Egypt. But he did so only so as to challenge his more secular Arab nationalists by disassociating ancient civilizations from the real rupture represented in the time of Muhammad and the founding of Islam. His famous line was that "the Muslim Brothers do not . . . advocate Pharaonism, Arabism, Phoenicianism, or Syrianism."[73] He was highly critical of any attempt to equate the ancient world with the main national inspiration of Egyptian "awakening" and clearly preferred to tie his identity to one heavily anchored in Islamic symbolisms. In his own words about ancient civilizations:

> There is nothing in any of this preventing us from being interested in the ancient history of Egypt, and all that the ancient Egyptians possessed in the way of knowledge and science. We welcome ancient Egypt as a history containing glory, science and learning. But we resist with all our strength . . . the program that seeks to recreate [ancient] Egypt after God gave Egypt the teachings of Islam

> … and provided her with honor and glory beyond that of [the ancient past], and rescued her from the filth of paganism, the rubbish of polytheism, and the habits of the *Jahiliyya*. … If what is meant by nationalism is: the revival of the customs of a pagan age [*jahiliyya*] that have been swept away; or the reconstitution of extinct mores that have disappeared; or the dissolution of the bonds of Islam under the banner of nationalism and racial pride (as some regimes have done, going so far as to destroy the traits of Islam and Arabism in names, script and expressions), so as to resurrect long-forgotten pagan customs; if this is the kind of nationalism that is meant, then it is despicable and harmful in its effect. It will lead the East to enormous ruin, cause the East to forfeit its tradition. It will cause a decline in its prestige, and cause it to lose its most special characteristics along with its most sacred traits of honor and nobility. Yet, this harms not God's religion: "If you turn your backs on Him, He will replace you with another people who will be unlike you" [Qur'an 47:38].[74]

Sayyid Qutb would even be more precise in delineating the stark contrast between ancient civilizations and the coming of Islam: "I have listened to those hollow [Pharaonic] anthems which provoke in us only a superficial zeal because they do not emanate from a genuine connection between [ancient] Egypt and us," repeating almost word for word al-Banna's criticism of Pharaonism. But at times he is more eloquent than his Islamist predecessor: "What are they but deafening clichés, whose content is hidden in a noisy clamor!"[75] As I mentioned, he, too, loved to read about the ancient civilizations and went so far as to advocate their inclusion into the school curriculum, but his intentions were radically different from those of more secular Egyptian nationalists:

> I propose that every literary fragment discovered from Ancient Egypt be translated into Arabic, that the images of [ancient] Egyptian life, in all of their shades, be drawn in the Arabic language, that a strong bond be forged between [ancient] Egyptian monuments and youths at every stage of their development, that life be breathed into those monuments and statues and histories by the creation of stories, myths, epics and information around them. I call for the lives of Ahmose, Tutmose, Ramses, Nefertiti and others like them to be within the grasp of every school child and advanced student and for [ancient Egyptian] myths to come alive in nurseries.[76]

His massive writings contain many allegorical stunts, making ancient Egypt a stand-in for all of the present secular regimes of the world. For him,

"Islam is not a historical event that once happened and then was left behind as history moved on.... The *Jahiliyya* is a condition, not a temporal, historical period. The *Jahiliyya* has driven its stakes into every corner of the world, in the diversity of beliefs, doctrines, political regimes and circumstances."[77] His message is loud and clear: The *jahiliyya* is still keeping us from realizing our true self, and if we are to move forward, we must decontaminate ourselves from its devious and corrupting power.

After Qutb's death, we would witness in the 1970s a realigning of political forces that allowed for his type of reading to penetrate the public sphere. The most famous character in the post-Qutbian period is undoubtedly Ayatollah Khomeini, who in the late 1970s would use the same allegorical stunts to challenge yet another Kemalist-like regime, that of the Shah of Iran. His clearest statement to this effect can be found in his 1979 denunciation of the Shah's decision to celebrate "2500 years of continuous monarchy," a discourse the Shah used that was reminiscent of those found under all of the other local modernist regimes. Khomeini would apply the same critique Qutb used to challenge Arab nationalists and proceeded to remind his fellow Iranians "that Muslims had nothing in common with the pre-Islamic heritage of Iran, and Islam had come to destroy the principle of hereditary monarchy":

> The second commandment which God gave to Moses was "remind people of the Days of God." ... The day that the great Prophet of Islam migrated to Medina ... the day that he conquered Mecca.... The day of Khawarej ... when Hazrat Ali unsheathed his sword and did away with these corrupt and cancerous tumors ... the fifteenth of Khordad (5 June 1963) when a people stood against a force and they did something which caused almost five months of martial law. But because the people had no power, they were not consolidated, they were not awake, they were defeated.... The seventeenth of Shahrivar (8 September 1978) was another one of the Days of God when a people, men, women, young people and older people, all stood up and, in order to get their rights, were martyred.... A nation which had nothing broke a force in such a way that nothing remained of it.... Empty-handed, a monarchical empire of 2500 years, 2,500 years of criminals was done away with.[78]

In all of these cases the idea is to disrupt the Eurocentric hold that the temporal narrative had on Arab nationalism and Kemalism so as to relinquish Islam as the central popular identity of the region. If the Pahlavi, Kemalist, and

Arab nationalist regimes were under the spell of Eurocentrism when producing their historical narratives of the nation, Islamists unabashedly rewrote the historical script and made Islam the defining moment in world history, one that they believed humanity should grab on to in order to improve the well-being of all. By (re)centering Islam into that narrative, they also decentered the Eurocentrism that underlies the script of their challengers.

Conclusion

It is apparent that in its efforts to challenge Eurocentrism, Islamism was only possible because of its ontological location within Eurocentrism. Islamism was inscribed into colonial modernity and learned how to manipulate Eurocentrism from within the latter's gaze so as to challenge local modernist regimes. In other words, Islamism is written into the text of colonial modernity simply because it was its radical antithesis. In the words of Hamid Dabashi, "the worst aspect of 'Islamic ideology' . . . was its consistent conversation with 'Western modernity,' its arch nemesis and thus its principle interlocutor."[79] In doing so they, too, were destroying the diversity of the region by their attempt to eliminate all of the divergent religious and intellectual practices that existed, so as to challenge Eurocentric colonial modernity.[80] The end result of all this was to bring yet another absolutist ideology into the region not unlike that of their predecessors. Because it was so dependent on colonial modernity, it, too, reproduced the essentialism that was embedded in Eurocentrism and proceeded to project a monolithic reading of Islam onto the population, which it judged as in a state of *jahiliyya* in need of a savior. To return to our time-traveling vehicle analogy, they hoped to remove the old drivers (Arab nationalists and Kemalists) and replace them with a new and improved operator, who is better situated to drive them toward the finish line.

Chapter 6

Women as the Sign of the Times

> The first step for women's liberation is to tear off the veil and totally wipe out its influence.... The qualities of the woman become characteristic of the family and are extended to the country. Thus a good mother is more useful to her species than a good man, while a corrupt mother is more harmful than a corrupt man.
>
> —*Qasim Amin 1900*

> The modest dress that the contemporary girl chooses to wear is not returning to a past but is doing something more progressive than even modernism. She has developed beyond education and formal knowledge. She has reached the stage of faith and commitment.... The Muslim woman is no longer a plaything in the hands of foreigners to be painted and dressed as they wish.
>
> —*Ali Shariati 1971*

IN THIS CHAPTER WE WILL EXPLORE how gender provides an opportunity to demonstrate the manner by which Kemalists, Arab nationalists, and Islamists all internalized the colonizer's notions of change and progress (what I call the colonizer's temporal script), with special attention to its effects on women. As we saw in the preceding chapters, colonial modernity was obsessed with the constant judgments of people in accordance to a racialized scheme of progress and regression, placing some as advanced and others as underdeveloped, where the West and its Others were positioned in a linear scale of civilizations, religions, and races. The colonized responded to this civilizational insult in a number of ways, but they all did so by positing that they had indigenous elites who had the cultural and intellectual characteristics that could move their backward nations forward. But this civilizational discourse between the colonized and colonizer was highly gendered, and the "woman question" was one of the defining markers in the evaluation of how civilized a people were designated. We will look, therefore, at the representation of Middle Eastern women in this gendered discourse.

By its constant negative reference to "Islamic civilization's" oppression of women and its handling of women's rights, the colonizer produced in the colonized a civilizational anxiety that they felt needed to be challenged. We will attempt to understand how the postcolonial intellectual of the Middle East approached this Western denunciation as they proceeded to either "modernize" or "Islamize" women. As we will see, the prominence of the woman question in the colonial encounter between the colonizer and the colonized forced the latter into a defensive reaction by either forcing women (in the case of Kemalist and secular Arab nationalists) to unveil and accept the colonizer's judgment of the superiority of the "modern Western woman" or (in the case of Islamists today) to demand that their women veil and represent an ideal version of an authentic Muslim woman.

In both cases, the woman question was seen as a measure of civilizational achievement and progress and, as such, simply followed in the footsteps the colonizer first imprinted into the Middle East with the coming of colonial modernity. As Leila Ahmed has argued, "why the contest over culture should center on women and the veil and why [both modernizers and Islamists] fastened upon those issues as the key to cultural and social transformation only becomes intelligible by reference to ideas imported into the local situation from the colonizing society."[1] This colonial importation, moreover, makes it clear that Kemalist, Arab nationalists, and Islamists all shared the same reactive impulses and proceeded to use the colonizer's temporal script as they maneuvered to respond to the ethnocentric and negative views the colonizer held of Islam and "its" handling of women.

Thus in response to the colonizer's insistence that Islam was a reactionary religion in its treatment of women, male nationalist elites in the Middle East seized upon the "women question" as one of their central ideological poles, where women became used as symbolic markers of progress by all three movements, each deploying their vision of the proper woman in the context of an evolutionary model of a developed and moral civilization. Kemalist and secular Arab nationalists understood the modern woman as a secular, unveiled, educated housewife, who could uplift the nation by raising modern, literate children, whereas Islamists held similar views about literacy and education but chose to clothe the woman more "authentically," as one who possesses the knowledge of Islamic morality and ethics in their role of raising the children of the nation. It was in this larger global contest between the colonized and the colonizer that the woman question came into prominence, with all three movements coalescing around the temporal script the colonizer brought to the region. This contest would impact Middle Eastern women as they became the boundary marker between the colonizer and the colonized and were seen as symbolic trophies for measuring the progress of the sovereign nation.

As a result of this colonial relationship, women, in the eyes of anticolonial political elites would become a political "developmental" project and were used as a form of symbolic capital toward their nationalist discourse of moral and political development. In the words of Nira Yuval-Davis, "Women's bodies function as 'symbolic border guards' toward the drawing of these boundaries of difference, and their protection of the state."[2] Women and the quality of their bodies and minds became a symbol of the nation's level of civilizational attainment. Yet in the end women remain, in all of these projects, nothing more than symbolic trophies, with their material and political needs rarely dealt with in any substantial way. By analyzing how gender was deployed by Arab nationalists—Kemalists and Islamists alike—we hope to highlight the limits of working within this colonizer's temporal template of development. In all three cases it will become apparent that the male elites of these movements, no matter if their intention was to modernize women in the Western image or to Islamize women in the image of an imagined utopian Islamic ideal, portrayed themselves "as the saviors who will liberate the body from its present confines and take it toward its deserved future," in effect furthering men "as the hero-body that has the power and will to liberate and take under its protection the female body."[3]

The chapter is divided into three sections. We will begin with the colonizer's insistence on pronouncing Muslim society as "backward" and moved gender and women's bodies to the center of national and cultural debate, causing them to become the symbolic markers of how (un)modern and (un)civilized the colonized were. We will then turn our attention to how liberal secular Arabs and Kemalist-inspired Turks accepted the colonizer's designation of their society's backwardness and proceeded to enact a nationalist project to "modernize" women, by appropriating the colonizer's use of "progress" on their women. Here we will analyze the important contributions of Qasim Amin and other "feminists" of secular Arab nationalism. Finally, we will explore how the Islamists challenged and reproduced both the West's judgment of what composes a "civilized" woman and their rejection of the liberal Arab and Kemalist acceptance of the colonizer's judgment. We'll look at the Iranian activist and Islamist scholar, Ali Shariati, to see how he deconstructed the Western judgment of the civilized woman in his attempt to show that only Islam can actually bring progress to women. But more generally, this chapter is intended to help us understand how Western elites, by negatively equating Islam—a religion that they construed as essentially oppressive of its women—and women's rights had the effect of making issues like veiling change from an unconsciously performed cultural practice in the Middle East to one of a hardened cultural identitarian artifact that had to be dealt with by either reform (secular Arab nationalists), compulsory enforcement (Islamists), or all-out removal (Kemalists). Child rearing, as we will see, was also central to this encounter, where women, as the keepers of the home, were now asked to be the caretakers of the nation's children and whose major responsibility was to provide the state with a future generation that would uplift the nation so that it could join the civilized nations of the world (Kemalists and Arab nationalists) or be in compliance with the moral utopia of an enlightened Islamic peoples (Islamist).

Colonial Feminism

Arguably, the veil has become for many in the West the most significant marker of the level of civilization and progress attained by a given country or culture when it comes to the constructed binary of Islam and the West. For those who cling to identifying themselves with this thing they call "the West," the veil is the ultimate signifier of the Otherness of Islam, marking Muslims, in their minds, as fully alien to "Western civilization." In becoming a civilizational marker, it creates an insurmountable barrier between the perceived antithetical civilizations. In this sense the veil functions as the most important of all symbols in the effort to identify and construct a pure Western identity. But as the postcolonial theorist Frantz Fanon recognized in the 1950s, in the context in which the colonized were overthrowing their colonial regimes, it can also be asserted as a symbol of resistance by the colonized in their battle against their colonial oppressor. In doing so they become fixated on it to the point that it moves from an unconscious practice to a solid, even hardened item of their imagined authentic national and civilizational identity. In the words of Fanon, it moves away from a historically flexible piece of clothing to one that comes to be weighed down heavily with cultural identity and authenticity:

> We shall see that this veil, one of the elements of the traditional Algerian garb, was to become the bone of contention in a grandiose battle, on account of which the occupation forces were to mobilize their most powerful and most varied resources, and in the course of which the colonized were to display a surprising force of inertia. Taken as a whole, colonial society, with its values, its areas of strength, and its philosophy, reacts to the veil in a rather homogeneous way.... The colonialist's relentlessness, his methods of struggle were bound to give rise to reactionary forms of behavior on the part of the colonized. In the face of the violence of the occupier, the colonized found himself defining a principled position with respect to a formerly inert element of the native cultural configuration. It was the colonialist's frenzy to unveil the Algerian woman, it was his gamble on winning the battle of the veil at whatever cost that were to provide the native's bristling resistance.[4]

We therefore need to evaluate how the colonizer's obsessive desire to denounce the veil and act as the benevolent caretaker of women's rights when speaking about the place of Islam in the hierarchy of world civilizations forced the anticolonial movements to place it at the center of their struggle for political and cultural sovereignty. Without understanding the colonizer's role in bringing a rigid understanding of the veil into the region, we would simply think it is a product of a cultural essence belonging to those Muslims "over there" without recognizing the role the colonial encounter had on this "cultural practice," a fallacy many Western commentators and scholars often repeat when speaking about the veil and Islam. In this sense, it is not a *tradition*, using the customary anthropological term that produced the discourse, but rather a repressive quality of the encounter the region has experienced under colonial modernity.

This can easily be observed in the manner by which both British and French colonial regimes of the nineteenth and twentieth centuries symbolically used the veil and women's rights as one of their fundamental ideological arsenals to legitimize their colonial rule. Not surprisingly, as Leila Ahmed has noted, the male elites of these colonial regimes devised their critiques of Islam and its handling of women by "capturing the language of feminism" in the service of colonialism and in denouncing the culture of brown men, even while on the home front, they opposed fundamental women's rights and at times became leaders of antifeminist organizations: "This champion of the unveiling of Egyptian women was, in England, founding member and sometime president of the Men's League for Opposing Women's Suffrage. Feminism on the home front and feminism directed against white men was to be resisted and suppressed; but taken abroad and directed against the cultures of colonized peoples, it could be promoted in ways that admirably served and furthered the project of the dominance of the white man."[5] She fittingly defines this form of feminism as "*Colonial Feminism.*"

The Columbian Exhibition Marginalized White Women, but at Least They Had a Building

But such hypocrisy in this form of colonial feminism had a logic to it that made it appear noncontradictory from the point of view of the colonizer. For these men of the late-nineteenth and early twentieth centuries, the temporal script of colonial Social Darwinism smoothed out the rough edges that might otherwise appear to be mere hypocrisy. For these Victorian-era colonial male elites, the higher races of all civilizations were white *men,* after all, and their white women were seen as their domesticated kin. Even though the Aryan race stood at the pinnacle of all world civilizations and races, the ideal measure of such a race was undoubtedly both white and male.

We can see this gendered Social Darwinism at work in our earlier example of the 1893 Chicago's World's Columbian Exhibition. As Gail Bederman has shown, although the exhibition placed white civilization apart from colored races, by placing the latter in the Midway Plaisance, they also placed white women in what we could call an in-between status. She concludes from this:

> The message was inescapable: The White City's civilization was built by men, only. Exhibiting men's achievements required the entire White City, while women's achievements could fit into the smallest exhibition hall at the fair....

> Segregating women's exhibits in one small building suggested that women's contributions to civilization were completely different from men's. Visitors were impressed mostly by the Women's Building's softness, compared to the masculine dynamos and technological marvels of the manly exhibits of the White City. For example, the *New York Times* suggested that "the achievements of man [are] in iron, steel, wood, and the baser and cruder products ... [whereas] in the Woman's Building one can note the distinct demarcation in the female successes in the more delicate and finer products of the loom, the needle, the brush, and more refined avenues of effort which culminate in the home, the hospital, the church, and in personal adornment. The lesson most people took from the Women's Building was that there was a "distinct demarcation" between men's contributions to civilization—machines, technology, commerce—and women's—needlework, beauty, domesticity.[6]

The men of less-developed races, on the other hand, were considered to be lacking manliness insofar as these Persian, Algerian, Egyptian, and Turkish males were forced to present themselves as unmanly by constantly showing no self-restraint and who could not help but respond to their sexual appetites as they "savor[ed] their countrywomen's sensuous dancing." Hence the logic here: The white male organizers of the Columbian Exhibition of 1893 not only placed colored men outside of their manly White City of Industry and Commerce and Parliament, but they situated the Women's Building at the very edge of the civilized portion of the exhibition, "far from the manly Court of Honor" but also situated "directly opposite the only exit to the *uncivilized* section of the fair, the Midway ... on the border between civilized and savage (as befit women who, according to scientists, were biologically more primitive than men)."[7] But, although white women were marginal on the white side of civilization, they nonetheless received a building hierarchically above those of the colored men. This was not the case for brown women, who were represented inside the Midway Plaisance as sensuous creatures—usually in the role of belly dancers—living under barbarism and who were abused by their unmanly colored men, with brown women depicted as living under sexual and indecent exploitation. Bederman concludes from this that "although few American women deigned to see the exotic belly dancers, they understood the message: White women's place in civilization might be marginal, but at least it was moral and safe. Under barbarism, however, women experienced not respect and equality but sexual danger and indecent exploitation."[8]

This is the gendered and racialized lens the male colonizer saw his world through, and it is the reason why male colonial feminists could be antifeminist at home while purporting to be serving the interest of women abroad. For them there was no hypocrisy in what seemingly appears to be contradictory stances from our contemporary point of view.

Cromer as the Quintessential Colonial Feminist

Saving brown women from the exploitation of Muslim men, thus, worked quite consistently with the male-centered aspect of colonial feminism. The British agent and consul-general Earl Cromer, who took administrative command over the occupation of Egypt between 1883 and 1907, for instance, most blatantly practiced this appropriation of colonial feminism. As was discussed in previous chapters, he had a lasting impact on colonial discourse and how Islam figured into the ideological mirror of colonial modernity. But what is most glaring about his views of Islam is precisely related to the way he felt obliged to speak on behalf of women's rights and the lack thereof in the "Muslim world," a view that remains to be pervasive today in the thinking of many political and intellectual elites interested in colonial escapades overseas.

In Cromer's gendered Social Darwinistic thinking, the woman question in Islam was central to understanding why "Mohammedan" nations stood so far behind European civilization: "The position of women in Egypt, and in Mohammedan countries generally," he warns his readers, "is, therefore, a fatal obstacle to the attainment of that elevation of thought and character which should accompany the introduction of European civilization, if that civilization is to produce its full measure of beneficial effect. The obvious remedy would appear to be to educate the women."[9] Indeed, it was inconceivable for Cromer to think that without the civilizing role of "modern Europe" on the Muslim world, especially in its mission to uplift the Muslim women from the bondage of their male-dominated religion, the "moral and material" advancement of Egypt and other "Mohammedan countries" was highly unlikely. The connection between the level of advancement of Islamic countries and their treatment of women, therefore, was a direct cause-and-effect relationship that could only be broken, in Cromer's mind, by a more superior civilization. Hence, the woman question becomes essential for this form of colonial reasoning, because it denies Muslim men the legitimacy of ruling over their territory and in effect places them and their religion into the time of the backward Other, who is not ready to rule until the higher race of colonial Europe sets them on the right path of development.

In Cromer's desire to rationalize British colonial rule, therefore, he had to put colonial feminism into motion so as to claim British rule over Egyptian men. This is why in his colonial (and very popular) text, *Modern Egypt* (2 vols.), he consistently fused the categories of Islam, male, and women's oppression and continued to argue notions like the reason "Islam as a social system failed" was owning "first and foremost" to the manner by which it treated its women: "The degradation of women in the East is a canker that begins its destructive work early in childhood, and has eaten into the whole system of Islam."[10] Unlike Christianity, which teaches civility and manly respect for its women, in which Christian, white European men have successfully "elevated" their women, Islam, with its regressive teachings about women, degraded not only the women of its followers but caused the entire society to become stagnant and unable to achieve the time of Christian Europe. Veiling and segregation of women were the most blatant indicators of its failures and are the main reasons why "the inferiority of Muslim men could be traced"[11] to this religion. Hence, placing the blame on the religion of Islam and its treatment of women created the ideological space for not only explaining why Muslim countries were "behind" Europe and the West but also for removing all blame for their backwardness from European colonial male rule. Indeed, he goes one step farther and makes a rationale for colonial rule by claiming Muslim males were not up to the task because they are racially inferior and indoctrinated by a religion that is permeated by a lack of reason and logic. Leila Ahmed's summary of Cromer's view on Islam, the veil, and low achievement of Islamic countries clearly highlights the implications of his thinking:

> The practices of veiling and seclusion exercised "a baneful effect on Eastern society".... It was essential that Egyptians "be persuaded or forced into imbibing the true spirit of western civilization," Cromer stated, and to achieve this, it was essential to change the position of women in Islam, for it was Islam's degradation of women, expressed in the practices of veiling and seclusion, that was "the fatal obstacle" to the Egyptian's "attainment of that elevation of thought and character which should accompany the introduction of Western civilization"; Only by abandoning those practices might they attain "the mental and moral development" which he [Cromer] desired for them.[12]

Notice also that by constantly focusing on women's bodies and the veil as the keys to emancipation from barbarism, Cromer, in his effort to rule over Egypt, sets in motion the colonial logic of culturalizing the struggle between the colonizer and the colonized male. By doing so, he forced these categories to the center of the struggle between British and Egyptian men and thereby solidified a rigid gendered ideological pole around which cultural identity must wrap itself. Because European men, with their superior civilization, was the only savior possible for both Egyptian women *and* men, the only possible route of resistance remaining for the colonized male became very limited: They either had to accept colonial logic and dress their women with modernity and its racialized aesthetic attire or negate the colonizer's devaluation of their religion and insist on the veiling of their women. Both of these revolved around the same temporal script of liberation and advancement, and the only difference between them was the way in which they managed and manipulated the female body and mind.

This is precisely what we mean by the gendered effects of colonial modernity. It focuses the mind of the colonized male to become attached to a signifier in the shape of a woman and a veil who stands in the way of the emancipation of the nation and religion. Thus, emancipating the nation from the French and British would not be enough to produce take-off into the future utopia, without also emancipating the nation from its backward treatment of the female body and mind. This is as true for secular Kemalist/Arab nationalists as it is for Islamists, who just reverse the logic by keeping the focus on the veil but emphasizing its implementation so as to protect the nation from immorality.

What is most striking about this colonial linkage of the veil, women's rights, and the stagnation of Muslim societies is that it determined the way in which resistance was expressed. In the politically astute words of Fanon: "The doctrinal assertions of colonialism in its attempt to justify the maintenance of its domination almost always push the colonized to the position of making uncompromising, rigid, static counter-proposals."[13] By doing so, it placed feminism in a difficult bind, by equating its use with that of colonialism itself, in which those who used it were accused of importing "Western ideals" at best or being collaborators at worse. This creates a sense that feminism was not only inauthentic to the region but harmful as well. As we will see, Kemalist and secular Arab nationalists didn't help to remedy this charge. Far from it, they were responsible for a good part of why many today equate feminism with imperialism. But to be fair, Islamists, even though they clothed their political discourse in an imagined authentic garb, were also largely dependent on the colonizer's social techniques of rule, because they, too, appropriated essentially the same gendered script as their foes but only superficially inverted it.

Kemalist Feminism

There were mainly two types of responses to Cromer's form of racialized feminism. The first, quite secular strain of Arab and Turkish feminism was the dominant form from the early twentieth century until quite recently. The later, more religious form of feminism, did not emerge until the last couple decades of the twentieth century, in an effort to challenge secular nationalists by positing an "alternative" discourse. In this section we will deal with the more secular strain that we will call, to simplify things, Kemalist, because this form of feminism shares many of the assumptions we covered in chapter 3. Under the colonizer's constant barrage of Orientalist representations of Islam and its veiled women being held in bondage in harems and accusations that Muslim men acted uncivilized in their treatment of women, many leaders of the emerging nationalist movements in the early twentieth century Middle East attempted to distance themselves, by accepting the colonizer's judgment and enacting policies aimed at "modernizing" and "emancipating" the "Muslim woman" from her "traditional" bondage. The image of choice was the "Western woman," who was depicted as wearing clothing appropriate for "modern times." It promoted a form of nationalist feminism that believed that a nation could not propel itself into modernity without first remaking its women into the image of a secular, domesticated, learned, and, most importantly, Westernized woman.

These formerly colonized elite men, exposed to the humiliation of the colonizer's gaze of being branded primitive male misogynists, used the symbol of the unveiled, modern woman to express the deep felt anxieties they had acquired under the colonial encounter. In the attempt to overturn the humiliation they experienced, they accepted the colonizer's judgment of Islam and its men and proceeded to eradicate any symbols that the Western colonizer identified as backward. In the fine words of Leila Ahmed, "theirs are the words and acts of men exposed to the Western discourse who have accepted its representation of their culture, the inferiority of its practices, and the meaning of the veil."[14] All of the major concerns about the rights of women, their level of education, the problems of seclusion, polygamy, and veiling were informed by equating the Eurocentric definitions of modernity and its discourse of the incompatibility of Islam and the West.[15] What was common to all of this talk of eradicating obsolete practices involved the spatial and temporal distancing from Islam as the only way to the emancipation of the nation and its women.

Kemal Ataturk and "The New Woman"

Thus the colonizer, by positing itself as the protector of the female body, led many elite anticolonial nationalists to respond by erecting a new state that had the capacity, unlike in Ottoman times, to protect and produce the "new woman." This was especially the case for Kemal Ataturk and Turkey from the 1920s until very recently, with the rise of the Islamic AKP Party. The woman question became synonymous with building the new Occidentalized state, all of which was full of rhetorical references to the "improvement" of women's bodies and minds, which filled both Turkey's airwaves and magazines. As a symbol, the "new woman" of Kemal Ataturk and his nationalist supporters would become one of the leading images used to show how far forward modern Turkey has traveled in time.

As Alev Cinar has pointed out, Ataturk personally took on this quest by showcasing his wife, Latife Hanim, and his adopted daughter, Afet Inan, and used them as symbolic trophies of his new modernist state in his public tours, ballroom dancing, and official ceremonies. Today, many Turkish feminists still equate emancipation with all things Western, especially when it comes to the veil, having fully internalized Kemalist representations of the modern and professional woman, who stands temporally distant from the backward female of the Islamic era. In 1920 Iran, under the reign of Reza Shah, this Occidentalization of women's bodies would be taken a step farther. The Shah issued a proclamation making it illegal for women to be in public wearing the veil and ordered the Iranian police to forcefully remove any headgear unless it was of a European style, all under the rationale of showing Iran to be a civilized society to the West. Many veiled women, under such threats, "chose to stay at home rather than venture outdoors and risk having their veils pulled off by the police."[16]

Notice here the meticulous nature of this temporal nationalist discourse. It was not enough to "modernize" the public sphere, the urban planning, science, and the school system. In order to launch successfully into the time of modernity, it was essential to these nationalists that women's bodies be radically made over, because it was believed that a certain kind of clothing was not proper for time traveling. To leave the time of barbarism entailed the penetration of "the lifestyle, public manners, gender behavior, body care, and the daily customs of the people, as well as their willingness to change their self-conception as Turks," all of which entailed going well beyond the modernization and Westernization of the external features of the society: "Photographs of women unveiled, of women in athletic competitions, of female pilots and professionals, and photographs of men and women 'miming' European lifestyles depicted the new modernist interpretations of a 'prestigious' life in the Turkish nation-state."[17] Kemal Ataturk made this type of makeover a high initiative of the state apparatus by denouncing the veil publicly and ridiculing the men of his assembly whose wives or daughters remained in Islamic attire:

> In some places I have seen women who put a piece of cloth or a towel or something like that over their heads to hide their faces, and who turn their backs or huddle themselves on the ground when a man passes by. What are the meaning and sense of this behavior? Gentlemen, can the mothers and daughters of a civilized nation adopt this strange manner, this barbarous posture? It is a spectacle that makes the nation an object of ridicule. It must be remedied at once.[18]

This gendered discourse was so pervasive that it radically impacted the aesthetics of public spaces like the coffee and tea salons, restaurants, and the market place, and women took special care to fit into this new state-sanctioned version of the "new woman" to such an extent that school classrooms, universities, and other such places became cleared of what Kemalists identified as a scourge upon their modern, up-to-date eyes. Turkish women, in this sense, had to carry the anxiety-ridden baggage of these men's shamed consciousness who grew up under the lens of Eurocentric eyes. Women's bodies became central to the sign of the nation and its movement toward the utopia of the modern. It was through this rhetorical practice that the veil came to symbolize for these Kemalists all that was backward and uncivilized, and the failure of the past

Ottoman/Muslim period to advance forward into modernity could only be undone if the citizens of the new modern republic unveiled and emancipated their women. Hence, in doing so, these men positioned themselves as the guardian of their weak sisters, who needed the protection of a strong manly state who could deliver the society to its deserved future utopia. As such this rhetorical device was political as well insofar as it marked the old political class as incompetent, patriarchal, barbaric, and lacking the proper mannerisms of manly modernity: "images of women in bathing suits were abundantly used in photographs, cartoons, and illustrations during the formative years of the republic.... The state-sponsored parade of images of women in their bathing suits was justified with a rhetoric of liberation of the body/nation from the oppressive authority of Islam."[19]

Qasim Amin: The Other Colonial Feminist

> The only remedy is to bring up our children to understand the important achievements of Western civilization and to grasp its principles, its influence, and its effects.
>
> —*Qasim Amin 1900*

The most influential figure in this form of feminism was arguably the Egyptian jurist and intellectual Qasim Amin (1863–1908), whose two books *The Liberation of Women* and *The New Woman* at the turn of the twentieth-century would set off a major debate in the Arab press that turned the veil from a residual, marginal clothing item to something that played a central role in all of the competing political ideologies, secular and religious. Qasim Amin was the Arab version of Kemal Ataturk and preceded him by a couple of decades. He was also a self-described feminist, who took Cromer's criticism of Islam and women to heart and urged Arabs, especially his fellow Egyptians, to immediately "unveil" their society from the clutches of barbarism and warned them that failure to adopt Western ways would mean the eventual conquest by a more superior Western civilization. Women were central to his plea to his Arab brethren and he identified women as the most significant agents of change in the efforts to create the Arab nation of the future.

For Qasim Amin, women were "the foundation of the towering constructs of modern civilization," and he looked to both Europe and America as the inspirational guide for Egyptian women to emulate. In his two books he constantly quotes American and European men as authority figures on the question of women. He believed that, as representatives of modernity in its pure form, only these countries could claim that "women have contributed shoulder to shoulder with men to every branch of trade and industry, to every branch of knowledge and the arts, to every philanthropic activity, and to every political event."[20] His text is highlighted by many of these references to the West: "Western man's respect for a woman's freedom.... Western households are based on firm principle."[21]

But most telling for us is the historicist method he chose for his books, which provided an academic style social-evolutionary perspective that presented itself as scientific and final, as a way to give him an authoritative voice over his competitors. For instance, Qasim Amin begins his book *The New Woman* with a chapter entitled "A Historical Perspective on Women," by making the claim for a historical, stageist type of analysis for understanding how familial and gender relations are the best variables for understanding the linear movement of society from its simple, backward childhood era to its modern, contemporary stage of adulthood: "It is impossible to understand women's present status without an adequate knowledge of their position in history. This is a basic principle of social research, which demands the understanding of various stages of change. In other words, we need to be familiar with our starting point, which will then enable us to predict the direction of change that will be facing us."[22] In doing so, he promises to make a survey of women in the world, by highlighting the evolution of mankind with the type of woman as the marker of the temporal distance the human family has marched from its most earliest days:

> We have briefly surveyed the life of women in the world, and can recapitulate our discussion in a few words. Women lived freely during the first period of history, while humanity was at its infancy. With the formation of the institution of the family, women fell into real slavery. When humanity began its journey on the road to civilization, women started gaining some of their dues. A woman, however, was still subject to man's tyranny, because he required she enjoy only those rights that he permitted her to have. As human civilization reached its climax, women received their complete freedom and most of the rights that men have. These are the four phases that reflect women's changing status in our world's civilization. Egyptian women today are in the third stage of that historical development.... This situation is a consequence of the political despotism to which we are subject.... This demonstrates the dominance of old customs that are still influencing our lives and actions.[23]

We should note here that one of the characteristics of those who argue for equating modernity with Westernization is this historicist, stageist, inevitable model, where man's journey through time comes prepackaged with a certain social, political, legal, and familial structure. Gender relations are viewed as intricately evolving in sync with all of these as well. Hence, rhetorically and politically it gives people like Amin and the academics he depends on the power and legitimacy to look and appear as neutral observers of a historical process that evolves over time. It gives his argument authority over others simply because the laws of history and evolution are objective, historical facts no less so than the law of gravity.

In his attempt to heighten his position over other Arab and Egyptian men, for instance, he collected a large number of scholarly voices to glue together a temporal script that modeled time in an evolutionary manner. Not only was it morally and ethically the responsibility of Egyptian society to liberate women from the clutches of barbarism, but it was the way nature intended change. Just like a plant evolves from a seed to a flower, so does human history move from simplicity and backwardness to complexity and advancement. To be sure, he used the metaphor of the infant child rising to become the mature adult, but the argument remains the same: "Moral development does not differ in its course from physical development. Before walking, a child crawls, gradually learning by holding on to the wall or by leaning against the arm of his nurse. He only masters walking through continuous practice for some time, during which he falls often. In the same way, humanity's moral development moves from one stage to another as a consequence of experimentation, which inevitably exposes it to much stumbling, confusion, and painful experiences. This is the law of nature. We cannot conceive that we will be able to rid ourselves of it or to run away from it. At the same time, it is not wise for us to turn back or to stop our forward progress."[24]

For Amin it didn't matter if it was God or Nature that was behind this law of change, only that we as humans need to get out of its way and remove those contaminating items that get in the way of its natural progress. He thus argued that Egypt, unfortunately, although successfully having removed the colonizer, was hopelessly out of tune with this law of nature, causing it to live "for generations under political tyranny, resulting in a general decline in all areas of life—the intellect, morality, and work. It is still declining lower and lower and has become weak, sick, and subdued, and is vegetating rather than living." Although it has "rid itself of servitude," it maintained the most primitive characteristics and had instead become "confused and did not know what to do with its new freedom."[25] Such things like veiling were singled out for special scrutiny, and he argued that the first step toward putting the nation back on the track of evolution was to liberate the woman and "to tear off the veil and totally wipe out its influence." In his summation, "veiling is the symbol of ancient ownership, and is one of the vestiges of the barbaric behavior that characterized human life for generations. It existed before it was realized that a person should not be owned simply because she was a female—just as people with black skin should not be slaves for the white man."[26]

But arguably the most controversial aspect of his thesis is that he places blame on what he believes is the inability of Muslims to let go of past obsolete systems of belief that are no longer applicable to modern times. Interestingly enough, this is reminiscent of our own time where people like Bernard Lewis and others congratulate Islam for serving an important function during its early phase but argue that it now somehow gets in the way of people's effort to transition into modernity. Amin similarly pats Islam on the back for its early role, where it was ahead of its time by infusing a nomadic, tribal society with a lifestyle appropriate for a premodern society, but although it created useful military bonds and established law and order, it did not infuse society with the proper scientific ethos it needed to progress any farther: "Since Islamic civilization began and ended before the principles of science were discovered, how can we continue to believe that it was a 'model of human perfection'? ... We must respect it, because it has affected and complimented humanity in its development. But we must also note that many of the external forms of this ancient civilization are inappropriate to our present social life."[27] In other words, those who challenge his argument are labeled as lost in the time of premodernity before the age of science and rationality, whereas he, on the other hand, is a man possessing the proper qualities of the modern, enlightened man who is able to do a historical, value-free, analysis of the evolution of society, culminating in the modern unveiled woman.

Qasim Amin and the Role of Mothers in Pulling The Arab out of Barbarism

But veiling was not the only thing he saw as being in the way of evolution. For too long the women of the Middle East have been totally ignorant and lacking all civilized traits that are essential for them to acquire if the Egyptian nation is to progress forward, especially given the fact that these women are directly responsible for socializing the next generations of change-makers. For successful modernization and development of society to occur, Amin claims, we need to bring women up to par with modernity, so that they are able to serve as *ministers of the interior* (this is the term used by Judith Newton in her discussion of British mid-nineteenth-century debates and used in Abu-Lughod 1989a). In the words of Lila Abu-Lughod, Amin's form of familial discourse can be understood as the professionalization of housewifery, where issues like child rearing become narrated in the nationalist project of "producing good sons" and, in her words, "may have initiated new coercive norms and subjected women to new forms of control and discipline, many self-imposed, even as they undermined other forms of patriarchy."[28] The quality of this child rearing is so central to the success of the nation that he worries that "in the face of the battle" between a superior Western civilization and the Egyptian nation, the only way Egyptians can come out of this unharmed is if it acquires "those intangible intellectual and education capabilities that are central to every type of power," by which he was referring to the quality of the family structure: "As such, for a nation to survive in the face of this form of competition, it must be 'concerned with the structure of its family, for the family is the foundation of a country. Consequently, since the mother is the foundation of the family, her intellectual development or underdevelopment becomes the primary factor in determining the development or underdevelopment of the country'."[29]

As we will also see in the case of the Islamist Ali Shariati, this modern mothering function would also introduce into the region a pervasive system of gendered discourses that went well beyond the veil to include an array of themes for the moral and material improvement of Muslim countries, especially those pertaining to child rearing practices and the productive functions of mothering, which places women, in both colonial and anticolonial thought, as the domestic productive force whose main function was "the development of a generation of morally upright, intellectually developed, and productive citizens."[30]

> The colonial project was marked by the intensive generation and elaboration of modes of knowledge production that would seek to contribute to the *moral and material* improvement of the native population. The discourse of uplifting an entire population onto a higher plane of material and moral well-being intersected with colonial representations and constructions of gender and segregation. Women, perceived as sequestered beings isolated from the machinery

> of "society," could be demarcated as "the locus of the country's backwardness" and would come to be instrumental in practices aimed at "social and politic discipline." Colonial policy sought to "penetrate that 'inaccessible' space ... and thus commence ... to 'work from the inside out'."[31]

As Shakry has commented on this type of argument, "children were posited as 'citizens of tomorrow' and a 'national asset' upon which 'the future of the country' ... depended."[32] Hence, mothers were labeled as "ignorant" and in large part blamed for the backwardness of the nation. The only way they could be redeemed was to go under a process of change where they would be equipped with the bourgeois traits of proper mothering and become the custodians of the future of the nation. In Qasim Amin's own account:

> Children, whether boys or girls, from birth to puberty are exposed primarily to the mother. They experience society through her, and the impressions they form are the result of what she has shared with them. The mother engraves on the blank sheet of the child's life whatever she wishes to engrave, a process, that goes on until the child is about fourteen years old, as Alphonse Daudet has said, after which it is impossible to add to or subtract from what has been etched on the mind of that child, except in the smallest detail.... Woman's work in society is important for building the moral character of a country, and moral character has a greater impact on a society's progress and organizations, laws, and religions.[33]

He goes on about this in length, "the qualities of the woman become characteristic of the family and are extended to the country. Thus a good mother is more useful to her species than a good man, while a corrupt mother is more harmful than a corrupt man."[34] At times he gets utterly disgusted with what he sees in the women of Egypt he knows: "If our women allotted to study one tenth of the time they spend today in idleness, foolish talk, and arguments, Egypt would make major advances thanks to them."[35] Sometimes his claims to be the guardian of women becomes even more difficult to swallow, for example, when he makes the following types of statements: "Most Egyptian women are not in the habit of combing their hair every day ... nor do they bathe more than once a week. They do not know how to use a toothbrush and do not attend to what is attractive in clothing, though their attractiveness and cleanliness strongly influence men's inclinations. They do not know how to rouse desire in their husband, nor how to retain his desire or to increase it.... If she tries to rouse a man, she will usually have the opposite effect."[36] This has led Leila Ahmed to correctly conclude, "Far from being the father of Arab feminism, then, Amin might more aptly be described as the son of Cromer and colonialism."[37]

Islamist Feminism

> Every new Algerian woman unveiled announced to the occupier an Algerian society whose systems of defense were in the process of dislocation, open and breached. Every veil that fell, every body that became liberated from the traditional embrace of the haik, every face that offered itself to the bold and impatient glance of the occupier, was a negative expression of the fact that Algeria was beginning to deny herself and was accepting the rape of the colonizer. Algerian society with every abandoned veil seemed to express its willingness to attend to the master's school and to decide to change its habits under the occupier's direction and patronage.
>
> —*Frantz Fanon (1965)*

The Islamists rejected the idea that the emancipation of women necessitates the adoption of Western modernity and proceeded instead to offer an alternative by dressing progress in Islamic attire and morality. But by doing so they remained trapped in its gendered and racial episteme. The Islamists, wary of the demeaning nature of the colonizer's denunciation of its Muslim men as premodern, uncivilized foes, searched to articulate a version of colonial modernity in which it was possible to portray Islam as the true protector of women, and that the future of the nation's advancement lay in how well the women of Islam stay on the straight path of Allah. In pointing to the morally corrupt nature of Western civilization to sexually use and abuse its women—using the same language of sexual exploitation the colonizer used against Muslim men—they aimed to reclaim the Muslim woman's body and mind as the ideal marker of modesty and morality. In Khomeini's take on this script, for instance, he presents Islam as a populist alternative "confronting the corrupt, 'Western-struck' (*gharbzadeh*) elite of the Shah era," with Western female clothing symbolizing "moral decay."[38] Hence, this form of anticolonial therapy attempted to relieve itself of shame, only to find itself holding on to the pain that it could not let go of, leaving women having to deal with its psycho-social dysfunctional consequences.

It's important to highlight how this form of analysis differs from the more typical method used in much mainstream literature on "Islam" and "women." First of all, I do not claim that this form of cultural dysfunctionality springs from some essential cultural source, or that it has its roots in some mystical, medieval text or tradition. Many of those types of arguments, which now unfortunately fill our bookstores, are simply attempting to clear the guilt of their conscience by refusing to place some of the blame on those very same "Western" forces whose destructive military, political, economic, and cultural escapades have laid havoc on the Middle East (and to which they pay their tax dollars). The Islamist's "return" to an Islamic aesthetic and the manner by which it desires to remake women is not the product of a temporally out-of-time religious ideology. Far from it being premodern, Islamism uses the same guideposts of modernity as its enemies and ideological opponents. Islamists simply attempt to challenge the colonizer's Eurocentrism, not by somehow providing a pre-given tradition, but instead by offering a traditionalized interpretation of a past utopia, so as to offer what they perceive as a morally and ethically superior modernity. Hence, the actual traditions offered as authenticity are mediated by the conflict itself, where the appropriation of texts and traditions are hermeneutically selected so as to give legitimacy to those Islamists offering a political challenge to the colonizer and his Middle Eastern protégés. Many Orientalist commentators mistake this challenge as a pre-given tradition, as though the behavior of Islamists can be found in some sort of textual and scriptural statements of "Jihad" or what the prophet said and did with this or that woman, or what a text says about the veil and so forth, as though such texts and traditions pop out of a book and automatically drive these men to perform suicide bombings or beat their women. What I offer here instead is a plea to dig our inquiry into the ground a bit and situate Islamist discourse in the rhetorical world of power that they reside in at the very moment in which they procure such traditions. What you will find is not a simple reproduction of a time-immemorial sacred ethos but men who are trying to position themselves as possessing a public face that has the capacity to produce some form of dignity and strength in a moment of colonial emasculation by stronger men, even as they oppress and demoralize others.

Again, Fanon is our best guide to understanding the psychological aspect of colonial modernity: "The colonized, in the face of the emphasis given by the colonialist to this or that aspect of his traditions, reacts very violently. The attention devoted to modifying this aspect, the emotion the conqueror puts into his pedagogical work, his prayers, his threats, weave a whole universe of resistances around this particular element of the culture."[39]

By showing how dependent Islamists are on the gendered aspect of the template the colonizer brought to them over a century ago, gifted feminist postcolonial scholars already highlighted how Islamists like Ali Shariati differ little from Cromer, Ataturk, and Amin, whom we have analyzed previously. Just like their appointed enemies, these Islamists, as we will see, were obsessed with measuring the uplift of their civilization or nation with how far they could remake their women, promoting in fact the very same issues of concern of their secular counterparts except orienting their identities toward the opposite side of the hegemonic pole. Islamists were just as concerned with the moral development of their women as Amin was, leading them to scrutinize the daily lives of women, what they wore, how they mothered and raised the nation's next generation, the quality of their minds, their style of presenting their sexual being to the public and to their husbands. As we have discussed, Kemalists and secular Arab nationalists participate in a reverse form of this coercive and disciplinary discourse. Far too few liberal and conservative Western commentators of "fundamentalists" recognize this fact and normally offer such criticisms only to Islamists. But dogmatic stances of Kemalists and secular Arab nationalists who were obsessed with upholding a tyrannical form of secularism and performing muscular "modernism" on their women are quite disciplinarian in their own right.

Thus, just as the Kemalist before them purified the public space by making it socially unpleasant and at times dangerous for a veiled Muslim girl or woman to sit in a café or university classroom, Islamist likewise made it difficult for a woman or girl who wears her dress (or even pants) too tight to hang out in cafés or walk the streets without being treated as sexually promiscuous. The pervasive power of this gendered nationalist and Islamist discourse penetrates the material world we live in so powerfully that an alien visiting Arab countries in the 1960s and visiting again at the end of the first decade of the twenty-first century would be utterly shocked at the social and aesthetic nature of the change. But if he took the time to analyze the situation more closely, he would recognize that what occurred was simply a flip of the switch and a quick visit to the backstage for a change of wardrobe—nothing more. The man with a beard and a Muslim cap who has restacked the theater's backstage collections has now replaced the man with the brimmed hat who used to write the staged performance and used to be in command of the prompts and the selection of wardrobe.

Although there is much more variation in the public square than the Orientalist would like us to think, there is, admittedly, some truth to its Islamization, but what is most shocking is the similar social techniques used to make this change possible. Whereas before the public spaces were coercively "Western" in nature, today they are "Islamic," giving a whole new meaning to the saying, "out with the old and in with the new." Whereas Kemalists shunned the "Islamic woman," today a woman is more likely to be accused of wearing "'too much' makeup, 'too short' a skirt, 'too tight' a pair of pants, 'too low-cut' a shirt" and could easily be subjected to the lashing of the collective moral gaze or be accused of being "too loose" with her sexuality, a woman "who laughed 'too loudly'," at times possibly even being accused in places like Iran of becoming like "the painted dolls of the Pahlavi regime."[40]

Ali Shariati: The Quintessential Modernist Islamist

We could use an easier target to demonstrate the depth to which Islamists reproduced the disciplinary techniques of their secular foes, but we chose Ali Shariati, because many designate him as a revolutionary figure unlike other Islamist men. But as we will discuss, Shariati was just as disciplinarian in his discourse as many of the leading political Islamists. From the late 1960s to his death in 1977, he represented an important Iranian dissident voice and courageously challenged the tyrannical policies of the Shah regime and was able to attract many university students to his fiery lectures, in which he skillfully denounced the regime as a colonial outpost, protecting the interest of Western-led Capitalism (for this theme, see especially his book *Marxism and Other Western Fallacies*). He has become designated "as the 'ideologue' of the revolution."[41] His rich text, which we will be covering in detail, is his important *Fatima Is Fatima*, in which he used the prophet's daughter as an example of the prototype of the revolutionary Islamic woman he'd like to see in the new Iran, whom he urgently wants to create. The most significant aspect of this book from our point of view is how Shariati appropriated the figure of Fatima not only as a symbol of resistance to the Shah but also the manner by which she came to signify the type of woman "who could resolve the current problem of how women could enter modernity and remake themselves as neither Western nor traditional" and who could represent "an alternative to the Pahlavi 'westoxicated' images of woman."[42]

Like many Islamists, he made it explicit that he was not interested in producing a "traditional" Muslim woman who practiced tradition in an unthoughtful, "uneducated" way by just simply imitating customs. Instead, he preferred the Muslim woman with a political and social consciousness, who knew the revolutionary significance of her acts. This type of woman for him was absolutely essential for overcoming an Iranian society that he saw as remaining in an underdeveloped, semifeudal state of existence. In his words:

> In an underdeveloped country every effort [must be] made to mobilize men and women as quickly as possible; it must guard against the danger of perpetuating the feudal tradition which holds sacred the superiority of the masculine element over the feminine. Women will have exactly the same places as men, not in the clauses of the constitution but in the life of every day: in the factory, at school, and in the parliament.[43]

To create this kind of woman (and the future society), he proposed a revolutionary method of what he described as "changing the content of tradition but transforming its form."[44]

He uses the example of the Prophet's last pilgrimage, in which Muhammad kept the polytheistic ritual of circling around the ka'aba but changed radically its content through the removal of the symbols of multiple deities, as an illustration of what he means:

> The Prophet, with his revolutionary stand, took the pilgrimage of the idol-worshipping tribes and changed it into a completely opposite rite. It was a revolutionary leap. As a result, the Arab people underwent no anguish, no loss of values or beliefs, but rather, revived the truth and cleansed an ancient custom. They moved easily from idol worship to unity. Suddenly they had left the past.... This revolutionary social method found within the Traditions of the Prophet preserved the outer form but changed its content. It maintained the container as a permanent element but changed and transformed the content.[45]

Shariati thus suggested that like the Prophet Muhammad's divine inspired method of bringing about change to seventh-century Mecca, Iranian revolutionaries, when likewise confronted by "outdated customs, ancient traditions, a dead culture and a stagnant religious and social order," could also adopt this method in their effort to bring about real change. He points out that the Prophet, because of his political and social intelligence and the intervention of the divine, knew that the best way to bring about real change is to leave some of the external manifestations of traditions in tact but radically change the actual content of the said practices. This is the best way to ensure, Shariati tells us, that the revolutionaries remain connected to the people and not be viewed as strangers, who otherwise "may turn and condemn him."[46]

Shariati Arguing Against Superstitious Religion

The first thing that captured my attention about his text "Fatima Is Fatima" was how similar his notion of time and evolution is to that of those he wishes to challenge. For instance, he points out that his generation is so far ahead of the older generation that, although it is only thirty years in actual "calendar time" in reality (or "society's point of view") it is more like thirty centuries: "The distance is the same as that which separated Cain and Abel from the electronic age and automobiles."[47] Those who are able to admit this "are people who know time moves. They know that society has a skin which it sheds."[48] Those who do not and prefer instead to cling to old customs in the name of faith and act as our guides "are also mistaken in trying to save forms inherited from the past. They try to preserve old customs and habits.... They turn away from anything new, from any change and from any re-birth.... They try to remain the same and hold onto things of the past forever." He complains that "this type of thinking tends to lead us astray ... [and] time itself will outrun us."[49] Indeed, if you inserted this paragraph into Qasim Amin's text, or had Ataturk said these same words in his speeches, it would take nothing away from their secularist, Occidentalized nationalist message. What makes it appear different is the symbol of Islam. Take that away, and you have literally the same temporal discourse.

When he finally turns his attention to women, he turns his criticism to the issues of his Kemalist predecessors. Literally in a plagiarized form, he also turns his scorn on the "incomplete and useless" domesticated lady of the Shah's regime, who is confined to the home and "who is missing a part of her brain and who is excluded from literacy, books, education, discipline, thought, culture, civilization and social manners." Can she, he asks, "be worthy of being the nourisher of tomorrow's generation?"[50] Here is Shariati speaking about this "bizarre woman" at length:

> The most bizarre woman ... who must be called "absurd", is the lady of the house. She is a frightening creature.... The absurd woman is the woman who sits at home and is good for nothing. As she can afford it, she has a maid, a cook, a nurse, and it is they who actually do the work. She is a woman who stays at home to take care of it, but others actually do the work for her. As she is not a village woman, she does not work and co-operate with her husband in the fields.... What does this living creature do? Nothing. What role does she play in the world? None! ... Really, what is her work? Who is this person? She is the lady of the house, Daddy's lady of the old days. What is her profession? Consuming and only consuming. How does she pass her time? Her time? As a matter of fact, she is very busy. She is busy night and day. She is a thousand times busier than the village woman. For instance, what does she do? She gossips, she develops jealousies, objections, affectations, ornamentation, rivalries, pride, false friendship. She complains, grumbles, ogles, has a mincing, full of coquetry and falsity. The lady of the house is always busy. In her type of society, and in her social relationships, she fills her frighteningly empty life.[51]

Notice how he, too, offers women "a revolutionary role" for the kind of society he wishes to create, but only after he condemns them as the symbol of corruption of the Shah's regime, marking women as responsible for the degradation of his beloved nation.

Indeed, if you directly compare Shariati's statements above critiquing the ladies of the Pahlavi regime to Qasim Amin's criticism of the uneducated Egyptian housewife, you'd be unable to tell them apart. Here is Qasim Amin a little more than seventy-five years before Shariati's essays, saying nearly the same thing:

> The best man to her is he who plays with her all day and night ... and who has money ... and buys her clothes and nice things. And the worst of men is he who spends his time working in his office; whenever she sees him ... reading ... she curses books and knowledge.[52]

We can see here the performative change in the concept of *Tarbiya,* or child rearing, that runs deep in Islamist literature. Just as in Shariati's gendered discourse, Amin is utterly disgusted by the quality of the women's body and mind and cautions that if society is to move forward in time it must first transform these grotesque females. Thus, just as secularists like Qasim Amin saw mothering as essential for Egyptian society to successfully catch up with the West, so do Islamists like Shariati want to reorganize the family "into a house of discipline for producing a new ... mentality."[53] Notice here that even though Islamists prefer a nonsecular model of development, they use the concept of renewal (*tajdid*) as a way to offer their own version of take-off from a state of degradation to a time in which true Islam is reached.[54] That is, through the proper forms of *tarbiya,* in which the woman performs her proper moral function and raises the children of the *umma* to the standards Allah and His messenger have prescribed, the triumph of the Islamic *umma* can finally be recognized. Again, as in the days of Qasim Amin and Kemal Ataturk, the woman takes on her shoulders the burden for the advancement (or the demise) of civilization. Hence, in both cases we observe the problematic notion that women's bodies and minds are the most important sites through which the nation stamps its journey, and it is they that are expected to discipline their bodies and minds for the nation's time travel. When men's bodies and minds are referred to, it just doesn't have the same collective and disciplinary bite to it. It becomes instead diluted as a form of individualistic pathology of the Shah and his protégés. I searched for this type of statement in a number of Shariati's works to see if he used similar styles when discussing men and was unable to find even one equivalent type of civilizational denunciation.

Admittedly, Shariati does criticize the treatment of women at the hands of abusive men, and he courageously goes out of his way to expose the fate of women who often have to be raised in the home of her husband or father "without breathing any free air" and who often are transferred from their fathers' homes to their new husbands', as though there was a transaction "between a buyer and a seller," becoming in the process nothing more than "a respectable servant": "A married man means someone who has a servant who works in his house.... She is a household laborer and a nurse ... without any wages; she has no rights."[55] But these sprinklings of important acknowledgment of abuse are literally overshadowed by his much heavier and lengthier overtures of constant back-and-forth efforts to signify the woman as both the ills and triumphs of the nation's future.

Women's Body as the Site of Struggle Between the Colonizer and the Colonized

Instead of seriously critiquing the Shah's regime for the way it handled the sexual and physical abuse of women, he turns it into a small issue in order to get to a project he has more interest in, namely, to take state power away from other men. That is, after all, his major project, not the protection and security of women, per se, but the use of women as a means to an end. As Fanon has already suggested in this chapter, women for men like Shariati serve as the time-traveling route through which the battle between the colonizer and the colonized takes place. In Shariati's chapter titled "What Role Did Women Play in the Attack?" for instance, he places the rape of women by the colonial regime as equivalent to "emptying the brain" of Eastern civilization, which the colonizer uses so that he may "plunder" the riches of Iran and fill its interiors with anything the colonizer wishes.[56] Shariati's major concern is with the removal of the Shah's regime, which, for him, acts as the handmaiden of the colonizer, with women doing nothing more than playing a rhetorical function toward that end. Women thus become ideological arsenal in his struggle against the (colonized) regime. He uses the symbol of the "weak creature of the house ... who has not been educated" and without the means to "develop her child's sense of completeness," as a way to accuse other men of exploiting their women in an unmanly, uncivilized way, so as to mark these men as incompetent rulers.[57]

This use of women as a means to an end is most evident when he turns to ask the Leninist question, "What should we do?" He recommends, first of all, that the women that the revolution needs is "not the traditional woman asleep in her quiet, tame, ancient mould nor is it the new woman, the modern doll who has assumed the mould of the enemy." These are the women that represent the old, tired, morally corrupt social order. In other words, they symbolize all that is wrong in the present state of things, everything from the ritualistic, unthinking conservatism of the traditional folk of the nation, to the materialistic, wealthy, rich and autocratic and "Westoxified" regime of the Shah. Women stand in as the site in which all of these become marked as the regressive state of the present system. But the "new women" he proposes "is not satisfied with old advice." Instead she is a woman who pushes herself on the question of "Who am I? Who should I be?"[58] He describes the "new woman" of the revolution as the one who "says no to western colonialism and European styles.... 'You cannot change me! You cannot transform and negate my social, historical and cultural values'."[59] In Sullivan's concise conclusion of Shariati's text "Fatima Is Fatima," it "offered a new and revolutionary model of Islamic womanhood; but it is also a text that once again uses the body of the woman as the site on which to compose national and ethical values. Woman, for Shariati, is at once the greatest hope for and the greatest threat to revolutionary possibility."[60] I can only imagine what a burden that must be to carry on your shoulders.

Conclusion

In this chapter we can see the detrimental effects that this alluring temporal script has had on the colonized, allowing male elites to narrate their own versions of domination over others. In that sense, this temporal script is a flexible tool that can be fitted into a number of contexts, which different actors use for all sorts of projects. Although I have limited myself, quite problematically I admit, to studying male elites, it would add much to our analysis if we had included a chapter discussing how women in different political and rhetorical locations attempted to bend this template in different ways. But because we are interested in what we could call an ethnography of the colonial and nationalist state, we limited our focus to male elites. This allows us to analyze the way power penetrates colonial discourse between men struggling to gain advantage over each other, but it does not help us understand how women negotiated their own struggles through this same template. That would take another chapter, which I wish to write in the near future.

The advantage of looking at men, however, should not be overlooked. It allows us to see how the gendered discourse of Kemalist and secular Arab men did not differ much from their designated Islamist enemies, a fact that very few scholars have noted. With the exception of a small number of postcolonial scholars, whom we have borrowed heavily from for our own analysis here, most academics focus on either secular nationalist or Islamists, without seeing the depth to which both movements share the colonial gendered epistemology of their past colonial masters. Islamists simply replace the Kemalist image of the barbaric women of Islam with that of the morally corrupt seductress of the "painted dolls" of the West. Thus, whereas Qasim Amin and Kemal Ataturk blamed the traditional superstitious veiled woman of Islam for the backwardness of their nation, Islamists simply reversed the logic a bit and used the Kemalist-corrupted and Westoxified woman to stand as the symbol for the moral corruption of their beloved civilization and nation. In both cases, women's bodies and the quality of their mothering became the sites through which the nation falls or rises. In this way, she is positioned to take the ultimate responsibility for the eventual failure of the project, no matter if it is Kemalists or Islamists who hold the keys to power. Because, when the nation surely fails to reach the moral and advanced future utopia that these male elites have set out to create, *she* will be to blame for seducing the morality of the nation, and it will be *her* failure to produce the proper child needed for true civilization. Women thus become the means to ensure that the male elite remains blameless for the state's inability to bring a healthy, standard of living and justice to the nation's shantytowns.

Conclusion

Thinking Outside the Time-Space Box of Colonial Modernity

> I, the man of color, want only this: That the tool never possess the man. Was my freedom not given to me then in order to build the world of the You. At the conclusion of this study, I want the world to recognize, with me, the open door of every consciousness.
>
> —*Frantz Fanon*

THE MAJOR POINT OF THIS BOOK should now be clear. It suggests that if we want to politically engage our world, we will first have to seriously take note of the social and political imaginary we have now lived under for at least two centuries. As we have extensively discussed, the colonizer's temporal template gives the deceptive notion that we live in a world of multiple space-time containers, leading us to imagine a radically altered understanding of "us" and "them," creating a political divide that is ultimately unjust and violent. The book also implicitly suggests that we need to construct a social and political imaginary in which such a divide is restructured so that it is aimed at placing pressure on its hegemonic agents rather than placing the blame on its global subalterns. To remain committed to this highly racialized temporal epistemology of the globe is a sure way to maintain a global system of inequality and injustice. The best way to undo it is to start tearing down the lens and tools through which the hegemon rules. I will propose here that there are at least three ways of thinking outside the time-space box of colonial modernity.

Time-Space Containers Are Produced by Human Political Imagineers and Thus Can Be Unmade

The first thing to note when thinking about offering an alternative social and political imaginary is that the hegemon desires that we remain focused on a unit of political and social analysis that places global difference into neat boxes. Many of us are so implicated in this vision of the world that we don't know how to politically think outside of such boxes and offer solutions that stay committed to them as though they were made of compounds that were produced by some intelligent design, outside of our own making. These containers are a product of political projects whose intentions were to provide the colonial and nationalist hegemon with a tool to rule over their Others. We cannot respond by appropriating those same tools with which they rule and must instead articulate a political project that allows for "us" and "them" to merge into a politics that makes it difficult for the makers of the time machine to pull more levers.

This will require our intellectuals and cultural workers to produce works of art, history, literature, museums, sociologies, anthropologies, archaeologies, theologies, and sexualities that places subjects into a field of politics that makes it difficult for the hegemon to rule. Notice that the movements we discussed in this book worked within the given constraints provided to them by the colonizer's gaze, to force the Other into a faraway time and place. Indeed, the method these movements used to assert their own identity had already been narrated long before the appearance of any of these movements. What Occidentalizers like Herzl and Ataturk, and Islamists like Qutb, Khomenei, and bin Laden did was simply to take the constructions provided by the Orientalist system and tug on one or the other side, recreating the images of what they understood to be their authentic self. The only difference between them is which side of the rope they tugged on. Herzl and Ataturk used every muscle in their bodies to tug their "nation" *out of the Orient*, whereas the Islamists, with the help of the Almighty, did everything possible to *pull the Umma back toward Medina and Mecca*—one side desiring to remove the Orient and the other cleansing Islam from the toxins of the Occident. The cultural schizophrenia of the Arab nationalists stood in the middle and was unsure which side of the rope to pull on, but it knew, deep down, that it must do something in order to "improve" its subjects. Yet, in all three cases "the West," in some mysterious way, remained solidly in place. As Leila Ahmed has persuasively argued, even the most radical sounding narratives never seem to break free from the Orientalist categories to which they are responding. Rather, they tend to "appropriate, in order to negate, the symbolic terms of the original narrative. Standing in relation of antithesis to thesis, the resistance narrative thus reverse—but thereby also accept—the terms set in the first place by the colonizers."[1]

But given that we can now see the limits of working within the worldview that the colonizer taught us to inhabit, we must look for ways to articulate a self that allows our collective egos to dissipate a bit and become calmed by noting the actual interconnected space and time of Self and Other. Here we will need to explore how some intellectuals and cultural producers are turning away from the time machine so as to live in a world not determined by a standard of measurement that is highly judgmental and insulting, but one that is inhabited by a compassionate Being that allows all of us to live free of the tools of an obsessed collective mind to transform us into an image of development. This will mean that we will have to open ourselves to multiple types of cultural producers, some who may be secular and others who may be religious or spiritual. But most of all, this means we must permit the acts of resistance to live in a situational field that is not determined by a normalizing container. Colonial and nationalist hegemons, as we have seen in this book, love containers. It makes it easy for them to rule and divide, to segregate and appropriate land of Others, to unequally distribute resources, to remunerate one gender and not the other, to psychologically uplift the Self and to demean the Other (what W. E. B. DuBois calls the "psychological wage of whiteness"[2]), and so on.

Civilizational Talk Can Only Reproduce the Fault Lines of Colonial Modernity

Secondly, the hegemon creates the social and political imaginary that makes it appear we live an individualistic existence, with a clear I and you, but in reality the two constitute each other. Power surely has much to do with this relationship, but it works its way so as to create an image of these identities as separate, Robinson Crusoe-types of islands, so that it can sequester the power it seeks. This will mean that we will have to write and produce works of art and history that negate the lens through which the hegemon wants us to see Self and Other and turn to a new way of seeing that blurs the binaries and permits us instead to see the constitutive nature of our identities, so that, in fact, "we" and "them" belong to one unequal global system that constitutes our identities in order to exploit natural and human resources. This is why I continuously repeated the thesis of this book—that we do not live in separate space-time islands. To hold that view would allow the hegemon easier access to our consent for his rule.

This does not mean the end of binaries, for surely politics would come to a stop and a new form of hegemony would be created. But what it does mean is that the binaries must be focused on a non-time-space axiom that negates the sort we discussed in this book and in their place creates a political divide that produces new political subjects, whose major objectives are to be meticulous about maintaining their focus on the hegemon rather than the subaltern Other. Although there is no doubt we are creatures who have skin and bodies, we need to recognize as well that we are incredibly absorbing social beings who live in no one body.

This will mean that we will need to challenge the Thomas Friedmans and Samuel Huntingtons of the world, who use a mode of historical analysis in which the political and economic failures "over there" are posited as originating from some deep Arabian tribal system or some mysterious or deep civilizational ethos. This means we offer up a different social and political imaginary than the one they provide. In resisting their cultural talk, we must simply refuse to compare "our" island with "their" island, because in the act of placing them side-by-side as though they were two different species with separate time-space bodies, we reproduce the imaginary lens through which the hegemon wants us to see the world. This means we must not fall victim to the urge of evaluating and comparing "their" gender systems, human rights, civic and democratic participation with "ours," without first understanding the effects that an intercontinental constitutive system of power, with its structured asymmetrical relationship, have had on shaping those differences in the first place. To do so would be similar to allowing an upstairs neighbor with a plumbing problem, whose sewage leaks into your home, to blame you for your inability to maintain a sanitary environment, instead of acknowledging their culpability in producing the mess.

As we become critical of the civilizational talk of the colonizer and his colonized elites, we should resist as well the urge to turn to the Koran in our attempt to answer the Huntingtons of the world on whether or not Islam is about peace, democracy, or respect for women, even though the intentions are usually well-meaning. Responding to Islamophobes by offering up Hadiths or Koranic verses to demonstrate a "peaceful Islam" is quite limiting, because it keeps the focus of people's political imaginaries fixated on an "Islam" and the "West" binary and further naturalizes global identities through the separation of the Self from its Other. For this does nothing more than reproduce the boxes and constrict the debate around issues of faith and culture rather than issues of power. Leaving it at this level is a sure way of providing the hegemon with the means to maintain his time-space containers of difference. Instead we have to offer a new social and political imaginary that permits us to see in ways that articulate nonessentialist forms of politics.

So as not to be misunderstood, I need to make myself clear. I am not saying that we don't look at some of the problems "over there." Indeed we must do that if we are to have any real effects on our world. But when we look "over there" it must not be in a way that insists the Other exists in his own time-space container, separate and detached from our own. Our world, however unequal, is so economically, politically, and culturally intertwined that to divide it by some civilizational logic keeps us from seeing our own complicity in the problems of "that part of the world." That is, when looking at the "Muslim world" and trying to enforce human rights issues, for instance, creating time-space categories like honor killing does nothing more than produce a template for the hegemon to rule from. Indeed, such activists, rather than helping the victim of abuse "over there," are in fact aiding a social and political imaginary that elites "here" and "there" can now use against their weaker subjects. Instead of using culturalized categories like "honor cultures," we need to find an activist epistemology that frames the issues in such a way that they cannot be activated by elites "over here," who want to bash immigrants in Denmark or elites "over there," who want to have a cultural resource to legitimize the killing of daughters and other females.[3] This requires that we stop using the colonizer's time-space containers and look for a form of politics that is hard for the hegemon, both "here" and "there," to grab and beat its Others with. In other words, we need a new epistemology of resistance.

The Epistemology of Resistance Must Remain Flexible to Change as the Hegemon Shifts Its Gaze, So as to Incorporate Agents of Resistance

Our third and final suggestion is to note that one of the defining features of hegemony, be it colonial or nationalist, is its chameleon-like quality, which allows it to engage politics through no one ideological lens. There are no ideological scripts that it cannot absorb. Similarly, it has no essential ideology of its own. It shifts every time we offer up a new epistemology of resisting it, incorporating many of our beloved political stands of the past, so that it can continue to create and reproduce its power over a newly defined Other. Indeed, at the very moment we think we have successfully created the political space for human rights, including women's and gay rights, the hegemon maneuvers to absorb them as well and then uses them against a defined Other, reproducing an old or new social and global divide. This means we have to be diligent and ready to constantly shift our political discourse so that we maintain our focus on the hegemon. When our given social and political imaginary becomes part of the hegemonic discourse, we must be willing to alter it so as to maintain our resistance to the eye of power rather than being used to further pounce on the hegemon's enemy. This requires that we always be a step ahead of the hegemon in keeping our radar of power scrutinizing the hegemon's digestion of our earlier liberatory texts. Given the hegemon's unquenchable appetite for power, it can devour anything we throw at it, even the most basic rights we as humans can think of. It does this because it is an expert at producing political scripts that divide the Self from its Others. So we, too, have to become chameleon-like and constantly shift our political discourse so as to offer a new epistemology of resistance it has not yet learned to digest. This is a never-ending process that can never result in some utopian future.

That is the message of this book. If there is anything to learn from the historical analysis that we have provided here, it is surely that we have to be politically diligent and constantly on the lookout for how our liberatory political discourses are being used by the hegemonic powers of our world. This will require first and foremost the refusal to reproduce the time-space boxes that the hegemon produced as the fundamental template it uses to rule over both "us" and "them."

Notes

Introduction

1. Meltem Ahiska, "Occidentalism, The Historical Fantasy of the Modern" In Sibel Irzik and Guven Guzeldere, *Relocating the Fault Line,* special issue of *The south Atlantic Quarterly* 102:2/3 (Spring/Summer 2003), 354.

2. Immanuel Wallerstein. *Unthinking Social Science: The Limits of the Nineteenth Century Paradigm* (Cambridge, MA: Polity Press, 1991), 83.

3. Bobby Sayyid. "Sign O' Times: Kaffirs and Infidels Fighting the Ninth Crusade." In Ernesto Laclau, ed., *The Making of Political Identities* (London: Verso Press, 1994), 68.

4. On Islam and popular culture in Turkey, see the fine selection of essays in Kandiyoti and Saktanber. *Fragments of Culture: The Everyday of Modern Turkey* (New Brunswick: Rutgers University Press, 2002).

5. Sibel Bozdogan and Resat Kasaba. *Rethinking Modernity and National Identity in Turkey* (Seattle: University of Washington Press, 1997).

6. See Benedict Anderson, *Imagined Communities* (London: Verso, 1983).

7. Edward Said, *Orientalism* (New York: Vintage Books, 1979), 116.

8. Said, ibid., 42.

9. Said, ibid., 93–94.

10. Said, ibid., 42.

11. Said, ibid.

12. Partha Chatterjee. *Nationalist Thought and the Colonial World: A Derivative Discourse.* (Minneapolis: University of Minnesota Press, 1993a), 6.

Chapter 1

1. Ali Mirsepassi, *Intellectual Discourse and the Politics of Modernization: Negotiating Modernity in Iran* (Cambridge: Cambridge University Press, 2000), 8.

2. Edward Said, *Orientalism* (New York: Vintage Books, 1979), 177.

3. See Timothy Mitchell, *Rule of Experts: Egypt, Techno-Politics, Modernity* (Berkeley: University of California Press, 2002), 123–152.

4. Gail Bederman, *Manliness and Civilization: The Cultural History of Gender and Race in the United States, 1880–1917* (Chicago: University of Chicago Press, 1996), 31, 35.

5. This analysis is borrowed from Joseph Massad's adaptation in his study of Jordanian nationalism, from Johannes Fabian's analysis of anthropology. Joseph Massad *Colonial Effects: The Making of National Identity in Jordan* (New York: Columbia University Press, 2001), 77–78; Johannes Fabian, *Time and the Other* (New York: Columbia University Press, 2002).

6. Joseph Massad, *Colonial Effects: The Making of National Identity in Jordan* (New York: Columbia University Press, 2001), 78.

7. Quoted in Mathew Jacobson, *Barbarian Virtues: The United States Encounters Foreign Peoples At Home and Abroad, 1876–1917* (New York: Hill & Wang, 2000), 142.

8. Quoted in Jacobson, *Barvarian Virtues,* 116.

9. Raymond Corbey, "Ethnographic Showcases, 1870–1930," in Jan Nerveen Pieterse and Bhikhu Parekh, eds., *The Decolonization of Imagination: Culture, Knowledge, and Power* (London: Zed Books, 1995), 60.

10. Corbey, "Ethnographic Showcases," 72.

11. Emphasis added. Elizabeth Marshall Thomas, *The Old Way: A Story of the First People* (New York: Farrar Straus Giroux, 2006), 6.

12. Bederman, *Manliness and Civilization,* 31.

13. Michael Adas, *Machines as the Measure of Men: Science, Technology, and Ideologies of Western Dominance* (Ithaca, NY: Cornell University Press, 1989); David C. Engerman et al., *Staging Growth: Modernization, Development, and the Cold War* (Amherst: University of Massachusetts Press, 2003).

14. Bederman, *Manliness and Civilization,* 31.

15. Joeseph Massad, *Desiring Arabs* (Chicago: The University of Chicago Press, 2007).

16. Fabian, *Time and the Other,* 111–112.

17. Spencer cited in Jacobson, *Barbarian Virtues,* 142.

18. Bederman, *Manliness and Civilization,* 29.

19. Hegel cited in Mirsepassi, *Intellectual Discourse,* 31.

20. Paul Mendes-Flohr, *Divided Passions: Jewish Intellectuals and the Experience of Modernity* (Detroit: Wayne State University Press, 1991), 81.

21. Hegel cited in Mendes-Flohr, *Divided Passions,* 81.

22. Jacobson, *Barbarian Virtues,* 113.

23. Ibid., 119.

24. Ibid., 142.

25. Michael Adas. "Modernization Theory and the American Revival of the Scientific and Technological Standards of Social Achievement and Human Worth," in David C. Engerman, et al., *Staging Growth: Modernization, Development, and the Global Cold War* (Amherst: University of Massachusetts Press, 2003), 27.

26. Jacobson, *Barbarian Virtues,* 50.

27. Dipesh Chakrabarty, *Provincializing Europe: Postcolonial Thought and Historical Difference* (Princeton, NJ: Princeton University Press, 2008), 9.

28. Fabian, *Time and the Other.*

29. Bikkhu Parekh, "Liberalism and Colonialism: A Critique of Locke and Mill," in Nederveen Pieterse and Bhikhu Parekh, *The Decolonization of Imagination: Culture, Knowledge, and Power* (London: Zed Books, 1995), 81–98.

30. John Stuart Mill, cited in Chakrabarty, *Provincializing Europe,* 8.

31. Parekh, *Decolonization of Imagination,* 93.

32. Pieterse and Parekh, *The Decolonization of Imagination,* 93–94.

33. Adas, *Machines as the Measure of Men.*

34. Bernard Lewis's answer to the question "Why do they hate us?" is posited in terms of the "Islamic mind," located deep in doctrinal ideas, and represents a "return" to "the classical Islamic view" in which "the duty of God's soldiers is to dispatch God's enemies as quickly as possible to the place where God will chastise them—that is to say, the afterlife" (Lewis cited in Mirsepassi, *Intellectual Discourse,* 43). As Ali Mirsepassi argues (*Intellectual Discourse,* 44), "the venturing of the 'clash of civilization' thesis depends upon the assertion that the hatred felt by Muslims has relatively little to do with any violation on the part of the West, and a great deal more to do with an ancient and almost supernatural form of enmity." Edward Said's now classic response to Lewis and Huntington is also recommended, "The Clash of Definitions," in Edward Said, *Reflections on Exile* (Cambridge: Harvard University Press, 2000), 569–590.

35. Thomas Friedman, *New York Times,* October 30, 2003 "It's No Vietnam."

36. Thomas Friedman, *The New York Times,* November 8, 2006, "Tolerable or Awful: The Roads Left in Iraq."

37. Thomas Friedman, *The New York Times,* November 29, 2006, "Ten Months or Ten Years."

38. Ibid.

39. Ibid.

40. Said, *Orientalism,* 172.

41. Friedman, "Tolerable or Awful."

42. Lauren Langman and Douglas Morris, "The Roots of Terror," in Michael J. Thompson, *Islam and the West: Critical Perspectives on Modernity* (United Kingdom:

Rowman & Littlefield Publishers, 2003), 49–74. The schizophrenic mode of analysis of Langmann and Morris's essay brings up many Orientalist assumptions, ripe for a world-system's critique. Langman and Morris are struggling to devise a radical revision for the roots of terrorism and the rise of Islamic movements, including mentioning the need for a "larger social-historical context" and the rise and fall of global hegemonies. But in the end, the entire edifice of their argument is directly taken from Bernard Lewis's book, *Islam and the West,* including this quote, with which they are in full agreement: "The highly advanced Islamic pursuits of science, medicine, and philosophy ceased to develop [after the collapse of the Almohad Empire]. 'Independent inquiry virtually came to an end, and science was for the most part reduced to a veneration of a corpus of approved knowledge'" (p. 61). They continue down this path by arguing that "Asian 'tigers' have prospered, as has Israel—while Islamic countries have remained poor, backward, and stagnant," leaving us with the intentional impression that it has something to do with the ethic of Islamic culture. The "left" here meets Bernard Lewis in its crudest form. It reminds us very much of the argument leveled against African Americans: "Jews, Koreans, and Chinese made it, so what's wrong with you? Is it the dysfunctional, matriarchical family system now run by single parent families?"

43. Mirsepassi, *Intellectual Discourse,* 40.

44. Hegel, cited in Susan Bordo, *Twilight Zone: The Hidden Life of Cultural Images from Plato to O. J.* (Berkeley: University of California Press, 1990), 76.

45. Clementine Eck's arguments, made during a discussion between Eck and Jordanian journalist Rana Husseini, discussing honor killing on an Amsterdam radio station. http://www.nrc.nl/podcast/article1873652.ece/Eerwraak

46. Norma Khoury, *Honor Lost: Love and Death in Modern-Day Jordan* (New York: Washington Square Press, 2003), 1–2.

47. Massad, *Desiring Arabs,* 173.

48. Ibid., 175, 178.

49. Georg Simmel, quoted in Michel Warschawski, *On the Border* (Cambridge, MA: South End Press, 2005), xvi.

50. Dipesh Chakrabarty makes a similar argument, *Provincializing Europe,* 6–11.

51. Michael Adas, "Modernization Theory and the American Revival of the Scientific and Technological Standards of Social Achievement and Human Worth." In David C. Engerman, et al., *Staging Growth: Modernization, Development, and the Global Cold War* (Amherst: University of Massachusetts Press, 2003), 36.

52. Michael Latham, "Introduction," in David C. Engerman, et al., *Staging Growth: Modernization, Development, and the Global Cold War* (Amherst: University of Massachusetts Press, 2003), 9.

53. Ernesto Laclau and Chantal Mouffe, *Hegemony and Socialist Strategy: Towards a Radical Democratic Politics* (London: Verso Press, 2001).

54. Bederman, *Manliness and Civilization,* 23.

55. Pieterse and Parekh, *The Decolonization of Imagination,* 3.

Chapter 2

1. Ivan Davidson Kalmar and Derek J. Penslar, eds., *Orientalism and the Jews* (Waltham, MA: Brandeis University Press, 2005), xxxvi.

2. See, for instance, how Thomas Cahill, author of *The Gifts of the Jews* (New York: Anchor Books, 1998), revises the origins of modern Western civilization to argue that it was all made possible by Judaism and Jews.

3. Nissin Rejwan, in ibid., 115.

4. Cited in ibid., 115.

5. Cited in ibid., 115.

6. The citations of Herder, Schopenhauer, Sombart, and Rathenau are all taken from Ritchie Robertson, *The "Jewish Question" in German Literature, 1749–1939* (New York: Oxford University Press, 1999), 429.

7. Cited in ibid., 437.

8. Cited in ibid., 430.

9. Cited in Aziza Khazzoom, "The Great Chain of Orientalism: Jewish Identity, Stigma Management, and Ethnic Exclusion in Israel," in *American Sociological Review,* Vol. 68, August 2003 491.

10. Max Naumann, cited in Noah Isenberg, "To Pray Like a Dervish: Orientalist Discourse in Arnold Zweig's *The Face of East European Jewry,*" in Kalmar and Penslar, eds., *Orientalism and the Jews,* 104.

11. Cited in Jonathan Hess, *Germans, Jews and the Claims of Modernity* (New Haven, CT: Yale University Press, 2002), 2.

12. Grattenauer, cited in Paul Mendes-Flohr, *Divided Passions: Jewish Intellectuals and the Experience of Modernity* (Detroit, MI: Wayne State University Press, 1991), 81.

13. Isenberg, "To Pray Like a Dervish," 100.

14. Hess, *Germans, Jews, and the Claims,* 2.

15. Nissim Rejwan, *Israeli's Place in the Middle East: A Pluralist Perspective* (Gainesville: University Press of Florida, 1999), 95.

16. Khazzoom, "The Great Chain," 489.

17. Hess, *Germans, Jews, and the Claims,* 4.

18. Khazzoom, "The Great Chain," 491.

19. Daniel Boyarin, *Unheroic Conduct: The Rise of Heterosexuality and the Invention of the Jewish Man* (Berkeley: University of California Press, 1997), 279.

20. Quoted in Hess, *Germans, Jews, and the Claims,* 3.

21. Ibid., 52.

22. Ibid., 52–53.

23. James Pasto, "Islam's 'Strange Secret Sharer': Orientalism, Judaism, and the Jewish Question," in *Comparative Studies in Society and History,* Vol. 40, No. 3 (July 1998), 461.

24. Michaelis, quoted in Hess, *Germans, Jews, and the Claims,* 53.

25. Ibid., 53.

26. Hess, Ibid.

27. Pastor Schwager, cited in Pasto, "Islam's 'Strange Secret Sharer'," 453.

28. Hess, *Germans, Jews, and the Claims,* 67.

29. Ibid., 52.

30. Pasto, "Islam's 'Strange Secret Sharer'," 453–454.

31. Hess, *Germans, Jews, and the Claims,* 59–60.

32. For a similar argument, see Pasto, "Islam's 'Strange Secret Sharer'," 461.

33. Hess, *Germans, Jews, and the Claims,* 61.

34. Pasto, "Islam's 'Strange Secret Sharer'," 467.

35. The last two quotes are from Dalia Manor, "Orientalism and Jewish National Art: The Case of Bezalel," in Ivan Davidson Kalmar and Derek J. Penslar, eds., *Orientalism and the Jews,* Waltham, MA: Brandeis University Press, 2005, 155.

36. Manor, "Orientalism and Jewish National Art," 142–161.

37. Ammon Raz-Krakotzkin, "The Zionist Return to the West and the Mizrahi Jewish Perspective," in Ivan Davidson Kalmar and Derek J. Penslar, eds., *Orientalism and the Jews* (Waltham, MA: Brandeis University Press, 2005), 172.

38. Zweig, cited in Isenberg, "To Pray Like a Dervish," 100.

39. Zweig, cited in ibid., 98–99, emphasis added.

40. Rathenau, cited in Mendes-Flohr, *Divided Passions,* 82.

41. Kalmar and Penslar, *Orientalism and the Jews,* xxxvi.

42. Raz-Krakotzkin, "The Zionist Return to the West," 165.

43. Raz-Krakotzkin, "The Zionist Return to the West," 166.

44. Jacques Kornberg, *Theodor Herzl: From Assimilation to Zionism* (Bloomington: Indiana University Press, 1993), 160.

45. Boyarin, *Unheroic Conduct,* 280–282.

46. Theodor Herzl, *The Jewish State* (New Jersey: Dover Publications, 1988 (1896).

47. Boyarin, *Unheroic Conduct,* 287.

48. Herzl, cited in Boyarin, *Unheroic Conduct,* 283–284.

49. Herzl, cited in Kornberg, *Theodor Herzl*, 178.
50. Kornberg, *Theodor Herzl*, 178.
51. Herzl, cited in Boyarin, *Unheroic Conduct*, 298.
52. Kornberg, *Theodor Herzl*, 160.
53. Ibid., 179.
54. Boyarin, *Unheroic Conduct*, 280.
55. Raz-Krakotzkin, "The Zionist Return to the West," 170.
56. Theodor Herzl, *Old New Land*, translated from German by Lotta Levensohn, (New York: M. Weiner, 1960), 42.
57. Herzl, *Old New Land*, 42.
58. Ibid., 43.
59. Ibid., 56–59.
60. Ibid., 59–61, emphasis added.
61. Theodor Herzl, *The Complete Diaries of Theodor Herzl*, 1895, 5 Vols.: 1:114.
62. Herzl, *The Jewish State*, 135.
63. Herzl, *The Jewish State*, 82.
64. Herzl, cited in Kornberg, *Theodor Herzl*, 179.
65. Noel Ignatiev, *How the Irish Became White* (New York: Routledge, 1995), 2.
66. This idea comes from David Roediger. *The Wages of Whiteness* (London; New York: Verso, 1991): "White labour does not just receive and resist racist ideas but embraces, adopts and, at times, murderously acts upon those ideas. The problem is not just that the white working class is at critical junctures manipulated into racism, but that it comes to think of itself and its interests as white" (p. 12).
67. For a contemporary view of what I call Occidentalization, see Thomas Cahill's book (1998) in which he continually refers to the Jews as the inventors of Western Civilization: "By 'we' I mean the usual 'we' of the late-twentieth-century." He directly links "we" with "our" Western civilization on numerous occasions, as, for example, here: "The people of the Western World, whose peculiar but vital mentality has come to infect every culture on earth, so that, in a startlingly precise sense, all humanity is now willy-nilly caught up in this 'we'. For better or worse, the role of the West in humanity's history is singular. Because of this, the role of the Jews, the inventors of Western culture, is also singular." Thomas Cahill, *The Gift of the Jews: How a Tribe of Desert Nomads Changed the Way Everyone Feels* (New York: Anchor Books, 1998), 3.
68. Frank Kaplan, "Between East and West: Zionist Revisionism as a Mediterranean Ideology," in Kalmar and Penslar, eds., *Orientalism and the Jews*, 125–141.
69. Ibid., 127.
70. Cited in Raz-Krakotzkin, "The Zionist Return to the West," 170.
71. Cited in Khazzoom, "The Great Chain of Orientalism," 501.

72. Joseph Massad, *The Persistence of the Palestinian Question: Essays on Zionism and the Palestinians* (London: Routledge, 2006), 26.

73. Khazoom, "The Great Chain of Orientalism."

74. David Ben Gurion. 1954. *Rebirth and Destiny of Israel.* New York: Philosophical Library, 489; G. H. Jansen, *Zionism, Israel, and Asian Nationalism* (Beirut: Institute for Palestine Studies, 1971), 219. Indeed, David Ben-Gurion wrote an article for the French paper *Le Monde* in 1958 entitled, "Israel, Etat Occidental."

75. Boyarin, *Unheroic Conduct,* 303).

76. Khazzoom, "The Great Chain of Orientalism," 489.

77. James Gelvin, *The Israel-Palestine Conflict: One Hundred Years of War* (New York: Cambridge University Press, 2005a), 69; see also Gershon Shafir. *Land, Labor, and the Origins of the Israeli-Palestinian Conflict, 1882–1914* (Berkeley: University of California Press, 1996).

78. Theodor Herzl, in Raphael Patai, ed., *The Complete Diaries of Theodor Herzl* (New York: Herzl Press, 1960), 87–88), cited in Michael Prior, *The Bible and Colonialism: A Moral Critique* (Sheffield, Eng.: Sheffield Academic Press, 1997), 113.

79. Ben-Gurion, cited in Tom Segev, *1949: The First Israelis* (New York: Owl Books, 1998), 28.

80. Raz-Krakotzkin, "The Zionist Return to the West," 169–170.

81. Ibid., 166.

82. Jabotinsky, cited in Massad, *The Persistence of the Palestinian Question,* 58.

83. Ibid., 36; see also Segev, *1949: The First Israelis,* chapters 2 to 4.

84. Shahak, cited in Massad, *The Persistence of the Palestinian Question,* 39.

85. Ibid., 39.

86. Cited in Segev, *1949: The First Israelis,* 69.

87. Ibid., 72.

88. Ibid., 73.

89. Ibid., 81.

90. Ibid., 85.

91. Ibid., 75.

92. Rhoda Kanaaneh, *Birthing the Nation: Strategies of Palestinian Women in Israel* (Berkeley: University of California Press, 2002), 44; Nira Yuval-Davis, *Gender and Nation* (London: Sage Publications, 1997), 70.

93. Kanaaneh, *Birthing the Nation* 52.

94. Ibid., 38.

95. Massad, *The Persistence of the Palestinian Question,* 148.

96. Ahmad Sa'di, "Modernization as an Explanatory Discourse of Zionist-Palestinian Relations," in *The British Journal of Middle Eastern Studies,* Vol. 24, No. 1 (May 1997), 28.

97. Raz-Krakotzkin, "The Zionist Return to the West," 170.
98. Herzl, *The Old New Land*, 124.
99. Novel, cited in Sa'di, "Modernization as an Explanatory Discourse," 31.
100. Cited in ibid., 28.
101. Raz-Krakotzkin, "The Zionist Return to the West," 166.
102. Sa'di, "Modernization as an Explanatory Discourse," 29.
103. Gelvin, *The Israel-Palestine Conflict*, 147.
104. Cited in ibid., 149.
105. Ibid., 145–150.
106. Ibid., 149–150.
107. Donald Harman Akenson, *God's People: Covenant and Land in South Africa, Israel, and Ulster* (Ithaca, NY: Cornell University Press, 1992), 152.
108. Edward Said, "Introduction," in Edward Said and Christopher Hitchens, "A Profile of the Palestinian People," in Edward Said and Christopher Hitchens, *Blaming the Victim: Spurious Scholarship and the Palestinian Question* (London: Verso Press, 1989), 1.
109. Michael Prior, *Zionism and the State of Israel* (London: Routledge, 1999), 140.
110. Barbara R. Rossing, *The Rapture Exposed: The Message of Hope in the Book of Revelation* (New York: Basic Books, 2004), 49.
111. Regina Sharif, *Non-Jewish Zionism: Its Roots in Western History* (London: Zed Press, 1983).
112. Walter Eytan, *The First Ten Years, A Diplomatic History of Israel* (New York: Simon and Schuster, 1958), 181.
113. Sharif, *Non-Jewish Zionism*, 74.
114. See Don Wagner, "Beyond Armageddon," in *The Link*, Vol. 25, No. 4 (1992: 1–13); Prior, *Zionism and the State of Israel*, 140.
115. Rossing, *The Rapture Exposed*, 51.
116. Prior, *Zionism and the State of Israel*, 136.
117. Rossing, *The Rapture Exposed*, 65.
118. Prior, *Zionism and the State of Israel*, 138.
119. Raz-Krakotzkin, "The Zionist Return to the West," 168.
120. Massad, *The Persistence of the Palestinian Question*, 39.
121. Raz-Krakotzkin, "The Zionist Return to the West," 169.
122. Ibid., 169.
123. Ibid., 171.
124. Ella Shohat, "The Invention of the Mizrahim," in *Journal of Palestine Studies*, Vol. 29, No. 1 (Autumn 1999), 8.
125. Raz-Krakotzkin, "The Zionist Return to the West," 171.

126. This is a topic to which some recent writers are beginning to engage. See especially Nissim Rejwan, *Arabs Face the Modern World: Religious, Cultural, and Political Responses to the West* (Gainesville: University Press of Florida, 1998). and Ammiel Alcalay, *After Jews and Arabs: Remaking Levantine Culture* (Minneapolis: University of Minnesota Press, 1993.

127. Shohat, "The Invention of the Mizrahim," 7.

128. Raz-Krakotzkin, "The Zionist Return to the West," 173.

129. S. D. Goiten's comment is found in Raz-Krakotzkin (2004: 74); Mark Cohen, *Under Crescent and Cross: The Jews in the Middle Ages* (Princeton, NJ: Princeton University Press, 1994), 126.

130. Maria Rosa Menocal, *The Arabic Role in Medieval Literary History: A Forgotten Heritage* (Philadelphia: University of Pennsylvania Press, 2004), 21.

131. Alcalay, *After Jews and Arabs*, 8.

132. Ella Shohat, "Sephardim in Israel: Zionism from the Standpoint of Its Jewish Victims," in Anne McClintock, ed., *Dangerous Liasons: Gender, Nation, and Postcolonial Perspectives* (Minneapolis: University of Minnesota Press, 1997), 45.

133. Ibid., 44.

134. Citation from Robertson, *The "Jewish Question,"* 489.

135. Quoted in Massad, *The Persistence of the Palestinian Question*, 58.

136. Segev, *1949: The First Isrelis*, 157.

137. Raz-Krakotzkin, "The Zionist Return to the West," 172.

138. Shohat, "The Invention of the Mizrahim," 12; Abbas Shiblak, *The Lure of Zion: The Case of the Iraqi Jews* (London: Saqi Books, 1986); G. N. Giladi, *Discord in Zion: Conflict Between Ashkenazi and Sephardi Jews in Israel* (London: Scorpion, 1990).

139. Raz-Krakotzkin, "The Zionist Return to the West," 172.

140. Sa'di, "Modernization as an Explanatory Discourse," 34.

141. Massad, *The Persistence of the Palestinian Question*, 60.

142. Shohat, "Sephardim in Israel," 49.

143. Ibid., 50.

144. Manor, "Orientalism and Jewish National Art," 158–160.

145. Segev, *1949: The First Isrelis*, 159.

146. Ibid., 159–161.

147. Ben-Gurion, cited in Massad, *The Persistence of the Palestinian Question*, 61.

148. Eban and Meir, cited in Shohat, "Sephardim in Israel," 42.

149. Cited in Segev, *1949: The First Isrelis*, 170.

150. Khazzoom, "the Great Chain of Orientalism," 501.

151. Gabriel Piterberg, "Domestic Orientalism: The Representation of 'Oriental' Jews," in *British Journal of Middle Eastern Studies* (November 1996) Vol. 23, Issue 2 125–146.

152. Shohat, "Sephardim in Israel," 40.
153. Cited in Piterberg, "Domestic Orientalism," 136.
154. Shohat, "Sephardim in Israel," 43–44.
155. Ibid., 45.
156. Raz-Krakotzkin, "The Zionist Return to the West," 174.

Chapter 3

1. Edward Said, *Orientalism* (New York: Vintage Books, 1979) 45–46.

2. Maxine Rodinson, *Europe and the Mystique of Islam* (Seattle: University of Washington Press, 1987), 35.

3. Hichem Djait, *Europe and Islam: Cultures and Modernity* (Berkeley: University of California Press, 1985, 13.

4. Albert Hourani, *Islam in European Thought* (New York: Cambridge University Press, 1991), 10.

5. Rodinson, *Europe and the Mystique of Islam,* 26.

6. Albert Hourani, *Europe and the Middle East* (Berkeley: University of California Press, 1980), 10.

7. Djait, *Europe and Islam,* 12–13.

8. Rodinson, *Europe and the Mystique of Islam,* 60–61.

9. Djait, *Europe and Islam,* 19.

10. Said, *Orientalism,* 12–21.

11. Djait, *Europe and Islam,* 51.

12. Immanuel Wallerstein, *European Universalism: The Rhetoric of Power* (New York: The New Press, 2006), 33.

13. Ibrahim Kalin, "Roots of Misconception: Euro-American Perceptions of Islam Before and After September 11," in Joseph E. B. Lumbard, ed., *Islam, Fundamentalism, and the Betrayal of Tradition,* (Bloomington, IN: World Wisdom, (2004), 154–155.

14. See Bernard Lewis, "The Roots of Muslim Rage," *The Atlantic Monthly* 266 (September 1990): 49.

15. Djait, *Europe and Islam,* 24.

16. Volney, cited in Djait, *Europe and Islam,* 25. Emphasis added.

17. Hourani, *Europe and the Middle East,* 11.

18. Ibid., 13, 57.

19. Albert Hourani, *Islam in European Thought,* 26–27.

20. Ibid., 29.

21. Hourani, *Europe and the Middle East,* 61; Joeseph Massad, *Desiring Arabs* (Chicago: The University of Chicago Press, 2007 12–13.

22. Renan, cited in Hichem Djait, *Europe and Islam: Cultures and Modernity* (Berkeley: University of California Press, 1985), 44.

23. Renan, cited in Kalin, "Roots of Misconception," 171 Emphasis added by Kalin.

24. Renan, cited in Albert Hourani, *Arabic Thought in the Liberal Age, 1789–1939* (Cambridge: Cambridge University Press, 2002) 11–12.

25. Renan, cited in Said, *Orientalism* 149.

26. Djait, *Europe and Islam,* 51.

27. Hourani, *Europe and the Middle East,* 55.

28. Ibid., 12–13.

29. Weber, cited in ibid., 70.

30. Max Weber, cited in ibid., 70.

31. Dietrich Jung and Wolgango Piccoli, *Turkey at the Crossroads: Ottoman Legacies and a Greater Middle East* (London: Zed Press, 2001), 73.

32. Fatma Gocek, *Social Constructions of Nationalism in the Middle East* (Albany: State University of New York Press, 2002), 24; Leo Stavrianos, *Global Rift: The Third World Comes of Age* (New York: William Morrow and Company, 1981), 205–229.

33. Meltem Ahiska, "Occidentalism, the Historical Fantasy of the Modern," in Sibel Irzik and Guven Guzeldere, *Relocating the Fault Line: Turkey Beyond the East-West Divide,* special issue of *The South Atlantic Quarterly,* 102:2/3 (Spring/Summer 2003), 353.

34. Ibid., 367.

35. Resat Kasaba, "Kemalist Certainties and Modern Ambiguities," in Sibel Bozdogan et al., Rethinking Modernity and National Identity in Turkey (Seattle: University of Washington Press, 1997), 25.

36. Ibid., 25.

37. Bryan Turner, cited in Bobby Sayyid, *A Fundamental Fear: Eurocentrism and the Emergence of Islamism* (London: Zed Press, 1997), 68.

38. Ibid.

39. Jung and Piccoli, *Turkey at the Crossroads,* 60.

40. Ibid., 60.

41. Kemal Ataturk, cited in Alev Cinar, *Modernity, Islam, and Secularism in Turkey: Bodies, Places, and Time* (Minneapolis: University of Minnesota Press, 2005), 5.

42. Gokalp, cited in Jung and Piccoli, *Turkey at the Crossroads,* 61.

43. Ataturk, cited in Ernesto Laclau, *On Populist Reason* (London: Verso, 2007), 213.

44. Both Ataturk and Gokalp, cited in Ahiska, "Oxidentalism," 367.

45. For an example of this trend in thinking, see Leonard W. Doob, *Becoming*

More Civilized: A Psychological Exploration (New Haven, CT: Yale University Press, 1960).

46. Ataturk, cited in Andrew Mango, *Ataturk: The Biography of the Founder of Modern Turkey* (Woodstock, NY: The Overlook Press, 2002), 479.

47. Ataturk, cited in Mango, *Ataturk,* 371.

48. Kemal Ataturk, *The Great Speech* (Ankara, Turkey: Ataturk Research Center, 2005 [1927]).

49. Ataturk, *The Great Speech,* cited in Mango (2002), 367.

50. Ataturk, cited in Kasaba, "Kemalist Certainties," 25.

51. Cited in ibid., 27.

52. Cited in ibid., 25.

53. Cinar, *Modernity, Islam,* 8.

54. Sayyid, *A Fundamental Fear,* 68.

55. Meral Ozbeck, "Arabesk Culture: A Case of Modernization and Popular Identity," in Sibel Bozdogan et al., *Rethinking Modernity and National Identity in Turkey* (Seattle: University of Washington Press, 1997), 225.

56. Cinar, *Modernity, Islam,* 113.

57. Yael Navaro-Yashin, *Faces of the State: Secularism and Public Life in Turkey* (Princeton, NJ: Princeton University Press, 2002), 19–20).

58. Ataturk, cited in Cinar.(2005), 68.

59. Ataturk, *The Great Speech,* cited in Mango (2002), 435.

60. Cinar, *Modernity, Islam,* 69.

61. Ataturk, cited in Cinar, *Modernity, Islam,* 68.

62. Deniz Kandiyoti, "Gendering the Modern," in Sibel Bozdogan and Resat Kasaba, *Rethinking Modernity and National Identity in Turkey* (Seattle: University of Washington Press, 1997), 122.

63. Ibid (1997), 122.

64. Jung and Piccoli, *Turkey at the Crossroads,* 74.

65. Kandiyoti, "Gendering the Modern," 119.

66. See Sibel Bozdogan for Istanbul and James Scott for Le Corbusier and Brazilia: Sibel Bozdogan and Resat Kasaba, *Rethinking Modernity and National Identity in Turkey* (Seattle: University of Washington Press, 1997; James C. Scott, *Seeing Like a State: How Certain Schemes to Improve the Human Condition Have Failed* (New Haven, CT: Yale University Press, 1998.

67. The last two quotes are from Cinar, *Modernity, Islam,* 104.

68. Ibid., 111–112.

69. Ibid., 112.

70. Jung and Piccoli, *Turkey at the Crossroads,* 61.

71. Navaro-Yashin, *Faces of the State,* 49.

72. Cinar, *Modernity, Islam,* 147–148.

73. Ataturk, *The Great Speech.* Cited in Kasaba (1997), 26.

Chapter 4

1. Muhammad Haykal, cited in Charles D. Smith, "The Crisis of Orientation: The Shift of Egyptian Intellectuals to Islamic Subjects in the 1930s," *International Journal of Middle Eastern Studies,* 4 (1973: 404.

2. King Abdal-Aziz in a discussion with an American ambassador, cited in John O. Voll, "Islamic Renewal and the 'Failure of the West'," in Richard Antoun and Mary Elaine Hegland, *Religious Resurgence: Contemporary Cases in Islam, Christianity and Judaism* (Syracuse, New York: Syracuse University Press, 1987), 130.

3. All the quotes of Nazik al-Malaika above cited in Nissim Rejwan, *Nasserist Ideology: Its Exponents and Critics* (New York: John Wiley & Sons, (1974), 136–138.

4. James Gelvin, *The Modern Middle East: A History* (New York: Oxford University Press, 2005b), 128.

5. Hisham Sharabi, *Arab Intellectuals and the West: The Formative Years* (Baltimore: The Johns Hopkins Press, 1970), 27.

6. Nissim Rejwan, *Arabs Face the Modern World: Religious, Cultural, and Political Responses to the West* (Gainesville: University Press of Florida, 1998), 18.

7. Frantz Fanon, *The Wretched of the Earth* (New York: Grove Press, 2004), 160.

8. Hamid Dabashi, *Islamic Liberation Theology: Resisting the Empire* (London: Routledge, 2008), 13.

9. Fanon, *The Wretched,* 17.

10. Partha Chatterjee, *The Nation and Its Fragments: Colonial and Postcolonial Histories* (Princeton, NJ: Princeton University Press, 1993b), 5–6.

11. Joseph Massad, *Colonial Effects: The Making of National Identity in Jordan* (New York: Columbia University Press, 2001), 7.

12. Ibid.

13. Haykal, cited in Israel Gershoni and James P. Jankowski, *Egypt, Islam, and the Arabs: The Search for Egyptian Nationhood, 1900–1930* (New York: Oxford University Press, 1986), 82–83.

14. Mazhar, cited in ibid., 83.

15. Smith, "The Crisis of Orientation," 391.

16. Albert Hourani, *Arabic Thought in the Liberal Age, 1789–1939* (Cambridge: Cambridge University Press, 2002), 326.

17. Israel Gershoni and James P. Jankowski, *Redefining the Egyptian Nation, 1939–1945* (Cambridge: Cambridge University Press, 1995), 51.

18. Taha Husayn, *The Future of Culture in Egypt* (Cairo: American Council of Learned Societies, 1975 [1954]), 4–5.

19. Taha Husayn, cited in Smith, "The Crisis of Orientation," 397.

20. Hourani, *Arabic Thought,* 329.

21. Taha Husayn, cited in ibid., 329–330.

22. Taha Husayn, *The Future of Culture in Egypt,* 9.

23. Ibid., 11.

24. Taha Husayn, cited in Hourani, *Arabic Thought,* 330.

25. Taha Husayn, *The Future of Culture in Egypt,* 1–2.

26. Hakim, cited in Gershoni and Jankowski, *Egypt, Islam, and the Arabs,* 98.

27. Hasan Arif, cited in ibid., 99.

28. Asher Kaufman, *Reviving Phoenicia: In Search of Identity in Lebanon* (London: I. B. Tauris, 2004), 13.

29. Rejwan, *Arabs Face the Modern World,* 35.

30. Mohammed Bamyeh "Hermeneutics Against Instrumental Reason: National and Post-national Islam in the Twentieth Century." *Third World Quarterly* Vol. 29, No. 3 (Spring 2008).

31. Donald Malcolm Reid, *Whose Pharaohs?: Archaeology, Museums, and Egyptian National Identity from Napolean to World War I* (Berkeley: University of California Press, 2002), 87.

32. Massad, *Colonial Effects.*

33. Jonathan Hess, *Germans, Jews and the Claims of Modernity* (New Haven, CT: Yale University Press, 2002), 63.

34. Ronald Hawker, "Imagining a Bedouin Past: Stereotypes and Cultural Representation in the Contemporary United Arab Emirates," unpublished, 4.

35. Michaelis, cited in Jonathan Hess, *Germans, Jews,* 70.

36. Michaelis, cited in ibid., 63.

37. Carsten Niebuhr, cited in ibid., 69–70.

38. Massad, *Colonial Effects,* 101–102; 117–118.

39. Ibid., 77.

40. Hawker, "Imagining a Bedouin Past," 1.

41. Ibid., 7.

42. Massad, *Colonial Effects,* 297.

43. Immanuel Wallerstein, *European Universalism: The Rhetoric of Power* (New York: The New Press, 2006), 31–33.

44. Melanie McAlister, *Epic Encounters: Culture, Media, & U.S. Interests in the Middle East since 1945* (Berkeley: University of California Press, 2005), 130.

45. Ibid., 132.

46. Ibid., 129.

47. Reid, *Whose Pharaohs?*, 2–3.

48. Reid, *Whose Pharaohs?*, 8.

49. Ahmad Husayn, cited in Elliott Colla, *Conflicted Antiquities: Egyptology, Egyptomania, Egyptian Modernity* (Durham, NC: Duke University Press, 2007), 157.

50. Ahmad Husayn, cited in ibid., 157–158.

51. Ahmad Husayn, cited in ibid., 158.

52. Albert Hourani, cited in John Voll, "Islamic Renewal," 136.

53. Smith, "The Crisis of Orientation," 383.

54. Nashshar, cited in Rejwan, *Nasserist Ideology*, 20.

55. Azzam, cited in Israel Gershoni and James Jankowski, *Redefining the Egyptian Nation, 1939–1945* (Cambridge: Cambridge University Press, 1995), 29.

56. Kaufman, *Reviving Phoenicia*, 14.

57. C. R. Pennell, *Morocco Since 1830: A History* (New York: NYU Press, 2000), 83.

58. See Khaldoun Samman, *Cities of God and Nationalism: Mecca, Jerusalem, and Rome as Contested Sacred Cities* (Boulder, CO: Paradigm Publishers,2007), chapter 3.

59. "Considering this view may help illustrate why it was so important for France, through the medium of its missionaries, geographers, scholars and politicians, to emphasize the distinct features of the Christians in Lebanon ... " (Kaufman, *Reviving Phoenicia*, 14–15). "[In Morocco] The 1930 ruling [Berber *dahir* (decree)] established a double standard: the Arab population would continue to fall under Islamic law, but Berbers (who are also Muslims) would be subject to French law.... It was clearly a divide-and-rule maneuver, which reinforced nationalist sentiments and angered the rest of the Islamic world" (Marvine Howe, *Morocco: The Islamist Awakening and Other Challenges* [Oxford: Oxford University Press, 2005] 68); Ernest Gellner, *Saints of the Atlas* [Chicago: University of Chicago Press, 1969], 18). "Jews, who once acted as the Sultan's merchants, now found greater benefits by working for Europeans.... Rich Jews flocked to the protection of the Europeans and most of those who naturalized as Europeans were Jews.... [The Alliance Israelite Universelle (AIU)] was set up in Paris in 1860 by some of the most influential Jews in France, who included Alphonse Cremieux, a republican lawyer who had lobbied to extend French citizenship to the Jews of Algeria. Consequently, the AIU was often identified as an agent of French influence" (Pennell, *Morocco Since 1830*, 83).

60. Colla, *Conflicted Antiquities*, 78.

61. Ahmad Amin, cited in Gershoni and Jankowski, *Redefining the Egyptian Nation*, 39–40.

62. Gelvin, *The Modern Middle East,* 137.

63. Hourani, *Arabic Thought,* 123.

64. Ibid., 145.

65. Gershoni and Jankowski, *Redefining the Egyptian Nation,* 65.

66. Sharabi, *Arab Intellectuals,* 26–27.

67. Haykal, cited in Gershoni and Jankowski, *Redefining the Egyptian Nation,* 42–43.

68. Haykal, cited in Smith, "The Crisis of Orientation," 404–405.

69. Arslan, cited in William Cleveland, *Islam Against the West: Shakib Arslan and the Campaign for Islamic Nationalism* (Austin: University of Texas Press, 1985), 121.

70. Arslan, cited in ibid., 122.

71. Hourani, *Arabic Thought,* 115.

72. Afghani, cited in Rejwan, *Arabs Face the Modern World,* 7.

73. Roxanne Euben, *Enemy in the Mirror: Islamic Fundamentalism and the Limits of Modern Rationalism* (Princeton, NJ: Princeton University Press, 1999), 97.

74. Ibid., 98.

75. Smith, "The Crisis of Orientation," 386.

76. Jamal Mohammed Ahmed, *The Intellectual Origins of Egyptian Nationalism* (London: Oxford University Press, 1960), 41–42.

77. Abduh, cited in ibid., 41–42.

78. Abduh, cited in Hourani, *Arabic Thought,* 141.

79. Dabashi, *Islamic Liberation Theology,* 17.

80. Ibid., 17.

81. Gabriel Piterberg, "The Tropes of Stagnation and Awakening in nationalist Historical Consciousness: The Egyptian Case," in James P. Jankowski and Israel Gershoni, *Rethinking Nationalism in the Arab Middle East* (New York: Columbia University Press, 1997), 43.

82. Joseph Massad, *Desiring Arabs* (Chicago: The University of Chicago Press, 2007), 25.

Chapter 5

1. A large number of publications highlight Islam as the most backward and troublesome religion in the world. See especially Christopher Hitchens's *God Is Not Great* and Sam Harris's *The End of Faith: Religion, Terror, and the Future of Reason.*

2. Richard Sennett and Jonathan Cobb, *The Hidden Injuries of Class* (New York: Vintage Books, 1993).

3. Bobby Sayyid, *A Fundamental Fear: Eurocentrism and the Emergence of Islamism* (London: Zed Press, 1997), 96.

4. Sayyid, *A Fundamental Fear,* 90.

5. Elliott Colla, *Conflicted Antiquities: Egyptology, Egyptomania, Egyptian Modernity* (Durham, NC: Duke University Press, 2007), 238.

6. Sayyid, *A Fundamental Fear,* 84.

7. Colla, *Conflicted Antiquities,* 245.

8. Immanuel Wallerstein, *The Decline of American Power* (London: The New Press, 2003), 112.

9. Mark Juergensmeyer, *The New Cold War? Religious Nationalism Confronts the Secular State* (Berkeley: University of California Press, 1993), 11.

10. Juergensmeyer, *The New Cold War?,* 23.

11. Wallerstein, *The Decline of American Power,* 115–116.

12. Sayyid, *A Fundamental Fear,* 88.

13. Qutb, cited in Yvonne Haddad, "Sayyid Qutb: Ideologue of Islamic Revival," in John L. Esposito, ed., *Voices of Resurgent Islam* (New York: Oxford University Press, 1983), 72.

14. Qutb, cited in Haddad, "Sayyid Qutb," 73).

15. Khomeini, cited in Michael Fischer, "Imam Khomeini: Four Levels of Understanding," in John Esposito, ed., *Voices of Resurgent Islam* (New York: Oxford University Press, 1983), 168.

16. Qutb, cited in Ibrahim Abu-Rabi, *Intellectual Origins of Islamic Resurgence in the Modern Arab World* (Albany: SUNY Press, 1996), 130–131.

17. Sayyid Qutb, *Milestones* (Indianapolis, IN: American trust Publications, 1990), 6.

18. John Calvert and William Shepard, "Translators' Introduction," in Sayyid Qutb, *A Child from the Village* (Syracuse, NY: Syracuse University Press, 2004), xiv.

19. Roxanne L. Euben, *Enemy in the Mirror: Islamic Fundamentalism and the Limits of Modern Rationalism* (Princeton, NJ: Princeton University Press, 1999), 56.

20. Samir Amin, *Delinking: Towards a Polycentric World* (United Kingdom: Zed Press, 1990), 177.

21. Abu Rabi argues that for Sayyid Qutb, "the complete secularization and Westernization of Turkey at the hand of Ataturk is just the beginning of the battle to attack Islamic symbols all over the Muslim world." Abu-Rabi, *Intellectual Origins,* 143.

22. Qutb, *Milestones,* 84.

23. Qutb, cited in Abu-Rabi, *Intellectual Origins,* 214.

24. Abu-Rabi, *Intellectual Origins,* 134.

25. Qutb, *Milestones,* 5.

26. Ibid.

27. Ibid., 6.
28. Ibid., 117–118.
29. Ibid., 118.
30. Qutb, cited in Haddad, "Sayyid Qutb," 71–72.
31. Qutb, cited in Abu-Rabi, *Intellectual Origins,* 206.
32. Ali Mirsepassi, *Intellectual Discourse and the Politics of Modernization: Negotiating Modernity in Iran* (United Kingdom: Cambridge University Press, 2000), 94.
33. Abu-Rabi, *Intellectual Origins,* 167.
34. Qutb, cited in ibid., 206.
35. Abu-Rabi, *Intellectual Origins,* 93.
36. Ibid., 103.
37. Ibid., 99.
38. Qutb, *Milestones,* 80
39. Malice Ruthven, *A Fury for God: The Islamist Attack on America* (London: Granta Books, 2002), 79.
40. All of the above Qutb citations are cited in ibid., 79–80.
41. Qutb, cited in Euben, *Enemy in the Mirror,* 58.
42. Qutb, *Milestones,* 120.
43. Ibid.
44. Ibid., 5–6.
45. Qutb, *Milestones,* 115
46. Qutb, cited in Abu-Rabi, *Intellectual Origins,* 133.
47. Qutb, cited in Euben, *Enemy in the Mirror,* 57.
48. Qutb, cited in Haddad, "Sayyid Qutb," 85.
49. Qutb, *Milestones,* 116.
50. Ibid.
51. Qutb, *Milestones,* 34.
52. Ibid., 32.
53. Qutb, cited in Haddad, "Sayyid Qutb," 76.
54. Qutb, cited in ibid., 77.
55. Qutb, cited in Abu-Rabi, *Intellectual Origins,* 143.
56. Qutb, cited in Haddad, "Sayyid Qutb," 75.
57. Qutb, cited in Haddad, "Sayyid Qutb," 81.
58: Qutb, *Milestones,* 6.
59. Ibid., 101–102.
60. John Voll, "Islamic Renewal and the 'Failure of the West'," in Richard Antoun and Mary Heglan, *Religious Resurgence: Contemporary Cases in Islam, Christianity, and Judaism* (Syracuse, NY: Syracuse University Press, 1987), 137.
61. Fischer, "Imam Khomeini," 169.
62. Ali Ahmad, quoted in Mirsepassi, Intellectual Discourse, 105.

63. Khomeini cited in Fischer, "Imam Khomeini," 168.

64. Cited in Ziad Abu-Amr, *Islamic Fundamentalism in the West Bank and Gaza* (Bloomington: Indiana University Press, 1994), 105–106.

65. Alev Cinar, *Modernity, Islam, and Secularism in Turkey: Bodies, Places, and Time* (Minneapolis: University of Minnesota Press, 2005), 117.

66. Colla, *Conflicted Antiquities,* 235.

67. Cinar, *Modernity,* 102.

68. Colla, *Conflicted Antiquities,* 238.

69. Ibid., 77–79.

70. Ibid., 239.

71. Cinar, *Modernity,* 103.

72. The Web site, cited in Cinar, *Modernity,* 123–125.

73. Banna, cited in Colla, *Conflicted Antiquities,* 245.

74. Banna, cited in Colla, *Conflicted Antiquities,* 248–249.

75. All quotes of Qutb in this paragraph cited in Colla, *Conflicted Antiquities,* 235.

76. Ibid., 236.

77. Ibid., 234.

78. Khomeini, cited in Fischer, "Imam Khomeini," 168–169.

79. Hamid Dabashi, *Islamic Liberation Theology: Resisting the Empire* (London: Routledge, 2008), 15.

80. Ibid., 13.

Chapter 6

1. Leila Ahmed, *Women and Gender in Islam: Historical Roots of a Modern Debate,* New Haven, CT: Yale University Press, 1992), 149.

2. Nira Yuval-Davis, cited in Alev Cinar, *Modernity, Islam, and Secularism in Turkey* (Minneapolis: University of Minnesota Press, 2005), 60.

3. Alev Cinar, *Modernity, Islam, and Secularism in Turkey: Bodies, Places, and Time* (Minneapolis: University of Minnesota Press, 2005), 54.

4. Frantz Fanon, *A Dying Colonialism* (New York: Monthly Review Press, 1965), 36–37; 46–47.

5. Ahmed, *Women and Gender,* 153.

6. Gail Bederman, *Manliness and Civilization: The Cultural History of Gender and Race in the United States, 1880–1917* (Chicago: University of Chicago Press, 1996), 34.

7. Bederman, *Manliness and Civilization,* 34–35.

8. Ibid., 35–36.

9. Cromer, cited in Omnia Shakry, "Schooled Mothers and Structured Play: Child Rearing in Turn-of-the-Century Egypt," in Lila Abu-Lughod, ed., *Remaking Women: Feminism and Modernity in the Middle East* (Princeton, NJ: Princeton University Press, 1998a), 128–129.

10. Cromer cited in Ahmed, *Women and Gender,* 152.

11. Cromer, paraphrased by Ahmed, *Women and Gender,* 153.

12. Ibid., 152–153.

13. Fanon, *A Dying Colonialism,* 63.

14. Ahmed, *Women and Gender,* 165.

15. Deniz Kandiyoti, "Women, Islam and the State," in Deniz Kandiyoti, ed., *Women, Islam and the State* (Philadelphia, PA: Temple University Press, 1991) 3.

16. Ahmed, *Women and Gender,* 164–165.

17. Nilufer Gole, *The Forbidden Modern: Civilization and Veiling* (Ann Arbor: University of Michigan Press, 1996), 14.

18. Ataturk, cited in Ahmed, *Women and Gender,* 164.

19. Cinar, *Modernity,* 63.

20. The two quotes of Qasim Amin are cited in Lila Abu-Lughod, "The marriage of Feminism and Islamism in Egypt: Selective Repudiation as a Dynamic of Postcolonial Cultural Politics," in Lila Abu-Lughod, ed., *Remaking Women: Feminism and Modernity in the Middle East* (Princeton, NJ: Princeton University press, 1998b), 256.

21. Qasim Amin, *The Liberation of Women/The New Woman: Two Documents in the History of Egyptian Feminism* (Cairo, Egypt: The University of Cairo Press, 2000 [1900]), 144.

22. Ibid., 119.

23. Ibid., 126–127.

24. Ibid., 146.

25. Ibid., 145.

26. Ibid., 134.

27. Ibid., 186.

28. Lila Abu-Lughod, "Introduction," in Abu-Lughod, *Remaking Women,* 9.

29. Shakry, "Schooled Mothers," 132.

30. Ibid., 129.

31. Ibid., 128.

32. Shakry, "Schooled Mothers," 133.

33. Amin, *The Liberation,* 165–166.

34. Ibid., 180.

35. Ibid., 181.

36. Amin, cited in Ahmed, *Women and Gender,* 157.

37. Ahmed, *Women and Gender,* 162–163.

38. Kandiyoti, "Women, Islam and the State," 8.

39. Fanon, *A Dying Colonialism*, 47.

40. Afsaneh Najmabadi, "Hazards of Modernity and Morality: Women, State and Ideology in Contemporary Iran," in Kandiyoti, ed., *Women, Islam*, 65.

41. Zohreh Sullivan, "Eluding the Feminist, Overthrowing the Modern? Transformations in Twentieth-Century Iran," in Abu-Lughod, ed., *Remaking Women*, 217.

42. Ibid.

43. Shariati, cited in ibid., 218.

44. Ali Shariati, "Fatima Is Fatima," in Ali Shariati, *Shariati on Shariati and the Muslim Woman* (Chicago, IL: ABC International Group, 1996b), 105.

45. Ibid., 105.

46. Ibid., 106.

47. Ibid., 100–101.

48. Ibid., 116.

49. Ibid., 101.

50. Shariati, cited in Sullivan, "Eluding the Feminist," 218.

51. Shariati, "Fatima Is Fatima, 140.

52. Amin, cited in Ahmed, *Women and Gender*, 158.

53. Abu-Lughod, "The Marriage of Feminism," 256.

54. Shakry, "Schooled Mothers, 150.

55. Shariati, "Fatima Is Fatima," 137–138.

56. Ibid., 134.

57. Ibid., 137.

58. Ibid., 145–146.

59. Ali Shariati, "The Islamic Modest Dress," in Ali Shariati, *Shariati on Shariati and the Muslim Woman* (Chicago, IL: ABC International Group, 1996a), 46.

60. Sullivan, "Eluding the Feminist," 217.

Conclusion

1. Leila Ahmed, *Women and Gender in Islam: Historical Roots of a Modern Debate* (New Haven, CT: Yale University Press, 1992), 163–164.

2. On the "psychological wage of whiteness," see W. E. B. Du Bois, *Black Reconstruction* (New York: Maxwell Macmillan International, 1992). See also David Roediger, *Wages of Whiteness* (London: Verso, 1991).

3. For a critique of a culturalized understanding of domestic violence, see Uma Narayan, *Dislocating Cultures: Identities, Traditions, and Third World Feminism* (New York: Routledge, 1997), chapters 2 and 3.

Bibliography

Abu-Amr, Ziad. 1994. *Islamic Fundamentalism in the West Bank and Gaza.* Bloomington: Indiana University Press.

Abu-Rabi, Ibrahim M. 1996. *Intellectual Origins of Islamic Resurgence in the Modern Arab World.* Albany, NY: SUNY Press.

Abu El-Haj, Nadia. 2002. *Facts on the Ground: Archaeological Practice and Territorial Self-Fashioning in Israeli Society.* Chicago: University of Chicago Press.

Abu-Lughod, Lila. 1998a. "Introduction." In Lila Abu-Lughod, ed., *Remaking Women: Feminism and Modernity in the Middle East,* 3–31. Princeton, NJ: Princeton University Press.

———. 1998b. "The Marriage of Feminism and Islamism in Egypt: Selective Repudiation as a Dynamic of Postcolonial Cultural Politics" In Lila Abu-Lughod, ed., *Remaking Women: Feminism and Modernity in the Middle East,* 242–269. Princeton, NJ: Princeton University Press.

Adas, Michael. 1989. *Machines as the Measure of Men: Science, Technology, and Ideologies of Western Dominance.* Ithaca, NY: Cornell University Press.

———. 2003."Modernization Theory and the American Revival of the Scientific and Technological Standards of Social Achievement and Human Worth." In David C. Engerman, et al., *Staging Growth: Modernization, Development, and the Global Cold War,* 25–46. Amherst: University of Massachusetts Press.

Ahiska, Meltem. 2003. "Occidentalism, The Historical Fantasy of the Modern." In Sibel Irzik and Guven Guzeldere, *Relocating the Fault Line: Turkey Beyond the East-West Divide.* Special issue of *The South Atlantic Quarterly.* 102: 2/3. (Spring/Summer): 351–380.

Ahmed, Jamal Mohammed. 1960. *The Intellectual Origins of Egyptian Nationalism.* London: Oxford University Press.

Ahmed, Leila. 1992. *Women and Gender in Islam: Historical Roots of a Modern Debate.* New Haven, CT: Yale University Press.

Akenson, Donald Harman. 1992. *God's People: Covenant and Land in South Africa, Israel, and Ulster.* Ithaca, NY: Cornell University Press.

Alcalay, Ammiel. 1993. *After Jews and Arabs: Remaking Levantine Culture*, Minneapolis: University of Minnesota Press.

Amin, Qasim. 2000 [1899/1900]. *The Liberation of Women/ The New Woman: Two Documents in the History of Egyptian Feminism.* Cairo, Egypt: The University of Cairo Press.

Amin, Samir. 1990. *Delinking: Towards a Polycentric World.* United Kingdom: Zed Press.

Anderson, Benedict 1983, *Imagined Communities.* London; New York: Verso.

Ataturk, Kemal. 2005 [1927]. *The Great Speech.* Ankara: Ataturk Research Center.

Avalos, Hector. 2005. *Fighting Words: The Origins of Religious Violence.* Amherst, NY: Prometheus Books.

Bamyeh, Mohammed. 2008. "Hermeneutics Against Instrumental Reason: National and Post-national Islam in the Twentieth Century." *Third World Quarterly.* Vol. 29, No. 3. (Spring): 541–554.

Bederman, Gail. 1996. *Manliness and Civilization: The Cultural History of Gender and Race in the United States, 1880–1917.* Chicago, IL: University of Chicago Press.

Ben Gurion, David. 1954. *Rebirth and Destiny of Israel.* New York: Philosophical Library.

Bordo, Susan. 1990. *Twilight Zone: The Hidden Life of Cultural Images from Plato to O. J.* Berkeley: University of California Press.

Boyarin, Daniel. 1997. *Unheroic Conduct: The Rise of Heterosexuality and the Invention of the Jewish Man.* Berkeley: University of California Press.

Bozdogan, Sibel, and Resat Kasaba, eds. 1997. *Rethinking Modernity and National Identity in Turkey.* Seattle: University of Washington Press.

Brantlinger, Patrick. 1995. "'Dying Races': Rationalizing Genocide in the Nineteenth Century." In Nederveen Pieterse and Bhikhu Parekh, *The Decolonization of Imagination: Culture, Knowledge, and Power*,.43–56. London: Zed Books.

Cahill, Thomas. 1998. *The Gift of the Jews: How a Tribe of Desert Nomads Changed the Way Everyone Feels.* New York: Anchor Books.

Calvert, John, and William Shepard. 2004. "Translators' Introduction." In Sayyid Qutb (2004), *A Child from the Village*, Syracuse, NY: Syracuse University Press.

Chakrabarty, Dipesh. 2008. *Provincializing Europe: Postcolonial Thought and Historical Difference.* Princeton, NJ: Princeton University Press.

Chatterjee, Partha. 1993a. *Nationalist Thought and the Colonial World: A Derivative Discourse*, Minneapolis: University of Minnesota Press.

———. 1993b. *The Nation and Its Fragments: Colonial and Postcolonial Histories*, Princeton, NJ: Princeton University Press.

Cinar, Alev. 2005. *Modernity, Islam, and Secularism in Turkey: Bodies, Places, and Time.* Minneapolis: University of Minnesota Press.

Cleveland, William. 1985. *Islam Against the West: Shakib Arslan and the Campaign for Islamic Nationalism* Austin: University of Texas Press.
Cohen, Mark. 1994. *Under Crescent and Cross: The Jews in the Middle Ages.* Princeton, NJ: Princeton University Press.
Colla, Elliott. 2007. *Conflicted Antiquities: Egyptology, Egyptomania, Egyptian Modernity.* Durham, NC: Duke University Press.
Corbey, Raymond. 1995. "Ethnographic Showcases, 1870–1930." In Jan Nederveen Pieterse and Bhikhu Parekh, eds., *The Decolonization of Imagination: Culture, Knowledge, and Power,* 57–80. London: Zed Books.
Dabashi, Hamid. 2008. *Islamic Liberation Theology: Resisting the Empire.* London: Routledge.
Djait, Hichem. 1985. *Europe and Islam: Cultures and Modernity.* Berkeley: University of California Press.
Doob, Leonard W. 1960. *Becoming More Civilized: A Psychological Exploration.* New Haven, CT: Yale University Prell.
Du Bois, W. E. B. 1992. *Black Reconstruction.* New York: Maxwell Macmillan International.
Engerman, David C., et al. 2003. *Staging Growth: Modernization, Development, and the Cold War.* Amherst: University of Massachusetts Press.
Euben, Roxanne L. 1999. *Enemy in the Mirror: Islamic Fundamentalism and the Limits of Modern Rationalism.* Princeton, NJ: Princeton University Press.
Eytan, Walter. 1958. *The First Ten Years, A Diplomatic History of Israel.* New York: Simon & Schuster.
Fabian, Johannes. 2002. *Time and the Other.* New York: Columbia University Press.
Fanon, Frantz. 1965. *A Dying Colonialism.* New York: Monthly Review Press.
———. 2004. *The Wretched of the Earth.* New York: Grove Press.
Fischer, Michael. 1983. "Imam Khomeini: Four Levels of Understanding." In John Esposito, ed., *Voices of Resurgent Islam,* 150–174. New York: Oxford University Press.
Gellner, Ernest. 1969. *Saints of the Atlas.* Chicago: University of Chicago Press.
Gelvin, James. 2005a. *The Israel-Palestine Conflict: One Hundred Years of War.* New York: Cambridge University Press.
———. 2005b. *The Modern Middle East: A History.* New York: Oxford University Press.
Gershoni, Israel, and James P. Jankowski. 1986. *Egypt, Islam, and the Arabs: The Search for Egyptian Nationhood, 1900–1930.* New York: Oxford University Press.
———. 1995. *Redefining the Egyptian Nation, 1939–1945.* Cambridge: Cambridge University Press.

Giladi, G. N. 1990. *Discord in Zion: Conflict Between Ashkenazi and Sephardic Jews in Israel.* London: Scorpion.

Gilman, Nils. 2003a. *Mandarins of the Future: Modernization Theory in Cold War America.* Baltimore, MD: The Johns Hopkins University Press.

———. 2003b. "Modernization Theory: The Highest Stage of American Intellectual History." In David C. Engerman, et al., *Staging Growth: Modernization, Development, and the Global Cold War,* 47–80. Amherst: University of Massachusetts Press.

Gocek, Fatma Muge. 2002. *Social Constructions of Nationalism in the Middle East,* Albany: State University of New York Press.

Gole, Nilufer. 1996. *The Forbidden Modern: Civilization and Veiling.* Ann Arbor: University of Michigan Press.

Haddad, Yvonne. 1983. "Sayyid Qutb: Ideologue of Islamic Revival." In John L. Esposito, ed., *Voices of Resurgent Islam,* 67–98. New York: Oxford University Press.

Harris, Sam. 2005. *The End of Faith: Religion, Terror, and the Future of Reason.* New York: W. W. Norton.

Hawker, R. W. "Imagining a Bedouin Past: Stereotypes and Cultural Representation in the Contemporary United Arab Emirates." Unpublished: http://74.125.45.132/search?q=cache:cm4qsQjYT5IJ:inhouse.lau.edu.lb/bima/papers/R_W_Hawker.pdf+hawker+imagining+a+bedouin+past&hl=en&ct=clnk&cd=1&gl=us&client=firefox-a

Herzl, Theodor. 1895. *The Complete Diaries of Theodor Herzl.* 5 Vols.: 1: 114.

———. 1960, 1997: 42. *Old New Land.* Translated from German by Lotta Levensohn. New York: M. Weiner.

———. 1988 [1896]. *The Jewish State.* Mineola, NY: Dover Publications.

Hess, Jonathan. 2002. *Germans, Jews and the Claims of Modernity.* New Haven, CT: Yale University Press.

Hitchens, Christopher. 2007. *God Is Not Great: How Religion Poisons Everything.* New York: Twelve.

Hourani, Albert. 1980. *Europe and the Middle East.* Berkeley: University of California Press.

———. 1991. *Islam in European Thought.* New York: Cambridge University Press.

———. 2002. *Arabic Thought in the Liberal Age, 1789–1939.* Cambridge: Cambridge University Press.

Howe, Marvine. 2005. *Morocco: The Islamist Awakening and Other Challenges.* Oxford: Oxford University Press.

Huntington, Samuel. 1993. "The Clash of Civilizations?" *Foreign Affairs,* Vol. 72, No. 3, (Summer): 22–49.

Husayn, Taha. 1975 [1954]. *The Future of Culture in Egypt.* Cairo, Egypt: American Council of Learned Societies.

Ignatiev, Noel, 1995. *How the Irish Became White.* New York: Routledge.

Isenberg, Noah. 2005. "To Pray Like a Dervish: Orientalist Discourse in Arnold Zweig's *The Face of East European Jewry.*" In Kalmar, Ivan Davidson, and Derek J. Penslar, eds., *Orientalism and the Jews,* 94–108. Waltham, MA: Brandeis University Press.

Jacobson, Mathew. 2000. *Barbarian Virtues: The United States Encounters Foreign Peoples at Home and Abroad, 1876–1917.* New York: Hill & Wang.

Juergensmeyer, Mark. 1993. *The New Cold War? Religious Nationalism Confronts the Secular State.* Berkeley: University of California Press.

Jung, Dietrich, and Wolgango Piccoli. 2001. *Turkey at the Crossroads: Ottoman Legacies and a Greater Middle East.* London: Zed Press.

Kalin, Ibrahim. 2004. "Roots of Misconception: Euro-American Perceptions of Islam Before and After September 11." In Joseph E. B. Lumbard, ed., *Islam, Fundamentalism, and the Betrayal of Tradition,* 143–187. Bloomington, IN: World Wisdom, Inc..

Kalmar, Ivan Davidson, and Derek J. Penslar. 2005. "Orientalism and the Jews: An Introduction." In Ivan D Kalmar and Derek J. Penslar, eds., *Orientalism and the Jews,* xiii–xl. Waltham, MA: Brandeis University Press.

———, eds. 2005. *Orientalism and the Jews.* Waltham, MA: Brandeis University Press.

Kanaaneh, Rhoda Ann. 2002. *Birthing the Nation: Strategies of Palestinian Women in Israel.* Berkeley: University of California Press.

Kandiyoti, Deniz. 1991. "Introduction." In Deniz Kandiyoti, ed., *Women, Islam and the State,* 1–21. Philadelphia: Temple University Press.

———. 1997. "Gendering the Modern." In Sibel Bozdogan and Resat Kasaba, *Rethinking Modernity and National Identity in Turkey,* 113–132. Seattle: University of Washington Press.

Kandiyoti, Deniz, and Ayse Saktanber, eds. 2002. *Fragments of Culture: The Everyday of Modern Turkey.* New Brunswick, NJ: Rutgers University Press.

Kaplan, Frank. 2005. "Between East and West: Zionist Revisionism as a Mediterranean Ideology." In Ivan D. Kalmar and Derek J. Penslar, eds., *Orientalism and the Jews,* 125–141. Waltham, MA: Brandeis University Press.

Kasaba, Resat. 1997. "Kemalist Certainties and Modern Ambiguities." In Sibel Bozdogan et al., *Rethinking Modernity and National Identity in Turkey,* 15–36. Seattle: University of Washington Press.

Kaufman, Asher. 2004. *Reviving Phoenicia: In Search of Identity in Lebanon.* London: I. B. Tauris.

Khazzoom, Aziza. 2003. "The Great Chain of Orientalism: Jewish Identity, Stigma Management, and Ethnic Exclusion in Israel." In *American Sociological Review.* Vol. 68. (August): 481–510.

Khoury, Norma. 2003. *Honor Lost: Love and Death in Modern-Day Jordan*. New York: Washington Square Press.

Kornberg, Jacques. 1993. *Theodor Herzl: From Assimilation to Zionism.* Bloomington: Indiana University Press.

Laclau, Ernest. 2007. *On Populist Reason.* London: Verso.

Laclau, Ernesto, and Chantal Mouffe. 2001. *Hegemony and Socialist Strategy: Towards a Radical Democratic Politics.* London: Verso Press.

Langman, Lauren, and Douglas Morris. 2003. "The Roots of Terror." In Michael J. Thompson, *Islam and the West: Critical Perspectives on Modernity,* 49–74. United Kingdom, Rowman & Littlefield.

Latham, Michael. 2000. *Modernization as Ideology: American Social Science and "Nation-Building" in the Kennedy Era.* Chapel Hill: University of North Carolina Press.

———. 2003. "Introduction." In David C. Engerman, et al., *Staging Growth: Modernization, Development, and the Global Cold War,* 1–23. Amherst: University of Massachusetts Press.

Lewis, Bernard. 1990. "The Roots of Muslim Rage." *The Atlantic Monthly,* Vol. 266. (September): 49.

Mango, Andrew. 2002. *Ataturk: The Biography of the Founder of Modern Turkey.* Woodstock, NY: The Overlook Press.

Manor, Dalia. 2005. "Orientalism and Jewish National Art: The Case of Bezalel." In Ivan D. Kalmar and Derek J. Penslar, eds., *Orientalism and the Jews,* 142–161. Waltham, MA: Brandeis University Press.

Massad, Joseph. 2001. *Colonial Effects: The Making of National Identity in Jordan.* New York: Columbia University Press.

———. 2006. *The Persistence of the Palestinian Question: Essays on Zionism and the Palestinians.* London: Routledge.

———. 2007. *Desiring Arabs.* Chicago: The University of Chicago Press.

McAlister, Melani. 2005. *Epic Encounters: Culture, Media, & U.S. Interests in the Middle East since 1945.* Berkeley: University of California Press.

Mendes-Flohr, Paul. 1991. *Divided Passions: Jewish Intellectuals and the Experience of Modernity.* Detroit, MI: Wayne State University Press.

Menocal, Maria Rosa. 2004. *The Arabic Role in Medieval Literary History: A Forgotten Heritage.* Philadelphia: University of Pennsylvania Press.

Mirsepassi, Ali. 2000. *Intellectual Discourse and the Politics of Modernization: Negotiating Modernity in Iran.* United Kingdom: Cambridge University Press.

Mitchell, Timothy. 1991. *Colonizing Egypt.* Berkeley: University of California Press.

———. 2002. *Rule of Experts: Egypt, Techno-Politics, Modernity.* Berkeley: University of California Press.

Najmabadi, Afsaneh. 1991. "Hazards of Modernity and Morality: Women, State and Ideology in Contemporary Iran." In Deniz Kandiyoti, ed., *Women, Islam and the State,* 48–76. Philadelphia: Temple University Press.

Narayan, Uma. 1997. *Dislocating Cultures: Identities, Traditions, and Third World Feminism.* New York: Routledge.

Navaro-Yashin, Yael. 2002. *Faces of the State: Secularism and Public Life in Turkey.* Princeton, NJ: Princeton University Press.

Ozbek, Meral. 1997. "Arabesk Culture: A Case of Modernization and Popular Identity." In Sibel Bozdogan, et al., *Rethinking Modernity and National Identity in Turkey,* 211–232. Seattle: University of Washington Press.

Parekh, Bikkhu. 1995. "Liberalism and Colonialism: A Critique of Locke and Mill." In Nederveen Pieterse and Bikkhu Parekh, eds., *The Decolonization of Imagination: Culture, Knowledge, and Power,* 81–98. London: Zed Books.

Pasto, James. 1998. "Islam's 'Strange Secret Sharer': Orientalism, Judaism, and the Jewish Question." In *Comparative Studies in Society and History.* Vol. 40, No. 3. (July): 437–474.

Pennell, C. R. 2000. *Morocco Since 1830: A History.* New York: NYU Press.

Pieterse, Nederveen, and Bhikhu Parekh. 1995. *The Decolonization of Imagination: Culture, Knowledge, and Power.* London: Zed Books.

Piterberg, Gabriel. 1996. "Domestic Orientalism: The Representation of 'Oriental' Jews." In *British Journal of Middle Eastern Studies* Vol. 23. Issue 2. (November): 125–146.

———. 1997. "The Tropes of Stagnation and Awakening in Nationalist Historical Consciousness: The Egyptian Case." In James P. Jankowski and Israel Gershoni, *Rethinking Nationalism in the Arab Middle East,* 42–62. New York: Columbia University Press.

Prior, Michael. 1997. *The Bible and Colonialism: A Moral Critique.* Sheffield, Eng.: Sheffield Academic Press.

———. 1999. *Zionism and the State of Israel.* London: Routledge.

Qutb, Sayyid. 1990. *Milestones.* Indianapolis, IN: American Trust Publications.

Raz-Krakotzkin, Amnon. 2005. "The Zionist Return to the West and the Mizrahi Jewish Perspective." In Ivan D. Kalmar and Derek J. Penslar, eds., *Orientalism and the Jews,* 163–181. Waltham, MA: Brandeis University Press.

Reid, Donald Malcolm. 2002. *Whose Pharaohs?: Archaeology, Museums, and Egyptian National Identity from Napoleon to World War I.* Berkeley: University of California Press.

Rejwan, Nissim. 1974. *Nasserist Ideology: Its Exponents and Critics*. New York: John Wiley & Sons.

———. 1998. *Arabs Face the Modern World: Religious, Cultural, and Political Responses to the West*. Gainesville: University Press of Florida.

———. 1999. *Israel's Place in the Middle East: A Pluralist Perspective*. Gainesville: University Press of Florida.

Robertson, Richie. 1999. *The "Jewish Question" in German Literature, 1749–1939*. New York: Oxford University Press.

Rodinson, Maxine. 1987. *Europe and the Mystique of Islam*. Seattle: University of Washington Press.

Roediger, David. 1991. *The Wages of Whiteness*. London: Verso.

Rossing, Barbara R. 2004. *The Rapture Exposed: The Message of Hope in the Book of Revelation*. New York: Basic Books.

Ruthven, Malice. 2002. *A Fury for God: The Islamist Attack on America*. London: Granta Books.

Sa'di, Ahmad, H. 1997. "Modernization as an Explanatory Discourse of Zionist-Palestinian Relations." In *The British Journal of Middle Eastern Studies*. Vol. 24. No. 1. (May): 25–48.

Said, Edward. 1979. *Orientalism*. New York: Vintage Books.

———. 1997. *Covering Islam: How the Media and Experts Determine How We See the Rest of the World*. New York: Vintage Books.

———. 2000. *Reflections on Exile*. Cambridge, MA: Harvard University Press.

Said, Edward, and Christopher Hitchens. 1989. "A Profile of the Palestinian People." In Edward Said and Christopher Hitchens, *Blaming the Victim: Spurious Scholarship and the Palestinian Question*, 207–234. London: Verso Press.

Samman, Khaldoun. 2007. *Cities of God and Nationalism: Mecca, Jerusalem, and Rome as Contested Sacred World Cities*. Boulder, CO.: Paradigm Publishers.

Sayyid, Bobby. 1994. "Sign O' Times: Kaffirs and Infidels Fighting the Ninth Crusade." In Ernesto Laclau, ed., *The Making of Political Identities*, 264–286. London: Verso Press.

———. 1997. *A Fundamental Fear: Eurocentrism and the Emergence of Islamism*. London: Zed Press.

Scott, James C. 1998. *Seeing Like a State: How Certain Schemes to Improve the Human Condition Have Failed*. New Haven, CT: Yale University Press.

Segev, Tom. 1998. *1949: The First Israelis*. New York: Owl Books.

Sennett, Richard, and Jonathan Cobb. 1993. *The Hidden Injuries of Class*. New York: Vintage Books.

Shafir, Gershon. 1996. *Land, Labor, and the Origins of the Israeli-Palestinian Conflict, 1882–1914*. Berkeley: University of California Press.

Shakry, Omnia. 1998. "Schooled Mothers and Structured Play: Child Rearing in Turn-of-the-Century Egypt." In Lila Abu-Lughod, ed., *Remaking Women: Feminism and Modernity in the Middle East,* 126–170. Princeton, NJ: Princeton University Press.

Sharabi, Hisham. 1970. *Arab Intellectuals and the West: The Formative Years.* Baltimore, MD: The Johns Hopkins Press.

Shariati, Ali. 1980. *Marxism and Other Western Fallacies: An Islamic Critique.* Berkeley, CA: Mizan Press.

———. 1996a. "The Islamic Modest Dress." In Ali Shariati, *Shariati on Shariati and the Muslim Woman,* 35–49. Chicago: ABC International Group.

———. 1996b. "Fatima Is Fatima." In Ali Shariati, *Shariati on Shariati and the Muslim Woman,* 75–213. Chicago: ABC International Group.

Sharif, Ragina. 1983. *Non-Jewish Zionism: Its Roots in Western History.* London: Zed Press.

Shiblak, Abbas. 1986. *The Lure of Zion.* London: Al Saqi Books.

Shohat, Ella. 1997. "Sephardim in Israel: Zionism from the Standpoint of Its Jewish Victims." In Anne McClintock, ed., *Dangerous Liaisons: Gender, Nation, and Postcolonial Perspectives,* 39–68. Minneapolis: University of Minnesota Press.

———. 1999. "The Invention of the Mizrahim." In *Journal of Palestine Studies.* Vol. 29. No 1. (Autumn): 5–20.

Smith, Charles D. 1973. "The Crisis of Orientation: The Shift of Egyptian Intellectuals to Islamic Subjects in the 1930s." In *International Journal of Middle Eastern Studies.* 4: 382–410.

Stavrianos, Leo S. 1981. *Global Rift: The Third World Comes of Age.* New York: William Morrow and Company.

Sullivan, Zohreh. 1998. "Eluding the Feminist, Overthrowing the Modern? Transformations in Twentieth-Century Iran." In Lila Abu-Lughod, ed., *Remaking Women: Feminism and Modernity in the Middle East,* 215–242. Princeton, NJ: Princeton University Press.

Thomas, Elizabeth Marshall. 2006. *The Old Way: A Story of the First People.* New York: Farrar Straus Giroux.

Trouillot, Michel-Rolph. 1995. *Silencing the Past: Power and the Production of History.* Boston, MA: Beacon Press.

Voll, John. 1987. "Islamic Renewal and the 'Failure of the West'." In Richard Antoun and Mary Heglan, *Religious Resurgence: Contemporary Cases in Islam, Christianity, and Judaism.* 127–144. Syracuse, NY: Syracuse University Press.

Wallerstein, Immanuel. 1991. *Unthinking Social Science: The Limits of the Nineteenth Century Paradigm.* Cambridge, MA: Polity Press.

———. 2003. *The Decline of American Power.* London: The New Press.

———. 2006. *European Universalism: The Rhetoric of Power.* New York: The New Press.

Wagner, Don. 1992. "Beyond Armageddon." In *The Link.* Vol. 25. No. 4:1–13.

Warschawski, Michel. 2005. *On the Border.* Cambridge, MA: South End Press.

Yuval-Davis, Nira. 1997. *Gender and Nation.* London: Sage Publications.

Index

About the Author

Khaldoun Samman, Associate Professor of Sociology at Macalester College in St. Paul, Minnesota, is the author of *Cities of God and Nationalism: Mecca, Jerusalem, and Rome as Contested World Cities* (Paradigm 2007) and, with Mazhar Al-Zo'by, coeditor of *Islam and the Orientalist World-System* (Paradigm 2008).